COLERIDGE'S WRITINGS

Coleridge's Writings

Volume 1

On Politics and Society

Edited by

JOHN MORROW

Princeton University Press
Princeton, New Jersey

© 1991 by John Morrow

Foreword © 1991 by John Beer

Published by
PRINCETON UNIVERSITY PRESS
41 William Street, Princeton,
New Jersey 08540

Printed in Great Britain

Library of Congress Cataloging-in-Publication Data
Coleridge, Samuel Taylor. 1772–1834.
On politics and society / edited by John Morrow.
p.   cm. — (Coleridge's writings : 1)
Includes bibliographical references and index.
ISBN 0–691–06887–9 (alk. paper) — ISBN 0–691–01503–1 (pbk. :
alk. paper)
1. State, The.   2. Political science.   I. Morrow, John. Ph. D.
II. Title.   III. Series: Coleridge, Samuel Taylor, 1722–1834.
Works.   Selections.   1990 : 1.
JC223.C65   1990
320′.01—dc20   90–8673   CIP

For my Father and Mother

Contents

Foreword

The appearance of hitherto unpublished material in the present century has brought out more fully the range and complexity of Coleridge's intelligence and knowledge. The *Notebooks* and *Collected Works*, both now well on the way to completion, together with the *Collected Letters*, have made it increasingly clear that this was the most extraordinary English mind of the time. The specialist or more general student who wishes to know what Coleridge had to say on a particular subject, however, may find the sheer mass of materials bewildering, since in his less formal writings Coleridge passed quickly from one subject to another. *Coleridge's Writings* is a series addressed to such readers. In each volume a particular area of Coleridge's interest is explored, with an attempt to present his most significant statements and to show the development of his thought on the subject in question.

The present volume, *On Politics and Society*, attempts to meet one of the most commonly encountered needs. Coleridge is often referred to as an important thinker on these questions, yet particular works read in isolation do not properly convey his achievement. The arrangement here, where short statements are interspersed among extended works, draws attention to the elements of development, while the commentary, tracing the cross-links between ideas, indicates his intellectual range.

Other features also emerge. Coleridge's style and his manner of ordering ideas changed from one period of his life to another; they could also vary according to his audience. His early political writing veers towards the declamatory and images are chosen with an eye to immediate effect. During his middle period his tone ranges between subtle reasoning and reproaches of the age that can be slightly querulous, while an elegiac note marks his later attempts to bring Church and state into a single, unified vision. Despite some unevennesses, however, the reader of these extracts will most often be struck by the energy of Coleridge's thinking throughout his life, the acuteness of his criticisms and distinctions, his instinctive sense of style. There was a quiet struggle, also, between the call to be a prophet and a larger sense of himself as reconciling priest; both roles can often be traced in the same piece. Dr Morrow's skill in selecting the most important statements highlights this interplay.

Further projected volumes will include Coleridge's writings on religion, on humanity and on nature. There will be no attempt at exhaustive presentation of Coleridge's writings on any of the subjects to be dealt with; for these, and for most other purposes the collected editions will remain indispensable. The purpose of the volumes in this series is to complement those more comprehensive presentations by drawing attention to his key statements and presenting them, with apposite commentary, in a full and coherent form.

J. B. B.
General Editor

Preface

In preparing the texts for inclusion in this volume I have attempted to cater primarily for the needs of the general reader, and graduate and undergraduate students; all readers, however, will wish to avail themselves of the definitive editing in the *Collected Works* of Samuel Taylor Coleridge (Princeton, NJ, 1969–), which is the standard edition, and to which much in the present volume is introductory. My greatest debt in compiling this volume is to the scholars involved in that project; I have depended heavily upon their work, and must record my thanks to them and to the Princeton University Press (the copyright-holders) for permitting this volume to benefit from it. Because most of the writings published here have already appeared in the *Collected Works*, it seemed sensible to base the texts on that source wherever possible. However, the works published in the present volume have been abridged somewhat, and I have supplied linking commentaries, notes, and English translations of Latin and Greek phrases; the translations appear in square brackets, as do any other intrusions into the texts. Some of Coleridge's notes have been retained as footnotes; the editor's textual notes are printed as end notes. Unless otherwise stated, all works cited in the notes and included in the Bibliography were published in London.

The extracts from Coleridge's correspondence which appear as items 2(f) and 6(i) are based on the texts in the *Collected Letters of Samuel Taylor Coleridge*, ed. Earl Leslie Griggs, 6 vols (Oxford, 1956–71); I am grateful to Oxford University Press for allowing me to use this material. I must also acknowledge the financial help of the Leave and Internal Research Committees of Victoria University, and assistance rendered by the staffs of the Cambridge and Victoria University Libraries. My stay in Cambridge was made very pleasant by a connection with Robinson College, and I am most grateful to the Warden and Council for electing me to a Bye Fellowship for the winter of 1984–5. I would also like to take this opportunity to record my thanks to Mark Francis of the University of Canterbury, New Zealand, and Paul Harris, Geoffrey Debnam, Chris Parkin and Arthur Pomeroy of Victoria University for their help in scholarly matters; to Marion Beardsmore, Jenny Berry and Coula Pastelides for their good-humoured and professional secretarial help, and to my wife, Diana, for all sorts of help and encourage-ment. Paul Harris and my wife very kindly shared the burden of checking the proofs. Professor John Beer's interest and advice and encouragement have been crucial. Carl Woodring, editor of the *Table Talk* for the *Collected Coleridge*, was kind enough to look at the relevant entries in proof and make one or two suggestions. In thanking these people for their help I must also acknowledge that final responsibility for any shortcomings rests with me.

Wellington, New Zealand   J. M.

List of Abbreviations

C & S	S. T. Coleridge, *On the Constitution of the Church and State According to the Idea of Each*, ed. John Colmer (1976), CC 10.
CC	*Collected Works of Samuel Taylor Coleridge*, gen. ed. Kathleen Coburn (Princeton, NJ, 1969–).
CL	*Collected Letters of Samuel Taylor Coleridge*, ed. Earl Leslie Griggs, 6 vols (Oxford, 1956–71).
CM	S. T. Coleridge, *Marginalia*, ed. George Whalley (1980–), CC 12.
CN	*Notebooks of Samuel Taylor Coleridge*, ed. Kathleen Coburn (New York and Princeton, NJ, 1957–).
DNB	*Dictionary of National Biography*.
EOT	S. T. Coleridge, *Essays on his Times*, ed. David V. Erdman, 3 vols (1978), CC 3.
Friend	S. T. Coleridge, *The Friend*, ed. Barbara E. Rooke, 2 vols (1969), CC 4.
JHI	*Journal of the History of Ideas*.
LS	S. T. Coleridge, *Lay Sermons*, ed. R. J. White (1972), CC 6.
Lectures 1795	S. T. Coleridge, *Lectures 1795: On Politics and Religion*, ed. Lewis Patton and Peter Mann (1971), CC 1.
OED	*Oxford English Dictionary*.
PW	*The Complete Poetical Works of Samuel Taylor Coleridge*, ed. E. H. Coleridge, 2 vols (Oxford, 1912).
Table Talk	*Specimens of the Table Talk of Samuel Taylor Coleridge*, ed. H. N. Coleridge (1835; 2nd edn, corrected, 1836).
WPW	*The Poetical Works of William Wordsworth*, ed. Ernest de Selincourt and Helen Darbishire, 5 vols (Oxford, 1940–9).

Coleridge's Life

The following outline shows some crucial events in Coleridge's career in relation to his social and political writings. Full chronologies are printed in the various volumes of the Princeton *Collected Works*.

1772   (21 Oct) Coleridge born.

1782–91   At school at Christ's Hospital.

1791–late 1794   At Jesus College, Cambridge (enlisted as a dragoon Dec 1793–April 1794).

1794   (June) Meeting with Southey at Oxford initiates pantisocratic scheme.

1795   (Jan) Bristol lectures begun.
(May–June) Six Lectures on Revealed Religion.
(Dec) *Conciones ad Populum; The Plot Discovered*.

1796   (Mar–May) *The Watchman*.

1797   (Nov) 'The Ancient Mariner' begun.

1798   (Mar) 'The Ancient Mariner' completed.
(Apr) 'Recantation' (later 'France: an Ode'); 'Fears in Solitude'.
(Sep) *Lyrical Ballads* published; to Germany with the Wordsworths.

1799   Attends lectures on literature, biblical criticism and physiology at Göttingen.
(July) Returns to England.
(Nov) In London writing for the *Morning Post* until April 1800.
(Dec) 'On the French Constitution'.

1801   (Nov) In London writing for the *Morning Post* until March 1802.

1802   (Sep–Oct) 'Comparison of France and Rome'.
(Oct) Letter of April to Sara Hutchinson published in revised form as 'Dejection'.
(From Sep) In London writing for the *Morning Post*.

1803   (July–Aug) 'The Men and the Times' in the *Morning Post*.
(Aug/Sep) Stuart sells and leaves the *Morning Post*.

1804   (Jan–Mar) In London, writing for *The Courier*.

1804–6   In Malta and Sicily, first as under-secretary to Alexander

Ball, British High Commissioner. Drafts 'Observations on Egypt'.

1805   Brief items for and in *The Courier*.
       (Jan) Acting Public Secretary in Malta.
       (Sep) To Sicily and Italy.
1806   (Aug) Returns to England.
1807   (Mar) Slave trade abolished.
1808   (July) Review of Clarkson, *History of the Abolition of the Slave-Trade*.
       (Nov) First prospectus of *The Friend*.
1809   (May) Wordsworth, *Convention of Cintra* pamphlet.
       (June) First number of *The Friend*.
1810   (Mar) Last number of *The Friend*.
1811   (Apr–Sep) On staff of *The Courier* as regular contributor.
1812   Second edition of *The Friend*.
       (Jan–May) Essays in *The Courier*.
1814   (Sep–Dec) 'Letters to Mr Justice Fletcher' in *The Courier*.
1815   (June) Battle of Waterloo.
1816   (May) 'Christabel', 'Kubla Khan' and 'The Pains of Sleep' published.
       (Dec) *The Statesman's Manual*.
1817   (Jan) *A Lay Sermon*.
       (July) *Biographia Literaria* and *Sibylline Leaves*.
       (Nov) *Zapolya*.
1818   (Jan) 'Treatise on Method' in *Encyclopaedia Metropolitana*.
       (Nov) New edition ('rifaccimento') of *The Friend*.
1818–19   (Dec–Mar) Lectures on the history of philosophy and on literature.
1825   *Aids to Reflection* published by 1 June. Work on *Church and State* begun.
1828   *Poetical Works* (3 vols).
1829   (Dec) *Church and State* (2nd edn 1830).
1832   (May) Reform Bill passed.
1834   (25 July) Death of Coleridge.

Introduction

Samuel Taylor Coleridge is, of course, remembered chiefly as a poet. But his poetic achievements were only part of a literary enterprise that began in 1793 (when his first poem was published) and ended with his death in 1834.[1] Writings on social and political matters form an important part of Coleridge's *corpus*, reflecting his enduring interest in day-to-day politics, and in the more fundamental issues raised by them. The present volume is intended to furnish modern readers with materials for the study of Coleridge's contributions to social and political theory. It does not collect all his writings in this area, but does include his major statements on questions about the goals and requirements of social and political life – particularly those questions that distinguish theory from commentary. In Coleridge's case, as in that of many other writers, the intellectual division of labour is not always very clearly demarcated, but it is possible to identify works which deal principally with the ends of politics, the nature of the state, and the bearing of these on institutions and behaviour.

I

As a Cambridge undergraduate in the early 1790s, Coleridge reacted favourably to the course of the French Revolution and was openly associated with the strong Unitarian current that flowed through Jesus College.[2] At times his views on the possibilities of human emancipation took on a millenarian flavour, as is apparent in some of his early poems, and in the utopian scheme which he and the young Robert Southey developed in the summer of 1794.[3] Southey and Coleridge planned to establish a colony of carefully picked friends in the wilds of the United States. The settlement was to be based on the principle of 'pantisocracy' (a Coleridgean coinage that means 'the equal government of all'), but it was also to incorporate 'aspheterism', or 'the generalisation of individual property'.[4] The communistic elements of the scheme were unusual at the time,[5] but neither these nor any other features of it were put to the test. By late 1794 the would-be emigrants were thinking of a truncated experiment in pantisocracy on a rented farm in Wales,

1

and the following year the project was abandoned altogether. However, there was one important practical consequence. The need to raise capital for the Welsh venture took Coleridge and Southey to Bristol, where they embarked on a series of radical political and religious lectures. Some of these lectures were published in 1795, Coleridge's first political writings to appear in print. They were quickly followed, in 1796, by *The Watchman*, a short-lived experiment in radical journalism.

Over the course of the next twenty-one years, Coleridge's political views and ideas were published in two daily newspapers, the *Morning Post* and *The Courier*, and in *The Friend*, his own venture into 'higher' journalism, which ran for ten issues between June 1809 and March 1810. In these publications Coleridge began to develop his mature theory, which was markedly at variance with the radical religion and radical politics that he had espoused in his early writings. His views reached full maturity in the two 'Lay Sermons' of 1816 and 1817, and in the more weighty *On the Constitution of the Church and State* of 1829.[6]

These works, like most of Coleridge's other writings, reflect his religious preoccupations: for that reason they are seen as parts of a continuing attempt to explore the relationship between states, societies and a Christian apprehension of human experience. However, while such a description would distinguish Coleridge from many modern writers and from a few of his contemporaries, it is too general to do any finer work. In what follows Coleridge's social and political theory will be discussed by reference to three sets of issues: his religious views; the value of social and political life and the sort of criteria appropriate to it; and the way Coleridge applied these criteria to existing ideas, institutions and practices. In his view, the true significance of politics lay in its potential for realising Christian values.

II

While Coleridge was an undergraduate at Cambridge, or shortly thereafter, he abandoned the orthodox Anglican views in which he had been brought up and became a Unitarian. The central tenet of Unitarianism is that Christ was merely the 'adopted' son of God, a human model that other humans should seek to copy and not, as Trinitarians believe, an object of worship. Unitarians reject the doctrine of the Atonement, whereby Christ's death was a sacrifice necessary to the salvation of mankind by virtue of its propitiatory effect on God. Further, they deny the Christian view of redemption. By following the moral example of Jesus, Christians can develop attitudes and feelings that will allow them to enjoy the afterlife. A rejection of the necessity for redemption is connected to a denial of inherited original sin. In general, Unitarians think that good conduct rather than correctness of belief is the key to salvation; human beings are creatures who have a high natural capacity for virtue and benevolence.[7]

These doctrines played an important role in Coleridge's earliest political writings, which were developed out of the lectures delivered in Bristol in 1795. Since original sin was not inherited, Coleridge did not see political and social institutions simply as necessary to regulate creatures whose characters are fatally flawed. On the contrary, he thought that such institutions were valuable in so far as they provided opportunities for the growth and exercise of moral feelings in accordance with precepts derived directly from the life of Jesus, and from the evidences of God's revelations in the Scriptures. Coleridge's early writings contain numerous examples of a very literal application of the Bible to social and political problems. In the 'Lectures on Revealed Religion' of 1795, for example, he deals with the 'Corruptions of Christianity' in relation to 'Doctrines' *and* 'in political applications'.[8] In these lectures, and in other writings from the same period, Coleridge regards political institutions as ways of facilitating and encouraging benevolent social interaction. They must respect the equal worth of God's creatures, and further its temporal expression by promoting social justice. At times Coleridge seriously doubted whether private property and any forms of political organisation were compatible with social justice, a scepticism that explains much about the form proposed for the pantisocratic settlement.[9] But throughout the Bristol lectures he was highly critical of patterns of political and social subordination which undermine equality, impose religious and secular forms of authority that substitute tyranny and servitude for benevolence, and impede the development of those moral feelings that provide the basis for human interaction.

Coleridge's faith in the possibility of universal benevolence was buttressed by his acceptance of David Hartley's theory of the association of ideas. This doctrine was thought to explain the growth of disinterested benevolence by showing how a concern for the well-being of those who gratify the self develops into a more disinterested and increasingly widely focused form of benevolence. Since one of the consequences of Hartley's theory for Coleridge was a belief that the growth of social sympathy starts with the practice of domestic virtues, he took exception to William Godwin's claim that particular affections are the source of narrow views that impede the growth of universal benevolence.

Coleridge also objected to Godwin's atheism, but in other respects the two writers shared common ground.[10] For example, Coleridge adopted Godwin's views about the generally harmful effect of closely relating public approbation to the possession of riches; it encourages luxury and makes other individuals willing to oppress their fellows in order to win esteem. In the context of pantisocracy, and in the more utopian sections of the 'Lectures on Revealed Religion', Coleridge went beyond Godwin and argued that private property itself is incompatible with equality and with the practice of Christian virtue.[11] For the most part, however, he concentrated on the connection between an excessive concern with wealth and social and political oppression. Coleridge also shared Godwin's concern with public enlightenment, and his dislike of social and political coercion as a means of winning assent for particular views. He placed great stress on the need to appeal to people's feelings and reason in order to instigate a process of enlightenment, which he saw as a prerequisite of any significant improvements in the quality of social life. Unlike Godwin, however, Coleridge regarded the Bible as an important source of such enlightenment – 'Go, preach the GOSPEL to the Poor'[12] – and this, combined with his warnings about the dangers of fermenting rebellion among an oppressed, ignorant and volatile population, sometimes gave his early writings the character of Christian moralising rather than radical theorising.[13] Nevertheless, Coleridge's position involved a clear, unequivocal challenge to a number of important received ideas, institutions and practices.

Coleridge's Unitarian connections and sympathies aligned him with a group whose unorthodox religious views were commonly identified with radical attitudes on political questions.[14] Unitarians, who saw the Church of England as the coercive purveyor of corrupt doctrines, firmly supported attempts to break the Anglican monopoly on important political offices by abolishing the doctrinal tests enshrined in the Test and Corporation Acts. In addition, they claimed that religious freedom was precarious without political rights, and therefore favoured some measure of parliamentary reform. Perhaps more important, however, was the fact that leading Unitarians were inclined to reject traditional views on the functions and justification of government. Joseph Priestley, 'the author of modern Unitarianism', argued that the purpose of government was to secure the happiness of the subject: 'if it fail in this essential character . . . no other property or title . . . ought to shelter it from the generous attack of the noble and daring patriot'. Richard Price, another leading light of English Unitarianism, incensed Edmund Burke with his suggestion that subjects could 'cashier' or dismiss their kings.[15]

The radical political implications of Unitarianism are apparent in a number of Coleridge's early political lectures. When Coleridge wrote of the importance of acting on the basis of principle, the 'grand and comprehensive Truth' involved was universal benevolence.[16] Burke, by contrast, recommended the virtues of 'opinion . . . bottomed upon solid principles of law and policy' – traditional, historically derived entities which generated value, not principles rationally deduced from an external criterion.[17] Moreover, although Coleridge insisted that it would be dangerous to make direct appeals to an ignorant, oppressed population, arguing that those who had the people's best interests at heart should seek to guide them towards enlightenment, he did not believe that traditional elites could be depended upon to fulfil that role. In the 'Introductory Address' to *Conciones ad Populum* he develops criteria for 'true friends of freedom' based upon temperance, selfless devotion to mankind, consistency of purpose and rationality.[18] These virtues depend on moral and intellectual attributes rather than on social standing. In opposition to such men as Samuel Horsley, Bishop of St David's (and later of Rochester), who wished to confine political discussion to political and social elites, Coleridge claimed that true 'friends of freedom' had a right to take an active role in public debate. Coleridge was neither a populist nor an incendiary, but he took a view of politics that was incompatible with the commonly held notions of hierarchy reflected in Horsley's dictum that the people of England had 'nothing to do with the laws, except to obey them'.[19]

Coleridge was particularly contemptuous of leadership claims made by, or on behalf of, the Church of England. Like other Unitarians he rejected the propriety of church establishments, regarding them as excrescences necessary only because the simple, original tenets of the Christian faith had been corrupted.[20] Through-out the Bristol lectures Coleridge portrays the Church of England in unflattering colours – it is an organ of theological obscurantism, an engine of oppression and a bastion of venality and undeserved privilege. In taking this line he identifies himself with radicals whose opposition to the Established Church was a direct and clearly understood challenge to the constitutional and social structure of the kingdom.

In 'On the Present War', the second part of *Conciones ad Populum*,[21] Coleridge treats the Church's support for the war against the revolutionary regime in France as a symptom of its corruption. He argues that the war is unjust because it aims to destroy the gains of the revolution, and unnecessary because it could have been avoided through negotiations. It is conducted in a barbarous manner, produces economic hardship for the poor at home and generates a climate of suspicion which is exacerbated by, yet serves to justify, government oppression and the use of spies. At a time when the anti-war sentiments of a tutor of Coleridge's college, the Unitarian William Frend, had precipitated his summons before the Vice-Chancellor's Court, and when opposition to the war was part of a critique of aristocratic influence in the state, Coleridge's anti-war arguments were a clear indication of the unorthodox character of his views.[22]

Furthermore, although Coleridge thought that public debate was valuable because of its beneficial effects on individual enlighten-ment, he also believed that it had significant political implications. In a critique of legislation that seriously restricted discussions of the Constitution, Coleridge argues that freedom of speech is necessary if the Constitution is to progress beyond the stage of 'government *with* the people' to that of 'government *by* the people'.[23] Although Coleridge's favourable references to the French Constitution suggest that he supported an extension of the fran-chise,[24] the details of his views on electoral reform are vague. It is quite clear, however, that he took a very sceptical attitude towards standard defences of the Constitution. He describes the present system of representation as 'corrupt' and refuses to accept Paley's claim that 'the people' are 'virtually represented' by those whom they had no say in electing.[25] Coleridge argues that in present circumstances freedom of expression is important if the population are to have any effect on a regime that is oligarchic in character, and essential if the Constitution is to advance from its less than perfect condition.

A number of features of Coleridge's earliest political writings were therefore closely connected to radical critiques of existing institutions and ideas. When Unitarian moral precepts – extolling freedom, social justice and equality – were brought to bear on existing institutions, they produced a radical critique of the theory and practice of English government, a rejection of the religious and political status of the Established Church, and stridently stated, but vaguely formulated, demands for social and political reform. Although Coleridge was not a proponent of popular insurrection in England, he thought that many of the central features of the social, political and religious structure of society were barriers to theological clarity, hindered the practice of disinterested benevolence, and frustrated the spread of moral and political enlightenment.

III

In the mid-1790s Coleridge's radical religious views provided the basis for his radical political theory; in later years, however, he began to adopt a more orthodox form of Christianity, and to develop political and social views that were compatible with it. Coleridge's reconciliation with Trinitarianism took place over a number of years, but the process was completed by 1806.[26] In the same years he came to accept the doctrine of the Atonement and with it ideas of original sin that weakened assumptions about man's natural capacity for benevolence and virtue, and for ordering his own existence without the help of political, social and religious authorities. Once Coleridge had ceased to regard Trinitarianism as a corruption of true Christianity, the way was open for him to become reconciled with the Church of England.

Before Coleridge formally returned to the Trinitarian fold his political theory had shown clear signs of moving in more orthodox channels. In the years 1798–1802 he abandoned his opposition to the war with France. His changed perspective on international affairs was accompanied by a growing suspicion of developments within France. The emergence of Napoleon (in the guise of First Consul) as the dominant force in French politics, and as a major threat to the security of the other European powers, also had an important impact, which first became apparent in two series of articles that Coleridge wrote for the *Morning Post* in 1799 and 1802. The first series discussed the new French Constitution of 1799 (the 'Constitution of the Year VIII'), while the second considered the validity of comparisons drawn between the late Roman Republic and the French Consulate.[27] Although these articles focused on developments in France, they had clear implications for Coleridge's political theory and for his views of English institutions. They are the most important statements of the theoretical implications of what David Erdman has termed Coleridge's 'disengagement' from the forces of radicalism at home.[28]

While Coleridge's articles on the French Constitution show that he had abandoned equality as a goal, they also indicate a continuing concern with the maintenance of public and private freedom. He claims that political equality is possible only in egalitarian societies such as the United States, and argues that European societies should seek to ensure that the 'artificial power' of wealth counteracts the 'physical power' of numbers.[29] He conceives of political systems as ways of providing a check on the power of numbers, claiming that this can be done in a generally beneficial way only if political power is proportionate to the possession of property. Coleridge criticises the new French Constitution for failing to maintain such proportionality, and for ensuring that the influence of property would be expressed in a corrupt and socially harmful manner. The Consulate had merely established a pseudo-republican façade for a regime based on the interests of a self-serving oligarchy and a military dictator.

During the course of his examination of the weaknesses of the French Constitution, Coleridge contrasts its failings with the virtues of the English system of government. In criticising the constitutional basis of the Consulate he is, therefore, also defending a particular conception of eighteenth-century English government.[30] Coleridge seems prepared to concede that the independence of the English Parliament could be threatened by a monied interest which, like the membership of the French Chambers, was financially dependent on the executive. However, the general thrust of his argument is that the English Constitution is generally superior to the French because it manages to preserve the independence of legislators. It does so by ensuring that they are drawn, for the most part, from a class of independent proprietors, and particularly from those who possess the most independent and secure form of wealth, that derived from landed property. This assessment of the constitutional importance of landed property is related to positive views of its social significance. Coleridge associates landed property not only with stability and a fixed interest in the fortunes of the country, but also with the maintenance of an aristocratic class imbued with an aristocratic spirit generating a 'delicate superstition of ancestry' which counteracts the dangers posed by the more modern and gross 'superstition of wealth'.[31]

Coleridge's favourable attitude towards the political and social roles of a landed aristocracy was developed further in his series of articles comparing France with Rome. The point of these articles is to show that France differs greatly from Rome, and that Roman history does not provide grounds for believing that the Napoleonic regime will last very long. Despotism, he argues, was inevitable in the polyglot empire of Rome, but not in France, where a common history and language provide the basis for combining stability with freedom. Among the advantages enjoyed by France, and, Coleridge implies, by England also, are sets of hierarchical and deferential relationships which make it possible for freedom to flourish in the absence of both equality and disorder. In 'those feudal institutions' France possesses that 'happy intertexture of the interests and property of the state, which was in vain to be sought for in the original Constitution of Rome, in which every rich proprietor was regarded as an illegal oppressor'.[32]

The arguments about property and independence that Coleridge uses in his critique of the French Constitution also lay behind his unfavourable reception of the Franco-Papal Concordat of 1802, and his related suggestion that an established church with its own property could help prevent religion from becoming an organ of state. Coleridge contrasts the independence enjoyed by the Church of England, by virtue of its possession of independent material resources, with the subservience of a state-salaried French Church, and claims that church establishments can prevent the misuse of religion for political purposes.[33]

These remarks, together with Coleridge's defence of English political and social institutions, show quite clearly that the radical perspective of the Bristol lectures had been dampened. It should be noted, however, that Coleridge's arguments reflect a continued concern with both public and private freedom; he defends English institutions and practices on the grounds that the recognition of the political claims of independent, and particularly landed, property help preserve these values. The reasons Coleridge gives for admiring the English Constitution are dependent, moreover, on a tradition of argument which was sceptical about certain features of eighteenth-century practice – particularly the tendency to fund government activity by way of debts. This had led to the emergence of a class of office-holders, financiers and contractors whose influence on the electoral system, and whose presence in the legislature, seemed to threaten the political role of independent proprietors. These reservations played an interesting role in subsequent developments in Coleridge's political and social theory. They also show that, although he had abandoned the radical stance of 1795, his theory did not promote a placid acceptance of the *status quo*.

IV

Coleridge's disengagement from the radical position advanced in 1795 had reached a fairly advanced stage by the time he launched *The Friend* in June 1809. The journal was intended to 'found true *Principles*, to oppose false *Principles*, in Criticism, Legislation, Philosophy, Morals, and International Law'.[34] It contains Coleridge's mature views on the relationship between religion, morals and politics, and his first reasonably systematic statement of a political philosophy.

The moral and political arguments of *The Friend* are structured round a consideration of two opposing views. The first, identified with William Paley, is held to empty both politics and morals of any distinctly moral element. The second (associated with Rousseau, but also attributed to contemporary English radicals such as Major Cartwright and William Cobbett) depends upon a conflation of morals and politics which resembles the position that Coleridge had taken in his early lectures. Coleridge argues that these writers' attempts to ground political rights on 'mere personality' confuses the basis of political and religious claims.[35]

Coleridge's moral theory depends upon a number of assumptions about the conjuncture of good and evil in human nature, the existence of conscience, and the necessity for free agency, or will, to enable people to act in ways which are consistent with their ideas of right or wrong. The moral point of view embodies the

Kantian principle that individuals should 'so act that [they might] be able without involving any contradiction to will that the Maxim of . . . [their] Conduct should be the Law of all intelligent Beings'.[36] Morality is not, as writers such as Paley claim, merely the utilitarian assessment of consequences, the gauging of the apparent outward effect of the act; it also examines the quality of the intention that produces the action in question. A moral person is one who acts as a free agent, one whose conduct is determined by his own will, and by a recognition of the moral status of other beings. For Coleridge, the characteristic which makes humans moral beings is their possession of 'reason', 'the power by which we become possessed of Principle . . . and of [such] Ideas . . . as [those of] . . . Justice, Holiness, Free Will'.[37] Since all men are endowed with reason they should all be accorded the same moral status.

In Coleridge's view, morality is inward, egalitarian and universal. It relates to the inward side of action, and reflects men's common capacity for acting freely and in accord with the ideas of justice. However, these characteristic features of reason restrict its role to matters having to do with the quality of intentions. It cannot be applied directly to the regulation of outward matters, since these, being affected by the vicissitudes of time and circumstances, necessarily fall within the province of the 'understanding', the discursive faculty which generalises from accumulated experience and determines the best way of translating intentions into actions.

Coleridge uses the distinction between reason and the understanding as a basis for distinguishing the sphere of politics from that of morality. Morality deals with the inward determinants of action, while politics deals with the outward side, and particularly with the regulation of human interaction. This distinction is nicely highlighted in Coleridge's description of Major Cartwright as a 'state moralist'.[38] Cartwright, a well-known proponent of parliamentary reform, assumed that political issues are open to exactly the same mode of treatment as moral problems, and imported moral principles into the assessment of political institutions and practices.

For Coleridge, morals and politics were distinct but they were not divorced from one another. Government should not only protect individuals, but also ensure that they have the opportunity to gain the material goods and the intellectual and moral capabilities that will facilitate the development and exercise of their personalities.[39] Moral considerations provide the grounds of obligation to political authority, even if the form that such authorities take depends upon circumstantial considerations which lie within the province of the understanding.

Coleridge's treatment of political obligation was developed by reference to three approaches. The first, attributed to Hobbes, explains obligation in terms of fear; the second, associated with Paley, depends wholly upon expediency; while the third grounds obligation on a theory of morality which is very similar to that advanced by Coleridge in his critique of Paley's moral theory. Coleridge attributes the third position to Rousseau, but presents it in a markedly Kantian guise. Hobbes's theory is rejected because it fails to accord with human experience, and because it implicitly denies any connection between morality and the grounds of obedience to political authorities. Coleridge claims that Hobbes failed to recognise any significant differences between human beings and beasts. Paley's notion of expediency is empty of any moral content, resting on a naturalistic conception of the subject matter of political philosophy that implies a debased view of humanity.[40] Rousseau, on the other hand, provides an account of obligation which recognises that individuals should be treated as moral ends rather than as means. Coleridge endorses Rousseau's account of the basis of obligation, but rejects his attempt to apply moral concerns to the framing and justification of particular institutional arrangements. He claims that such a procedure has the effect of undercutting the legitimacy of any regime that fails to uphold social and moral equality. The logical outcome of 'state moralism' is not manhood suffrage, as Rousseau and his followers claimed, but the most thoroughgoing leveller republic.[41]

Rousseau and his followers failed to recognise that judgements about the appropriateness of institutional forms involve a consideration of questions of degree, and have to take account of the fruits of human experience. The practice of politics, in other words, utilises the understanding. It involves calculations based on experience, and so, while there is every justification for treating men as moral equals, it is a moot point whether, in any given situation, they are equally well qualified for the exercise of political rights. In any case, the framing of political institutions and the distribution of political power within them are not matters to be dealt with in terms of moral discourse. They depend upon practical and circumstantial considerations, and are closely related to the distribution of property.

In *The Friend* Coleridge's treatment of the political significance of property rests on a distinction between the rationale of the state and the origins of government. The state's rationale is moral; it can be explained by reference to the characteristics and incidence of reason, but the development of political structures can not be accounted for in the same terms. Coleridge argues that government was created in order to protect men's property; reason can not, therefore, be said to play a direct role in its creation. While reason is equal in all men, property is held unequally. Its acquisition is significantly influenced by environmental considerations and by the varying capacities of different individuals. Coleridge acknowledges that the 'form' (or idea) of property can be deduced from reason alone, a point that he states more clearly in a contemporary notebook entry where the moral value of property in general is linked to the '*necessity* of individual action to moral agency, of an individual sphere to individual scheme[s] of action'.[42] But he insists that the moral basis of property is limited to its form; the *matter* of property rights and the extent of individual holdings are consequences of chance and of the varying capacities of individuals. Since government and human laws relate to property, and since property itself is not deducible from reason, it follows that it would be inappropriate to claim that universal rights based on moral personality should be recognised in relation to matters and institutions that are not the products of reason.

Coleridge's arguments about the historical origins of government in relation to property and reason provide a more developed basis for claims about the connection between property and political power which had appeared in his earlier critique of the French Constitution. Attempts to base claims to political rights on moral personality not only rest on a misunderstanding about the relationship between morality and politics, but also ignore the wisdom embodied in traditional institutions and practices. The experiences of the eighteenth century, and the fatal counter-example of the French Constitution of 1799, showed that systems of government which are based on the distribution of property are more likely to provide freedom and stability than are those which ignore it.

V

Coleridge's two major contributions to subsequent social and political thought are the 'Lay Sermons' of 1816 and 1817, and *On the Constitution of the Church and State*, which was first published at the close of 1829. These works build upon the moral and political theory developed in *The Friend* and seek to identify the behavioural, intellectual and institutional requirements of a political system which, while based upon property, would be justified by its capacity to contribute to the attainment of moral goals that combine a concern for moral agency with a recognition of the moral value of other individuals.

The 'Lay Sermons' were products of the years of economic hardship and political and social dislocation that immediately followed the conclusion of the war against France in 1815.[43] They were Coleridge's most elaborate contributions to contemporary debate about the causes of, and cures for, the post-war crisis. Addressed to the 'Higher' and 'Higher and Middle' classes respectively, each presents a different, although related, set of arguments. Their general purpose, however, was to make the upper classes see the intellectual, social and economic requirements of their position, and to encourage them to use their political power to alleviate rather than to aggravate the difficulties facing society.

In the first sermon, *The Statesman's Manual*, Coleridge attempts to persuade the upper classes to inform their actions by a 'philosophy of history' derived from reading the Bible in a 'spirit of prophecy'. He claims that such a perspective would provide a valuable corrective to much contemporary argument and analysis which, because it relied on the sophisms of Locke and Hume, ignored the rounded, more deeply informed views found in the Bible: 'by a derivative, indeed, but not a divided influence . . . the Sacred Book is worthily intitled *the* WORD OF GOD. Hence . . . its contents present to us the stream of time continuous as Life and a symbol of Eternity, inasmuch as the Past and Future are virtually contained in the Present.' A craving for novelty coupled with the belief that the Bible was already familiar discouraged the study of the Scriptures and the works of the 'red letter' names in the history of the human intellect – Thucydides, Tacitus, Machiavelli, Bacon and Harrington – whom Coleridge regards as admirable exponents of true, Platonic philosophy. He argues that a Platonised Christianity which transcends the realm of sense impression and gives men access to the 'infinite' provides the only escape from a system that is intellectually shallow, theologically barren and politically and socially disastrous. In the preceding century this philosophy and its 'red letter' exponents had been pushed aside by writers such as Hume and Paley whose historical and philosophical works were based on, and addressed to, the understanding and could not enlighten the reason or enliven the soul. To counteract this, Coleridge argues for a revival of 'austerer studies', principally philosophy and theology, among the educated classes. These studies would put men back in touch with a tradition from which they had been too long divorced and would provide the basis for an effective and morally viable response to prevailing difficulties.[44]

The second sermon, entitled *A Lay Sermon, Addressed to the Higher and Middle Classes* . . . , continues the attack on the intellectual basis of much contemporary argument. While critical of the dehumanising abstractions which were the stock-in-trade of contemporary exponents of the pseudo-science of political economy, it is equally harsh in its judgements on popular parliamentary reformers and agitators. Coleridge condemns their morals, motives and programmes, together with their attempts to associate all contemporary ills with taxation and other government fiscal practices. Although he is prepared to accept at least some of the features of commercial society, and even to repeat common arguments about the connection between the growth of commerce and expanding opportunities for the exercise of human freedom,[45] his primary aim is to ensure that these do not become universalised.

One of Coleridge's main concerns in *A Lay Sermon* is with the effect of what he called the 'spirit of commerce' on the landed classes.[46] He reiterates remarks he had made earlier about the role played by ideas of nobility as a 'counterpoise to the grosser superstition for wealth', and complains that 'ancient feelings of rank and ancestry' are revered less than in former times.[47] These ideas are being undermined by the landed classes themselves as a result of their growing tendency to embrace the 'commercial spirit', an ethos to which their social position, their upbringing and their *mores* should provide an effective counterweight. This development is directly relevant to the present crisis because the growing commercialisation of agriculture is undercutting the deference networks upon which the landed classes' social pre-eminence, and much of their social usefulness, depend.[48]

Coleridge looks to the upper classes themselves to resist the attractions of the commercial spirit. He opposes suggestions that property should be regulated by the state, since this would weaken the connection between property and free agency, and argues that only education and religion would provide counterweights compatible with a free recognition of the moral personalities of other beings. Much of *A Lay Sermon* is devoted to identifying forms of intellectual activity and intellectualised religion that would fulfil that function. The argument of the second 'Lay Sermon' thus joins hands with that of the first. Coleridge argues that philosophy and religion would provide a distraction from an excessive concern with wealth, and would also open the mind to those values which distinguish mankind from God's other creatures.[49] In concrete terms, this means that other human beings should be recognised as moral and religious equals, and treated as ends rather than means. Although the rationale of property limits the state's role in regulating rights, so far as landed property is concerned these rights continue to be morally dependent upon the fulfilment of obligations directly related to the underlying moral character of, and justification for, the state.

VI

Coleridge's arguments in *A Lay Sermon* place a great deal of stress upon the importance of the moral reform of individuals. However, he also maintains that individual efforts need to be guided and supported by agencies that would encourage individuals to recognise, and act in accordance with, the moral potentialities of their fellow human beings. In his last contribution to political theory, *On the Constitution of the Church and State*, he builds upon remarks in *A Lay Sermon* which suggest that a 'learned and philosophic public' requires the existence of 'an accredited, learned, and philosophical *Class*',[50] and argues that the production and nurturing of such a class provides the primary function of, and justification for, national churches, including, specifically, the Church of England.

The immediate context of *Church and State* was the late eighteenth- and early nineteenth-century debate over Roman Catholic emancipation,[51] but its arguments also applied to the threats posed by Protestant Dissenters as a result of the repeal of the Test and Corporation Acts. Opponents of these measures – one consequence of which would be the return of Catholics and Dissenters to Parliament – claimed that they would undermine the Anglican basis of the Constitution by making possible a legal assault upon the position of the Established Church. Coleridge's work attempts to defend the Church, and to ensure that it would not be damaged by Catholic emancipation, but he is not opposed to emancipation itself. However, because one of the issues at stake in the debate over Catholic emancipation was the character and functions of the Church of England, *Church and State* is not just a defence of the Church. It also, and necessarily, involves the development of a particular conception of what the Church is, or should be.

In *Church and State* Coleridge argues that the Church must be understood in relation to the social and political structure of which it forms a part. His argument depends upon a number of terminological distinctions. The first of these is between the Constitution as a body of law, and the Constitution as an 'idea', or 'that conception of a thing, which is not abstracted from any particular state, form, or mode, in which the thing may happen to exist at this or that time; nor yet generalized from any number or succession of such forms or modes; but which is given by the knowledge of *its ultimate aim*'.[52] This means that changes in the law would not necessarily affect the character of the Constitution. The second distinction draws attention to a wider and a narrower meaning of the term 'constitution'. The 'constitution of the state' includes the legislative and executive arms of government and the non-institutionalised forces related to them, but the 'constitution of the nation' also embraces the National Church.

Coleridge argues that such an 'idea' of the Constitution depends upon balancing different sorts of property – landed and commercial – in the legislative chambers. In that way, the community is able to reap the benefits of commercial activity and to give political recognition to the importance of this 'progressive interest' without losing the beneficial effects of the more stable, ethically directed values associated with landed proprietorship, or with what Coleridge now calls the 'forces of permanence'.[53]

In a presentation copy of *Church and State* Coleridge noted that the legislature represents 'interests' rather than the wishes of 'the People'.[54] This remark draws attention to the fact that the constitution of the state is based on property, but Coleridge's talk of 'interests' also relates to his frequently stated view that politics and the law are most directly concerned with non-personal values. The distinction between law and morality had been one of the major themes of *The Friend*, but in a notebook entry which is roughly contemporary with *Church and State* Coleridge relates this to the constitutional structure of the state:

> The proper object of a State is *Things*, the permanent *interests* that continue in the flux of its component Citizens, hence a distinction & if I might say so, a polarisation of ranks and orders is the very condition of its existence. . . . The aim of the . . . State is to preserve and defend the . . . difference between the integral parts of its total Body, by establishing and watching over the differential grounds, & causes and exponents of the difference . . . .[55]

The Crown plays a crucial role in balancing the proprietorial interests represented in the Lords and Commons. It serves as the 'beam' in the balance, and expresses the unity produced by the counterpoise between the interests of permanence and the interests of progress. Because the Crown is not an estate it represents not interests, but 'the majesty, or symbolic unity of the whole kingdom, both of the state and of the persons . . . , the cohesion by interdependence' of its constituent parts.[56]

The balance between the interests of permanence and those of progress is the main element in Coleridge's account of the constitution of the state. However, he claims that a healthy body politic also requires a correctly balanced relationship between institutionalised forces and the 'free powers or energies' that are not formally integrated in the constitutional structure, and between 'actual' and 'potential' powers throughout society.[57] With respect to the first, Coleridge was concerned to ensure that free energy which was not attached to property was kept out of the institutionalised structure of parliamentary representation, that the claims of those with property were properly recognised, and finally, that the free powers were enabled to vitalise the state by finding expression in extra-parliamentary activities. The aim was to prevent the state from falling victim to the free energies of the populace – as had happened in the Greek republics – while avoiding the ossification of institutionalised power that had fatally weakened the Venetian republic.

The distinction between 'actual' and 'potential' powers draws attention to those forces that are represented both in institutions and in the free activities of the populace, but are not exhausted by either. In particular, Coleridge has in mind the need for Parliament to restrain its law-making power where important values, such as those attached to religion, are concerned.[58] This part of Coleridge's argument was particularly relevant to the Catholic emancipation

issue, and it provides a bridge between his account of the constitution of the state and that of the constitution of the nation. In the
latter, the political forces and institutions of the country – all of
which are part of an elaborate system of balances – are themselves
balanced by a further set of institutions centred on the National
Church. The state and the Church are 'two poles of the same
magnet; the magnet itself, which is constituted by them, is the
CONSTITUTION of the nation'.[59]

Although much of what Coleridge wrote about the National
Church was based upon his understanding of the history of the
Church of England, he treats that institution, as he had treated
the constitution of the state, by reference to its idea. Moreover,
property plays as important a role in his account of the Church as
it had in relation to the state. The National Church is based on a
distinctive form of property, one that is reserved for the direct
fulfilment of *national* rather than *personal* purposes. Coleridge
emphasises the difference by a terminological distinction: the
property of the Church constitutes the 'Nationalty', while all kinds
of personal property are part of the 'Propriety'. The relationship
between these two forms of property is governed by the principle
of balance. 'These, the *Propriety* and the *Nationalty*, were the
two constituent factors, the opposite, but correspondent and
reciprocally supporting, counter-weights, of the *commonwealth*, the
existence of the one being the condition, and the perfecting, of the
rightfulness of the other.'[60]

Coleridge argues that a National Church based on its own
property is an essential feature of the state. It forms a *'third* great
venerable estate of the realm',[61] comparable in kind with the other
two estates, and designed to balance them. That is necessary
because personal property is under the control of its owners, and
so there is always the possibility that proprietors will neglect their
duties or misuse their property rights. The National Church
embraces the 'learned and philosophic class' of which Coleridge
had written in *A Lay Sermon*. Its control of the Nationalty is justified
because it contributes to the maintenance of an educated and
educational elite, or 'clerisy', who are independent of social and
political elites. They are thus able to nurture the intellectual and
religious values that are necessary to counteract the pervasive
effect of the spirit of commerce, and to encourage the pursuit of
ends that are national rather than connected with any particular
interest. The clerisy embody values that counteract the commercial

spirit, and enlighten the public so as to ensure that individuals avoid being completely absorbed by it. They are charged with the 'cultivation' of the population, with the 'harmonious development of those qualities and faculties that characterise our *humanity*'.[62]

In *The Friend* Coleridge had identified the enlightenment of the population as one of the ultimate ends of the state. The fact that he now assigned that role to a specific institution endowed with a portion of the nation's wealth explains why he considered the National Church an essential part of the constitution of the nation. His argument was designed to show why the question of Catholic emancipation had to be settled in a way that did not threaten the Church of England's position as the National Church. Coleridge adds a further strand to this argument when he claims that the status of the Church of England as a National Church is not dependent upon its Anglican character. National churches are independent of 'theological dogmata'; they are the 'Offspring of Human Law', and are not to be confused with what Coleridge called the 'Church of Christ'.[63] Although it is quite possible for a national church to contain a Christian church within it, the Church of Christ is not a 'KINGDOM, REALM . . . or STATE . . . of the WORLD'. It is a 'compensating counterforce' to states in general ('the *sustaining, correcting, befriending* opposite of the World!'[64]), and, while it modifies the evil *results* of political and social interaction, it does not seek to correct or change the structures of particular states. The Church of Christ is not connected to political institutions, and is based on quite different principles from those which are served by, and dictate the distribution of political power in, a body politic. It 'disregards all external accidents, and looks at men as individual persons, allowing no gradations of rank, but such as greater or lesser wisdom, learning and holiness ought to confer. A church is, therefore, in idea, the only pure democracy.'[65] A national church is, by contrast, part of a nation and has a material basis like other elements of the constitution.

The distinction between a national and Christian church serves two main functions in Coleridge's argument. In the first place, it allows him to claim that both churches could coexist beneficially without confusing law and religion. National churches are not necessarily Christian, but the advent of Christ had provided a 'providential boon, a grace of God, a mightly and faithful friend'. Coleridge likens the National Church to a vine whose fruit is improved by the close proximity of the olive tree of Christianity.[66]

For their part, national churches help prevent the intrusion of temporal power into the Church of Christ, and thus act as a bulwark against religious intolerance. If there were no national churches there would be a danger that an institution claiming to be *the* Church of Christ would seek to assume unregulated secular power on the basis of its claims to spiritual universality. Secondly, the distinction between Christian and national churches helps to justify the position of the latter by undercutting claims that the very existence of national churches involves an unwarranted and un-Christian intrusion of politics into religion. Because the Church of England is a national church, it is confined within legally defined limits, and is precluded from using its position to advance claims of a theological nature.

Coleridge's arguments about the essential nature of a national church, and his attempts to define and justify its role were designed to show why any measure of Catholic emancipation would have to contain safeguards (or 'securities', as contemporaries called them[67]) to guarantee the position of the Church of England. His attempts to distinguish between national and Christian churches contributed to the same goal, but had the additional advantage of showing that national churches were immune from the theological critiques levelled at them by those non-Anglican Protestants who might be tempted to combine with Roman Catholics in order to strip the Church of England of its property and its status as an established national church.

VII

Church and State marked the culmination of Coleridge's development as a social and political theorist and of his movement away from the radical position that had characterised his Bristol lectures of 1795. While there is much truth in John Stuart Mill's remark that Coleridge was primarily interested in asking what accepted ideas and institutions *meant*,[68] his mature theory involves more than an elaborate justification for 'things as they are'. Coleridge's conception of an idea provides a criterion for assessing current practices and institutions, and his treatment of the constitution of both Church and state contains a good deal of explicit and implicit criticism. Some of this critical energy is directed at the behaviour of political and social elites, but it also generates a more systematic criticism of the social and political structure. Coleridge's analysis of the 'spirit of commerce' and its effects on social and political life entails a very strict qualification of contemporary views about the viability of commercial societies, and of the desirability of fusing commercial and agricultural interests. He regarded the ethics of commerce as being largely incompatible with the pursuit of Christian values, and his arguments about balance were designed to strengthen the division between the landed and the commercial interests.

Moreover, Coleridge's understanding of the role of the National Church and his insistence that it is integral to the constitution of the nation were based upon a belief that neither of the major interests in society would, of themselves, produce a social, political or economic environment which would facilitate the attainment of Christian values. The implication of this was that the close connections between the Established Church and social and political elites would have to be broken; the Church could not fulfil its counteracting role if it was too closely identified with the state. Coleridge's theory therefore involves a critique of both modernising and traditional tendencies within English society and within contemporary political and social theory. This critique depended upon his views on the nature of religious experience, the relationship between religion, morals and politics, and the implications these had for the structuring of political relationships.

The key to the constructive part of Coleridge's programme lies in his belief that the social and political shortcomings of traditional, landed elites were due to moral and intellectual failings. The growth of commerce and the pervasive influence of its intellectual and moral corollaries made the basis of the traditional aristocratic order outmoded and inadequate, and Coleridge's mature theory provided a substitute for it. In place of a traditional culture based on inherited feelings, one that was self-sustaining and maintained through processes that were neither literate nor the products of intellectual endeavour, Coleridge enshrined a highly intellectualised Platonic conception of religion. The clerisy would induce the gentry to adhere to roles that were appropriate to their stations by instituting forms of upper-class education that were more spiritually and intellectually satisfying than Lockean materialism or Humean scepticism. The rediscovery of Platonism and the inculcation of its philosophy and moral values by the clerisy would form the intellectual basis of an aristocratic order in politics whose role would be defined by philosophy rather than by unreflective tradition. Landed property still lay at the heart of the state, but, because it now coalesced with commercially derived wealth, it needed something more than tradition to sustain it.[69]

1

The Politics of Radical Religion:
The Bristol Lectures of 1795

Coleridge's earliest political writings developed out of a series of lectures given in Bristol in 1795. These lectures were intended to provide a source of funds for the revised pantisocratic scheme, and many of the arguments advanced in them were closely connected to that scheme. Others were tailored more closely to English circumstances than to the special conditions that emigration would make possible, but the concern with liberty and equality that lay behind the pantisocratic proposal had a marked impact on Coleridge's view of the need for reform in contemporary society. In the extracts printed below, Coleridge is sharply critical of the political and religious establishments, condemns the war against France, and is favourably, although not uncritically, disposed towards recent political developments in that country. The three major themes that emerge from these writings are the need for reformers to act on the basis of fixed principles; the importance of enlightening those who are to be liberated; and the necessity for disinterested reformers to take a leading role in the process of enlightenment. Coleridge advances these claims in the context of analyses of the corruption and injustice which mark the structures and practices of politics and religion.

These themes are clearly enunciated in the first work printed below, the 'Introductory Address' from Conciones ad Populum.[1] *While Coleridge endorses the aims of the French Revolutionaries, he dissociates himself from many of their means, and treats the excesses of the Revolution as a warning to the 'friends of Freedom' in England. He then develops a typology of supporters of reform at home which is based upon the extent to which various groups act on fixed principles and seek to enlighten those they lead. Enlightenment, which is portrayed as being particularly important because of the misery and ignorance generated by the existing system of social and political relations, is seen as a necessary preliminary to institutional reform. While religion is treated as an essential part of that process of enlightenment, its effect on the moral character of the individual is given a distinctly political bearing. If he is poor, 'Religion will cheer his gloom with her promises, and by habituating his mind to anticipate an infinitely great Revolution hereafter, may prepare it even for the sudden reception of a less degree of amelioration in this World. But if we hope to instruct others, we should familiarise our own mind to some fixed and determinate principles of action.'[2]*

(a) *Conciones ad Populum*: "Introductory Address"

*For I am always a lover of Liberty, but in those who would appropriate
the Title, I find too many points destructive of liberty and hateful to
her genuine advocates.*[3]

When the Wind is fair and the Planks of the Vessel sound, we
may safely trust every thing to the management of professional
Mariners: in a Tempest and on board a crazy Bark, all must
contribute their Quota of Exertion. The Stripling is not exempted
from it by his Youth, nor the Passenger by his Inexperience. Even
so, in the present agitations of the public mind, every one ought
to consider his intellectual faculties as in a state of immediate
requisition. All may benefit Society in some degree. The exigencies
of the Times do not permit us to stay for the maturest years, lest
the opportunity be lost, while we are waiting for an increase of
power.

Companies resembling the present will, from a variety of circumstances, consist *chiefly* of the zealous Advocates for Freedom. It
will therefore be our endeavour, not so much to excite the torpid,
as to regulate the feelings of the ardent; and above all, to evince
the necessity of *bottoming* on fixed Principles, that so we may not
be the unstable Patriots of Passion or Accident, nor hurried away
by names of which we have not sifted the meaning, and by tenets
of which we have not examined the consequences. The Times are
trying; and in order to be prepared against their difficulties we
should have acquired a prompt facility of adverting in all our
doubts to some grand and comprehensive Truth. . . .

The Example of France is indeed a "Warning to Britain".[4] A
Nation wading to their Rights through Blood, and marking the
track of Freedom by Devastation! Yet let us not embattle our
Feelings against our Reason. Let us not indulge our malignant
Passions under the mask of Humanity. Instead of railing with
infuriate declamation against these excesses, we shall be more
profitably employed in developing the sources of them. French
Freedom is the Beacon, which while it guides to Equality, should
shew us the Dangers that throng the road.

The Annals of the French Revolution have recorded in Letters
of Blood, that the Knowledge of the Few cannot counteract the
Ignorance of the Many; that the Light of Philosophy, when it is
confined to a small Minority, points out the Possessors as the

Victims, rather than the Illuminators, of the Multitude. The Patriots of France either hastened into the dangerous and gigantic Error of making certain Evil the means of contingent Good, or were sacrificed by the Mob, with whose prejudices and ferocity their unbending Virtue forbade them to assimilate. Like Sampson, the People were strong – like Sampson, the People were blind. Those two massy Pillars of Oppression's Temple, the Monarchy and Aristocracy,

> With horrible Convulsion to and fro
> They tugg'd, they shook – till down they came and drew
> The whole Roof after them with burst of Thunder
> Upon the heads of all who sat beneath,
> Lords, Ladies, Captains, Counsellors, and Priests,
> Their choice Nobility![5]

There was not a Tyrant in Europe, who did not tremble on his Throne. Freedom herself heard the Crash aghast! –

The Girondists,[6] who were the first republicans in power, were men of enlarged views and great literary attainments; but they seem to have been deficient in that vigour and daring activity, which circumstances made necessary. . . . Brissot, the leader of the Gironde party, is entitled to the character of a virtuous man, and an eloquent speaker; but he was rather a sublime visionary, than a quick-eyed politician; and his excellences equally with his faults rendered him unfit for the helm, in the stormy hour of Revolution. Robespierre, who displaced him, possessed a glowing ardor that still remembered the *end*, and a cool ferocity that never either overlooked, or scrupled, the *means*. What that *end* was, is not known: that it was a wicked one, has by no means been proved. I rather think, that the distant prospect, to which he was travelling, appeared to him grand and beautiful; but that he fixed his eye on it with such intense eagerness as to neglect the foulness of the road. If however his first intentions were pure, his subsequent enormities yield us a melancholy proof, that it is not the character of the possessor which directs the power, but the power which shapes and depraves the character of the possessor. In Robespierre, its influence was assisted by the properties of his disposition. – Enthusiasm, even in the gentlest temper, will frequently generate sensations of an unkindly order. If we can clearly perceive any one thing to be of vast and infinite importance to ourselves and all mankind, our first feelings impel us to turn with angry contempt from those, who doubt and oppose it. The ardor of undisciplined benevolence seduces us into malignity: and whenever our hearts are warm, and our objects great and excellent, intolerance is the sin that does most easily beset us. But this enthusiasm in Robespierre was blended with gloom, and suspiciousness, and inordinate vanity. His dark imagination was still brooding over supposed plots against freedom – to prevent tyranny he became a Tyrant – and having realized the evils which he suspected, a wild and dreadful Tyrant. – Those loud-tongued adulators, the mob, overpowered the lone-whispered denunciations of conscience – he despotized in all the pomp of Patriotism, and masqueraded on the bloody stage of Revolution, a Caligula with the cap of Liberty on his head . . . .

Revolutions are sudden to the unthinking only. Political Disturbances happen not without their warning Harbingers. Strange Rumblings and confused Noises still precede these earthquakes and hurricanes of the moral World. The process of Revolution in France has been dreadful, and should incite us to examine with an anxious eye the motives and manners of those, whose conduct and opinions seem calculated to forward a similar event in our own country. The oppositionists to "things as they are," are divided into many and different classes. To delineate them with an unflattering accuracy may be a delicate, but it is a necessary Task, in order that we may enlighten, or at least beware of, the misguided Men who have enlisted under the banners of Liberty, from no principles or with bad ones: whether they be those, who

> admire they know not what,
> And know not whom, but as one leads the other:

or whether those,

> Whose end is private Hate, not help to Freedom,
> Adverse and turbulent when she would lead
> To Virtue.[7]

The majority of Democrats appear to me to have attained that portion of knowledge in politics, which Infidels possess in religion. I would by no means be supposed to imply, that the objections of both are equally unfounded, but that they both attribute to the system which they reject, all the evils existing under it; and that both contemplating truth and justice "in the nakedness of abstraction," condemn constitutions and dispensations without having sufficiently examined the natures, circumstances, and capacities of their recipients.

The first Class among the professed Friends of Liberty is composed of Men, who unaccustomed to the labour of thorough investigation, and not particularly oppressed by the Burthen of State, are yet impelled by their feelings to dissapprove of its grosser depravities, and prepared to give an indolent Vote in favour of Reform. Their sensibilities unbraced by the co-operation of fixed Principles, they offer no sacrifices to the divinity of active Virtue. Their political Opinions depend with weather-cock uncertainty on the winds of rumour, that blow from France. On the report of French victories they blaze into Republicanism, at a tale of French excesses they darken into Aristocrats;[8] and seek for shelter among those despicable adherents to fraud and tyranny, who ironically style themselves Constitutionalists. — These *dough-baked Patriots*[9] are not however useless. This oscillation of political opinion will retard the day of Revolution, and it will operate as a preventive to its excesses. Indecisiveness of character, though the effect of timidity, is almost always associated with benevolence.

Wilder features characterize the second class. Sufficiently possessed of natural sense to despise the Priest, and of natural feeling to hate the Oppressor, they listen only to the inflammatory harangues of some mad-headed Enthusiast, and imbibe from them Poison, not Food; Rage, not Liberty. Unillumined by Philosophy, and stimulated to a lust of revenge by aggravated wrongs, they would make the Altar of Freedom stream with blood, while the grass grew in the desolated halls of Justice. These men are the rude materials from which a detestable Minister manufactures conspiracies. Among these men he sends a brood of sly political monsters, in the character of sanguinary Demagogues, and like Satan of old, "the Tempter ere the Accuser,"[10] ensnares a few into Treason, that he may alarm the whole into Slavery. He, who has dark purposes to serve, must use dark means – light would discover, reason would expose him: he must endeavour to shut out both – or if this prove impracticable, make them appear frightful by giving them frightful names: for farther than Names the Vulgar enquire not. Religion and Reason are but poor substitutes for "Church and Constitution;" and the sable-vested Instigators of the

Birmingham riots well knew, that a Syllogism could not disarm a drunken Incendiary of his Firebrand, or a Demonstration *helmet* a Philosopher's head against a Brickbat.[11] But in the principles, which this Apostate has, by his emissaries, sown among a few blind zealots for Freedom, he has digged a pit into which he himself may perhaps be doomed to fall. We contemplate those principles with horror. Yet they possess a kind of wild Justice well calculated to spread them among the grossly ignorant. To unenlightened minds, there are terrible charms in the idea of Retribution, however savagely it be inculcated. The Groans of the Oppressors make fearful yet pleasant music to the ear of him, whose mind is darkness, and into whose soul the iron has entered.

This class, at present, is comparatively small – Yet soon to form an overwhelming majority, unless great and immediate efforts are used to lessen the intolerable grievances of our poorer brethren, and infuse into their sorely wounded hearts the healing qualities of knowledge. For can we wonder that men should want humanity, who want all the circumstances of life that humanize? Can we wonder that with the ignorance of Brutes they should unite their ferocity? peace and comfort be with these! But let us shudder to hear from Men of dissimilar opportunities sentiments of similar revengefulness. The purifying alchemy of Education may transmute the fierceness of an ignorant man into virtuous energy – but what remedy shall we apply to him, whom Plenty has not softened, whom Knowledge has not taught Benevolence? This is one among the many fatal effects which result from the want of fixed principles. Convinced that vice is error, we shall entertain sentiments of Pity for the vicious, not of indignation – and even with respect to that bad Man, to whom we have before alluded, altho' we are now groaning beneath the burthen of his misconduct, we shall harbour no sentiments of Revenge; but rather *condole* with him that his chaotic Iniquities have exhibited such a complication of extravagance, inconsistency, and rashness as may *alarm* him with apprehensions of approaching lunacy!

There are a third class among the friends of Freedom, who possess not the wavering character of the first description, nor the ferocity last delineated. They pursue the interests of Freedom steadily, but with narrow and self-centering views: they anticipate with exultation the abolition of privileged orders, and of Acts that persecute by exclusion from the right of citizenship. They are prepared to join in digging up the rubbish of mouldering Establishments, and stripping off the tawdry pageantry of Governments. Whatever is above them they are most willing to drag down; but every proposed alteration, that would elevate the ranks of our poorer brethren, they regard with suspicious jealousy, as the dreams of the visionary; as if there were any thing in the superiority of Lord to Gentleman, so mortifying in the barrier, so fatal to happiness in the consequences, as the more real distinction of master and servant, of rich man and of poor. Wherein am I made worse by my ennobled neighbour? Do the childish titles of Aristocracy detract from my domestic comforts, or prevent my intellectual acquisitions? But those institutions of Society which should condemn me to the necessity of twelve hours daily toil, would make my *soul* a slave, and sink the *rational* being in the mere animal. It is a mockery of our fellow creatures' wrongs to call them equal in rights, when by the bitter compulsion of their wants we make them inferior to us in all that can soften the heart, or dignify the understanding. Let us not say that this is the work of time – that it is impracticable at present, unless we each in our individual capacities do strenuously and perseveringly endeavour to diffuse among our domestics those comforts and that illumination which far beyond all political ordinances are the true equalizers of men.

We turn with pleasure to the contemplation of that small but glorious band, whom we may truly distinguish by the name of thinking and disinterested Patriots. These are the men who have encouraged the sympathetic passions till they have become irresistible habits, and made their duty a necessary part of their self-interest, by the long-continued cultivation of that moral taste which derives our most exquisite pleasures from the contemplation of possible perfection, and proportionate pain from the perception of existing *depravation*. Accustomed to regard all the affairs of man as a process, they never hurry and they never pause. Theirs is not that twilight of political knowledge which gives us just light enough to place one foot before the other; as they advance the scene still opens upon them, and they press right onward with a vast and various landscape of existence around them. Calmness and energy mark all their actions. Convinced that vice originates not in the man, but in the surrounding circumstances; not in the heart, but in the understanding; he is hopeless concerning no one – to correct a vice or generate a virtuous conduct he pollutes not his hands with the scourge of coercion; but by endeavouring to alter the circumstances would remove, or by strengthening the intellect, disarms, the temptation. The unhappy children of vice and folly, whose tempers are adverse to their own happiness as well as to the happiness of others, will at times awaken a natural pang; but he looks forward with gladdened heart to that glorious period when Justice shall have established the universal fraternity of Love. These soul-ennobling views bestow the virtues which they anticipate. He whose mind is habitually imprest with them soars above the present state of humanity, and may be justly said to dwell in the presence of the Most High . . . .

That general Illumination should precede Revolution, is a truth as obvious, as that the Vessel should be cleansed before we fill it with a pure Liquor. But the mode of diffusing it is not discoverable with equal facility. We certainly should never attempt to make Proselytes by appeals to the *selfish* feelings – and consequently, should plead *for* the Oppressed, not *to* them. The Author of an essay on political Justice considers private Societies as the sphere of real utility – that (each one illuminating those immediately beneath him,) Truth by a gradual descent may at last reach the lowest order.[12] But this is rather plausible than just or practicable. Society as at present constituted does not resemble a chain that ascends in a continuity of Links. – There are three ranks possessing an intercourse with each other: these are well comprized in the superscription of a Perfumer's advertisement which I lately saw – "the Nobility, Gentry, and People of Dress." But alas! between the Parlour and the Kitchen, the Tap and the Coffee-Room – there is a gulph that may not be passed. He would appear to me to have adopted the best as well as the most benevolent mode of diffusing Truth, who uniting the zeal of the Methodist with the views of the Philosopher, should be *personally* among the Poor, and teach them their *Duties* in order that he may render them susceptible of their *Rights*.

Yet by what means can the lower Classes be made to learn their Duties, and urged to practise them? The human Race may perhaps possess the capability of all excellence; and Truth, I doubt not, is omnipotent to a mind already disciplined for its reception; but assuredly the over-worked Labourer, skulking into an Ale-house, is not likely to exemplify the one, or prove the other. In that barbarous tumult of inimical Interests, which the present state of Society exhibits, *Religion* appears to offer the only means universally *efficient*. The perfectness of future Men is indeed a benevolent tenet, and may operate on a few Visionaries, whose studious habits supply them with employment, and seclude them from temptation. But a distant prospect, which we are never to reach, will seldom quicken our footsteps, however lovely it may appear; and a Blessing, which not ourselves but *posterity* are destined to enjoy, will scarcely influence the actions of *any* – still less of the ignorant, the prejudiced, and the selfish.

"Go, preach the GOSPEL to the Poor." By its Simplicity it will meet their comprehension, by its Benevolence soften their affections, by its Precepts it will direct their conduct, by the vastness of its Motives ensure their obedience. The situation of the Poor is perilous . . . . Prudential reasonings will in general be powerless with them . . . . They too, who live *from Hand to Mouth*, will most frequently become improvident. Possessing no *stock* of happiness they eagerly seize the gratifications of the moment, and snatch the froth from the wave as it passes by them. Nor is the desolate state of their families a restraining motive, unsoftened as they are by education, and benumbed into selfishness by the torpedo touch of extreme Want. Domestic affections depend on association. We love an object if, as often as we see or recollect it, an agreeable sensation arises in our minds. But alas! how should *he* glow with the charities of Father and Husband, who gaining scarcely more, than his own necessities demand, must have been accustomed to regard his wife and children, not as the Soothers of finished labour, but as Rivals for the insufficient meal! In a man so circumstanced the Tyranny of the *Present* can be overpowered only by the tenfold mightiness of the *Future*. Religion will cheer his gloom with her promises, and by habituating his mind to anticipate an infinitely great Revolution hereafter, may prepare it even for the sudden reception of a less degree of amelioration in this World.

But if we hope to instruct others, we should familiarize our own minds to some fixed and determinate principles of action. The World is a vast labyrinth, in which almost every one is running a different way, and almost every one manifesting hatred to those who do not run the same way. A few indeed stand motionless, and not seeking to lead themselves or others out of the maze laugh at the failures of their brethren. Yet with little reason: for more grossly than the most bewildered wanderer does *he* err, who never aims to go right. It is more honourable to the Head, as well as to the Heart, to be misled by our eagerness in the pursuit of Truth, than to be safe from blundering by contempt of it. The happiness of Mankind is the *end* of Virtue, and Truth is the Knowledge of the *means*; which he will never seriously attempt to discover, who has not habitually interested himself in the welfare of others. The searcher after Truth must love and be beloved; for general Benevolence is a necessary motive to constancy of pursuit; and this general Benevolence is begotten and rendered permanent by social and domestic affections. Let us beware of that proud Philosophy, which affects to inculcate Philanthropy while it denounces every home-born feeling, by which it is produced and nurtured. The paternal and filial duties discipline the Heart and prepare it for the love of all Mankind. The intensity of private attachments encourages, not prevents, universal Benevolence.[13] The nearer we approach to the Sun, the more intense his heat: yet what corner of the system does he not cheer and vivify?

The Man who would find Truth, must likewise seek it with an humble and simple Heart, otherwise he will be precipitant and overlook it; or he will be prejudiced, and refuse to see it. *To emancipate itself from the Tyranny of Association*,[14] is the most arduous effort of the mind, particularly in Religious and Political disquisitions. The asserter of the system has associated with it the preservation of Order, and public Virtue; the oppugner Imposture, and Wars, and Rapine. Hence, when they dispute, each trembles at the *consequences* of the other's opinions instead of attending to his train of arguments. Of this however we may be certain, whether we be Christians or Infidels, Aristocrats or Republicans, that our minds are in a state unsusceptible of Knowledge, when we feel an eagerness to detect the Falsehood of an Adversary's reasonings, not a sincere wish to discover if there be Truth in them; – when we examine an argument in order that we may answer it, instead of answering because we have examined it.

Our opponents are chiefly successful in confuting the Theory of Freedom by the practices of its Advocates: from our lives they draw the most forcible arguments against our doctrines. Nor have they adopted an unfair mode of reasoning. In a Science the evidence suffers neither diminution or increase from the actions of its professors; but the comparative wisdom of political systems depends necessarily on the manners and capacities of the recipients. Why should all things be thrown into confusion to acquire that liberty which a faction of sensualists and gamblers will neither be able or willing to preserve?

"The simplicity of wants and of pleasures may be taken as the criterion of Patriotism. Would you prove to me your Patriotism? Let me penetrate into the interior of your House. What! I see your antichamber full of insolent Lackies; they give you still those vain Titles, which Liberty treads under foot, and you suffer it and you call yourself a Patriot! I penetrate a little further; – your Ceilings are gilded – magnificent Vases adorn your Chimney-Pieces – I walk upon the richest Carpets – the most costly Wines, the most exquisite Dishes, cover your Table – a crowd of Servants surround it – you treat them with haughtiness; – No! you are not a Patriot. The most consummate pride reigns in your heart, the pride of Birth, of Riches, and of Talents. With this triple pride, a man never sincerely believes the doctrine of Equality: he may repeat its dogmas, but efficient Faith is not in him.". . .[15]

You reply . . . that these luxuries are the employment of industry, and the best means of circulating your property. Be it so. Renounce then the proud pretensions of democracy; do not profess Tenets which it is impossible for you surrounded by all the symbols of superiority to wish realized. But you plead, it seems, for equalization, of *Rights*, not of *Condition*. O mockery! All that can delight the poor man's senses or strengthen his understanding, you preclude; yet with generous condescension you would bid him exclaim "LIBERTY and EQUALITY!" because, forsooth, he should possess the same *Right* to an Hovel which you claim to a Palace. This the Laws have already given. And what more do *you* promise?

A system of fundamental Reform will scarcely be effected by massacres mechanized into Revolution. Yet rejected intreaty leads in its consequences to fierce coercion. And much as we deprecate the event, we have reason to conjecture that throughout all Europe it may not be far distant. The folly of the rulers of mankind grows daily more wild and ruinous: Oppression is grievous – the oppressed feel and are restless. Such things *may* happen. We cannot therefore inculcate on the minds of each other too often or with too great earnestness the necessity of cultivating benevolent affections. We should be cautious how we indulge the feelings even of virtuous indignation. Indignation is the handsome brother of Anger and Hatred. The Temple of Despotism, like that of Tescalipoca, the Mexican Deity, is built of human skulls, and cemented with human blood; – let us beware that we be not transported into revenge while we are levelling the loathsome Pile; lest when we erect the edifice of Freedom we but vary the stile of Architecture, not change the materials. Let us not wantonly offend even the prejudices of our weaker brethren, nor by ill-timed and vehement declarations of opinion excite in them malignant feelings towards us. The energies of mind are wasted in these intemperate effusions. Those materials of projectile force, which now carelessly scattered explode with an offensive and useless noise, directed by wisdom and union might heave Rocks from their base, – or perhaps (dismissing the metaphor) might produce the desired effect without the convulsion.

For this "subdued sobriety" of temper a practical faith in the doctrine of philosophical necessity seems the only preparative. That vice is the effect of error and the offspring of surrounding circumstances, the object therefore of condolence not of anger, is a proposition easily understood, and as easily demonstrated. But to make it spread from the understanding to the affections, to call it into action, not only in the great exertions of Patriotism, but in the daily and hourly occurrences of social life, requires the most watchful attentions of the most energetic mind. It is not enough that we have once swallowed these Truths – we must feed on them, as insects on a leaf, till the whole heart be coloured by their qualities, and shew its food in every the minutest fibre.

Finally, in the Words of an Apostle,

Watch ye! Stand fast in the principles of which ye have been convinced! Quit yourselves like Men! Be strong! Yet let all things be done in the spirit of Love.[16]

Coleridge's hostility to the Established Church is illustrated in the next two extracts. The first is taken from the second part of Conciones ad Populum, *'On the Present War'.*[17] *Coleridge argues that the war with France is unjust because unnecessary. Terrible in its consequences, it could have been avoided by negotiation, but that possibility had been overlooked by the administration, largely because it saw the war as providing an opportunity to destroy the gains of the French Revolution and return France to the yoke of* ancien régime *monarchism. Coleridge treats the Church's support for the war as a sure sign of its corrupt and un-Christian character.*

The second extract is taken from the fifth of the 'Lectures on Revealed Religion'.[18] *It contains Coleridge's views on church establishments and 'priestly' religions. They are identified with the corruption of true Christianity from its original and simple Unitarian form, and this, Coleridge claims, means there is little real difference between the Roman Catholic Church and the Church of England.*

(b) *Conciones ad Populum*: "On the Present War"

. . . If they, who mingled the cup of bitterness, drank its contents, we might look with a calm compassion on the wickedness of great Men. But alas! the storm which they raise, falls heaviest on the unprotected Innocent: and the Cottage of the poor Man is stripped of every Comfort, before the Oppressors, who send forth the mandate of Death, are amerced in one Luxury or one Vice. If a series of calamities succeed each, they deprecate the anger of Heaven by a FAST! – A word that implies, Prayers of Hate to the God of Love – and after these, a Turbot Feast for the rich, and their usual scanty Morsel to the poor, if indeed debarred from their usual labor they can procure even this.[19] But if Victory be the event,

> They o'er the ravag'd Earth,
> As at an Altar wet with human Blood
> And flaming with the Fires of Cities burnt,
> Sing their mad Hymns of Triumph, Hymns to God
> O'er the destruction of his gracious Works,
> Hymns to the Father o'er his slaughter'd Sons![20]

It is recorded in the shuddering hearts of Christians, that while Europe is reeking with Blood, and smoking with unextinguished Fires, in a contest of unexampled crimes and unexampled calamities, every Bishop but one voted for the continuance of the War.[21]

They deemed the fate of their Religion to be involved in the contest! – Not the Religion of Peace, my Brethren, not the Religion of the meek and lowly Jesus, which forbids to his Disciples all alliance with the powers of this World – but the Religion of Mitres and Mysteries, the Religion of Pluralities and Persecution, the Eighteen-Thousand-Pound-a-Year Religion* of Episcopacy. Instead of the Ministers of the Gospel, a Roman might recognize in these Dignitaries the High-priests of Mars – with this difference, that the Ancients fatted their Victims for the Altar, we prepare ours for sacrifice by leanness. . . .

(c) "Lectures on Revealed Religion, Its Corruptions and Political Views": Lecture 5

. . . What a man understands and can with little trouble do for himself, he will not pay another to do for him. We pay Physicians to heal us because we cannot heal ourselves – we fee Lawyers to

* Wherever Men's temporal interests depend on the general belief of disputed tenets, we must expect to find hypocrisy and a persecuting Spirit, a jealousy of investigation, and an endeavour to hold the minds of the people in submissive Ignorance. That pattern of Christian meekness, Bishop Horsley, has declared it to be the vice of the age and government that it has suffered a free and general investigation of the most solemn Truths that regard Society – and there is a remark in the last charge of the disinterested Bishop Prettyman, that the same busy spirit which inclines men to be Unitarians in Religion, drives them into Republicanism in Politics. And truly, the most exalted Forms of Society are cemented and preserved by the purest Notions of Religion. But whatever I may deem of the justice of their Lordships' observations, the prudence and policy of them have gained my immediate assent. Alas! what room would there be for Bishops or for Priests in a Religion where Deity is the only object of Reverence, and our Immortality the only article of Faith – Immortality made probable to us by the Light of Nature, and proved to us by the Resurrection of Jesus. Him the High Priests crucified; but he has left us a Religion, which shall prove fatal to every HIGH PRIEST – a Religion, of which every true Christian is the Priest, his own Heart the Altar, the Universe its Temple, and Errors and Vices its only Sacrifices. Ride on, mighty Jesus! because of thy words of Truth, of Love, and EQUALITY! The age of Priesthood will soon be no more – that of Philosophers and of Christians will succeed, and the torch of Superstition be extinguished for ever. Never, never more shall we behold that generous Loyalty to rank, which is prodigal of its own virtue and its own happiness to invest a few with unholy Splendors; – that subordination of the Heart, which keeps alive the spirit of Servitude amid the empty forms of boasted Liberty! This dear-bought Grace of Cathedrals, this costly defence of Despotism, this nurse of grovelling sentiment and cold-hearted Lip-worship, will be gone – it will be gone, that sensibility to interest, that jealous tenacity of Honors, which suspects in every argument a mortal wound; which inspires Oppression, while it prompts Servility; – which stains indelibly whatever it touches; and under which supple Dullness loses half its shame by wearing a Mitre where reason would have placed a Fool's-Cap. The age of Priesthood will be no more – Peace to its departing spirit! . . .

plead for us, because we do not understand the Law, but the Gospels are so obvious to the meanest Capacity that he who runs may read. He who knows his letters, may find in them everything necessary for him. Alas! he would learn too much, he would learn the rights of Man and the Imposture of Priests, the sovereignty of God, and the usurpation of unauthorized Vice-gerents – his attention must be kept from that dangerous Book – false Translations and lying Interpreters shall misrepresent and pervert it, and in return for the tenth of his Substance the Poor Man shall listen to some lilly-handed Sermonizer who gives him Seneca and Tully in lieu of Christ and St Paul, and substitutes schoolboy scraps stolen from the vain babbling of Pagan Philosophy for the pure precepts of revealed Wisdom – Who would talk to a Usurper on the duties of his situation? His first and indispensable Duty is to vacate it – To Priests we speak not, but it were to be wished that those who are desired by two or three to communicate stated Instruction should confine themselves to the reading and expounding of Scriptures – the Scriptures once understood, every man becomes his own Teacher. But these principles which I hope and trust, begin to spread among true Christians are so obnoxious to our spiritual Noblemen, that Bishop Horsley has declared to his Clergy, that Papists are more their brethren than Protestant Dissenters.[22] God forbid it should be otherwise. He who sees any real difference between the Church of Rome and the Church of England possesses optics which I do not possess – the mark of antichrist is on both of them. Have not both an intimate alliance with the powers of this World, which Jesus positively forbids? Are they not both decked with gold and precious stones? Is there not written on both their Foreheads Mystery! Do they not both SELL the Gospel – Nay, nay, they neither sell, nor is it the Gospel – they forcibly exchange Blasphemy for the first fruits, and snatching the scanty Bread from the poor Man's Mouth they cram their lying Legends down his Throat! The Right Reverend Priest did wisely in recommending to his Clergy a fraternizing spirit. It has been the fashion for the English Church to heap abuses on the Church of Rome and apply to her exclusively the prophetic Title of Babylon, the Mother of Abomination. Dr Horsley has attempted to reform this intemperance, and exclaims in the words of Holy Writ – "Ye be Brethren, fall not out by the Way" – Bishop Hurd in his late Life of Warburton alluding to the controversy between Horsley and the bishop making Arch-heretic observes of the former that he came forth against the enemy of the Church a champion of Orthodoxy clad in impenetrable armour from head to feet.[23] And truly Bishop Horsley did indeed defy the Children of Israel like Goliath, and like Goliath, he was armed in complete Brass! In one of his late works he observes of some Unitarian Pamphlet, that such Doctrines ought to be severely punished. Whosoever shall disbelieve that the Creator of the Universe became a creature, that the omnipresent God abode nine months in the Womb of a Woman, and the impassible Eternal suffered agonies and died on the Cross, whosoever shall disbelieve that The Father is one perfect God, the Son one perfect God, and the Holy Ghost one perfect God, yet that the three perfect Gods are but one Perfect God, and that this aggregated God is no greater than either of its three component parts, whoever shall disbelieve this which is the Catholic Faith, beyond all Doubt, he shall perish everlastingly, and what is of more consequence, by the Statutes of William and Mary yet unrepealed he is guilty of Felony without benefit of Clergy![24]

When Christians had permitted themselves to receive as Gospel the idolatrous doctrine of the Trinity, and the more pernicious dogma of Redemption, it is not wonderful, that an Episcopal Church should be raised, fit superstructure for such foundations!

An idea of Coleridge's early views on the Constitution and system of representation can be gained from The Plot Discovered, *the printed version of a 'Lecture of the Two Bills', given in late November 1795. The Bills in question had been introduced into the House of Lords by Lord Grenville and into the Commons by William Pitt, on 6 and 10 November 1795. Grenville's Bill (the 'Treason Bill') was meant to secure the King and government 'against Treasonable and Seditous Practices and Attempts', while Pitt's Bill (also known as the 'Convention Bill') was designed to prevent seditious meetings and assemblies. These acts widened the definition of treason and sedition to include criticisms of the Constitution, and placed public meetings and the drawing-up of petitions to Parliament under the effective control of local elites, particularly justices of the peace and lords lieutenant of counties. Coleridge shared the widely held view that these Bills would severely restrict liberty of speech, publication and assembly.*

In discussing these Bills Coleridge presents a progressive view of the Constitution. He attacks restrictions on freedom of speech and assembly because they will impede progression towards 'government by the people', and turn the British system of government into a despotism. Coleridge portrays the existing system of representation as corrupt, and argues that the only things that save Britain from despotism at present are those liberties of expression and assembly that are threatened by the two Bills.

(d) *The Plot Discovered; or An Address to the People, against Ministerial Treason*

. . . this clause [of the Treason Bill] is a gross libel on human nature, for it forbids all writings and all speeches that excite hatred or dislike of the Constitution; now the power of exciting hatred or dislike consists in this only, in shewing or appearing to shew that any person or thing is hostile to happiness. To forbid therefore this demonstration, or this attempt to demonstrate, that the Constitution is hostile to the happiness of man, argues (supposing the ministers acted on principle) that they already possess a prior demonstration that this Constitution affords the utmost possible quantity of happiness, the standing point of eternal and omnipresent good. Now if these ministers believe this, namely, that the Constitution as it at present exists is the best possible, they must likewise believe either that there is no God, or if there be a God, that he is not all-powerful or not benevolent. For this said summum bonum as it at present exists, doth evidently prevent little evil and produce much. An omnipotent Devil in a good humour would grant a much better extreme of possible good. But if the present Constitution be progressive, if its only excellence, if its whole endurableness consist in motion; if that which it is be only good as being the step and mode of arriving at something better; if these be truths (and Despotism shall dote on the wretch who dares call them falsehoods,) then are our ministers most unnaturally dwarfing what they dare not at once destroy. As ladies of high rank and sensibility give gin to young dogs, even so are they drenching the Constitution with a poison, to prevent its further growth and keep it a fit plaything for themselves to dandle. . . .

. . . These Bills are levelled against all who excite hatred or contempt of the Constitution and Government: that is, all who endeavour to prove the Constitution and Government defective, corrupt, or fraudulent. (For it has been before observed, that all detection of weakness, imposture, or abuse, necessarily tend to excite hatred or contempt.) Now the Constitution and Government are defective and corrupt, or they are not. If the former, the Bills are iniquitous, since they would *kill off* all who promulge truths necessary to the progression of human happiness: if the latter, (that is, if the Constitution and Government are perfect), the Bills are still iniquitous, for they destroy the sole boundary which divides that Government from Despotism, and *change* that Constitution, from whose present perfectness they derive their only possible justification. In order to prove these assertions, we must briefly examine the British Constitution or mode of Government.

Governments have assumed many different forms; but in their essence and properties, all possible modes of Government are reducible to these three: Government *by* the people, Government *over* the people, and Government *with* the people.

The Government is *by* the people, when the affairs of the whole are directed by all actually present; as among the American Tribes, and (perhaps [note omitted]) in Athens and some other of the ancient Grecian States, or by all *morally* present, that is, where every man is represented, and the representatives act according to instructions. Such, I trust, will be the Government of France. France! whose crimes and miseries posterity will impute to us. France! to whom posterity will impute their virtues and their happiness.

Government *over* the people is known by the name of Despotism, or arbitrary Government: which term does not necessarily imply that one man possesses exclusively the power and direction of the state, for this is no where the case. The Grand Seignior has his

DIVAN;* nor does even the King of Spain dare act in direct opposition to the wishes of the Priests and Grandees; who in *every* country influence the measures of the Government, and partake in its rapine. Despotism is that Government, in which the people at large have no voice in the legislature, and possess no other safe or established mode of political interference: in few words, where the majority are always acted upon, never acting.

The *third* mode is Government *with* the people. This ought to be *progressive* Government ascending from the *second* mode to the first: at least, it is bad or good according to its distance from, or proximity to, the first mode.

The Constitution and Government of Great Britain is evidently not the first mode, that is, a Government *by* the people. They who contend that it is the second mode, will detail from what the people at large are excluded: they, who would prove it to be the third or mixed mode, must point out to what the people are admitted. And for the honour of our country let these have the first hearing. We are astonished (these would say) at the audacity as well as the blindness of men who dare entertain a doubt on this subject. The English Constitution is the freest under heaven: our Liberty suffers restrictions only to acquire steadiness and security. The people by their proxies in the House of Commons, are a check on the nobility, and the nobility a check on the people; while the King is a check on both. The best disciplined people are subject to giddy moments, which will be most effectually resisted by the wisdom of men educated from their infancy for the senatorial office; whose privileges and even prejudices are an antidote against the epidemic disorders of discontent, and thirst of innovation. And what is the King, but the majestic guardian of Freedom, gifted with privileges that will incline, and prerogatives that enable him to prevent the legislative from assuming the executive power: the union of which is one distinguishing feature of tyranny? Such is the Constitution, concerning which it is asked whether or no it be Despotism!!!

Their opponents reply, it is very possible to sketch out an

---

* In reality the Government of Turkey is more free in its forms than the British. They have a Constitution, which determines the rights of the subject and of the Emperor; I mean, the Koran: and they have a grand national council, called the ULAMA, composed of some taken from the people, and of others, the Moulahs, the hereditary Counsellors of the state. If the grand Seignior violate the Constitution, the ULAMA have the right of deposing him: and without a decree of the ULAMA he cannot be deposed.

admirable theory of Government, and then *call* it the British Constitution. A philosopher, who should attack the Popish, or Abyssinian Creeds, would not be satisfied, if in answer to him the defendant should prove the excellence and perfectness of the Gospels. We do not ask what a British Constitution might be, nor what the British Constitution has been, we enquire what it now is. We affirm, that a Government, under which the people at large neither directly or indirectly exercise any sovereignty, is a Despotism. You have asserted that the people act by their proxies in the House of Commons: and Blackstone . . . says, "In England where the people do not debate in a collective body but by representation, the exercise of this sovereignty consists in the choice of representatives.["] If then it can be proved, that the people at large "have proxies," or "debate by representation," or have "the choice of representatives," the question will decide in your favour who assert the British Constitution to be the second or mixed mode of Government.[25] If these points cannot be proved, [the question will decide] in favour of us who suspect it to be a Despotism. Now we are of opinion, not only that such points cannot be made evident, but that the contrary may be demonstrated. The people (you say) exercise a legislative power by proxies, that is, by the majority in the House of Commons. But in the House of Commons three hundred and six are nominated or caused to be returned by one hundred and sixty [two] Peers and Commoners with the Treasury, and three hundred and six are more than a majority: the majority therefore of the House of Commons are the choice, and of course the proxies of the Treasury, and the one hundred and sixty two [note omitted]. Of the rest (that is, the minor number of the House of Commons) some are elected by corporate bodies, others through the undue practices of returning officers, and twenty eight have seats in parliament by *compromises*. And after . . . these are subtracted, with regard to the yet remaining members, it would be an insult to common sense to assert, they are elected by the people at large. The voters are so contemptibly few, that for this reason only they are almost or altogether useless: and from non-residence, taking up of freedoms, complicated rights, &c. &c. their charges for voting are so enormous, that they become worse than useless: since in order to be elected by them many men ruin themselves.[26] And for what? from public spirit? . . . If to all this you add the drunkenness, perjury, and murder that attend a general election, you must draw an unheightened picture which would make every honest man wish that the lesser number of the House of Commons were elected as the majority (or actual legislative power) that is, by the one hundred and sixty two Peers, Gentlemen, and Treasury. The right of election therefore, as it at present exists in England, must be considered not as an exception to Despotism, but as making it more operose and expensive from the increased necessity of corruption. The people at large exercise no sovereignty either personally, or by representation. Such would be the reply of those who might contend that the Government of England is Despotism. The Constitutionalists, those of them, I mean, who condescend to argue, would be forced to allow the truth of this statement: but they would attempt to do away the consequences. "If (they would say) men the most likely by their qualifications to know and promote the public interest, be actually returned to Parliament, it signifies little who return them. We *have* a House of Commons composed of 548 members, in which number are to be found the most considerable Landholders and Merchants of the kingdom; the heads of the Army, the Navy, and the Law; the occupiers of great offices in the State; together with many private individuals eminent by their knowledge, eloquence, or activity. Now if the Country be not safe in such hands, in whose may it confide its interests? If such a number of such men be liable to the influence of corrupt motives, what assembly of men will be secure from the same danger? the different *interests* are actually represented, and of course, the people *virtually*."[27] . . .

Such is Mr. Paley's solution. The plausibility of his reasonings amuses not satisfies the opponents. Struck (they say) with their ingenuity and acuteness, we thence infer that first among the first, the author himself must have detected their fallacy. Charity with unwilling ear half-listens to the report, that the reverent Moralist [note omitted] *cannot afford to keep a conscience.*[28] In whose hands can the public welfare be safely entrusted, if not to the heads of the Army, the Navy, and the Law? men receiving much and expecting more, men who must have cut and squared their notions and feelings to the grand scheme of *getting forward in the world?* to answer one question by another, in whose hands could it be worse intrusted? are not men who are the *servants* of Government out of the house, likely to prove its very convenient *friends* within the house? and *merchants!* has the Archdeacon never heard of *contracts*, and how judiciously they may be distributed![29] and "many individuals eminent by their abilities and eloquence!" that is, in plain language, needy young men of genius are occasionally picked up by one party or the other, presented with a title or a place, and then brought forwards as rhetorical gladiators for the amusement of the good people of England. A prize or two gained at Oxford sometimes proves an excellent advertisement to a young man who wants the lucrative office of an accommodating legislator. With regard to the independent landholders, they are indeed indepen- dent of the people. Their honesty is therefore an *accident*, and must not be admitted into calculation. When it occurs, it may ameliorate our service, but (unless the mode of representation be improved) it cannot make us freemen; I mean, that although it may occasionally procure good laws, it cannot secure to us the permanence of them. It is security which distinguishes liberty from a virtuous Despotism: and this security never exists unless when the legislative power is in the hands of those, whose worldly self-interests manifestly preponderate in favour of the incorrupt use of it. It has indeed been affirmed, that we are secure with the wealthy: since in impoverishing their Country they must injure themselves most of all, and that their wealth lifts them above the reach of temptation. We might quote in answer every page of the history of England for these last hundred years: but supposing the assertion not to have been confuted by facts, we yet deny the probability of it. For first, the taxes are not levied in equal proportions, so that without directly injuring himself a legislator may vote away the pittance of the poor: secondly, where the actual, efficient, independent legislators are so few, and the revenues of Government so immense, the administration can always put into a great man's pocket incalculably more than they take from his estate: thirdly, his wealth so far from lifting him above temptation exposes him to it. A man of large fortune lives in a splendour and luxury, which long habit makes him consider essential to happiness. He has perhaps a number of children, all of whom share his affection equally. He wishes that *all* his children should continue to live in the stile in which they have been brought up, but by the law of primogeniture the eldest only will possess the means of so doing. Hence, he seeks fortunes for the rest in the enormous patronage of the crown. A man of moderate wealth is not exposed to this temptation. His rank does not make industry disgraceful, and by industry all his children may be as well off as their father. Besides (though we would not dispeople St. Stephen's by such an exclusion-Bill [note omitted], as was passed in the days of Cromwell) yet while gaming is so much the rage, no man can be safely called wealthy, or supposed to be armed against temptation. Thus the actual possessors of power are few, and independent of the people: which is Despotism. And the manners of the Great are depraved, the sources of corruption incalculable, and consequently the temptations to private and public wickedness numerous and mighty: all which unite in precluding the probability of its proving a *virtuous* Despotism.

Hitherto nothing has been adduced that truly distinguishes our Government from Despotism: it seems to be a Government *over*, not *by*, or *with* people. But this conclusion we disavow. The Liberty of the Press, (a power resident in the people) gives us an *influential* sovereignty. By books necessary information may be dispersed; and by information the public will may be formed; and by the right of petitioning that will may be expressed; first, perhaps, in low and distant tones such as beseem the children of peace; but if corruption deafen power, gradually increasing till they swell into a deep and awful thunder, the VOICE OF GOD, which his vicegerants must hear, and hearing dare not disobey. This unrestricted right of over-awing the Oligarchy of Parliament by constitutional expression of the general will forms our liberty: it is the sole boundary that divides us from Despotism. . . .

By the almost winged communication of the Press, the whole nation becomes one grand Senate, fervent yet untumultuous. By the right of meeting together to petition (which, Milton says, is good old english for *requiring*[30]) the determinations of this Senate are embodied into legal form, and conveyed to the *executive* branch of Government, the Parliament. The present Bills annihilate this right. The *forms* of it indeed will remain; (the *forms* of the Roman republic were preserved under Tiberius and Nero) but the reality will have flown. No political information from the Press can previously enlighten the people; and if they meet, the deliberation must be engrossed by the hireling defenders of that scheme of cruelty and imposture, which the ministry chuse to call our Constitution. We can no longer consult in common on common grievances. Our assemblies will resemble a silent and sullen mob of discontented slaves who have surrounded the palace of some eastern tyrant. By the operation of Lord Grenville's Bill, the Press is made useless. Every town is insulated: the vast conductors are destroyed by the which the electric fluid of truth was conveyed from man to man, and nation to nation. A French Gentleman in

the reign of Lewis the fourteenth was comparing the French and
English writers with all the boastfulness of national prepossession.
Monsieur (replied an Englishman better versed in the principles
of freedoms than the canons of criticism) there are but two subjects
worthy the human intellect – Politics and Religion, our state
here, and our state hereafter: and on neither of these *dare* you
write! This spirited reproof may now be retorted on us. By Mr.
Pitt's Bill Britons are allowed to petition – with Justices of Peace at
their elbow! Justices of Peace invested with absolute censorial
power over the individuals, and the chance-right of military
domination over the assembly. British Liberty leaves her cell by
permission, and walks abroad to take the air between two jailors;
fettered, and handcuffed, and with a gagg in her mouth!!!

There are four things, which being combined constitute Despotism. 1. The confusion of the executive and legislative branches. 2.
The direct or indirect exclusion of all popular interference. 3. A
large military force kept separate from the people. 4. When the
punishments of state-offenders are determined and heavy, but
what constitutes state-offences left indefinite, that is, dependent
on the will of the minister, or the interpretation of the Judge. Let
the present Bills pass, and these four things will be *all* found in
the British Government. 1. By the enormous patronage of the
crown and the depravity of manners among the great, by the
immensity of the powers of corruption and the fewness of the
persons to be corrupted, the executive branch is actually the
legislative. 2. The Liberty of the Press abolished, and the right of
free discussion in petitioning assemblies, the people of Britain
will possess no greater controul over their governors than the
inhabitants in Russia. 3. A vast military force is maintained
throughout the kingdom for the purpose of intimidating the
disaffected; and that the soldiers may become in their notions and
feelings a body distinct from citizens they are placed in barracks,
instead of the constitutional mode of scattering them among their
countrymen. . . . 4. The Treason and Sedition Bills are so framed,
that they include all men who recommend reform by the only
possible mode of recommendation, the detection of a defectiveness
in our Constitution, and of iniquity and abuse in our Government.
The selection of particular persons for punishment depends entirely
on the minister. The Bills are a vast aviary, and all the honest are
incaged within it. . . .

2

The Retreat from Radicalism, 1798–1802

By late 1799 Coleridge had abandoned the radical reformist perspective that had been a feature of his early political writings. A growing hostility to France, resulting, by 1802, in support for war, and a determination to dissociate himself from oppositional and reformist politics in England, were practical results of Coleridge's reorientation. Early indications of Coleridge's changing perspective appeared in 1798. In March 1798 he admitted privately to his brother George that he regretted his association with democrats and radicals and that he had abandoned his earlier flirtation with anarchism.

(a) The Limitations of Political Change (letter of 1798)[1]

. . . I collect from your letter, that our opinions and feelings on political subjects are more nearly alike, than you imagine them to be. Equally with you . . . I deprecate the moral & intellectual habits of those men both in England & France, who have modestly assumed to themselves the exclusive title of Philosophers & Friends of Freedom. I think them at least *as* distant from greatness as from goodness. If I know my own opinions, they are utterly untainted with French Metaphysics, French Politics, French Ethics, & French Theology. – As to THE RULERS of France, I see in their views, speeches, & actions nothing that distinguishes them to their advantage from other animals of the same species. History has taught me, that RULERS are much the same in all ages & under all forms of government: they are as bad as they dare to be. The Vanity of Ruin & the curse of Blindness have clung to them, like an hereditary Leprosy. Of the French Revolution I can give my thoughts the most adequately in the words of Scripture – "A great & strong wind rent the mountains & brake in pieces the rocks *before* the Lord; but the Lord was not in the wind; and after the wind an earthquake; but the Lord was not in the earthquake: and after the earthquake a Fire – & the Lord was not in the fire:" and now (believing that no calamities are permitted but as the means of Good) I wrap my face in my mantle & wait with a subdued & patient thought, expecting to hear "the still small Voice,"[2] which is of God. – In America . . . the morals & domestic habits of the people are daily deteriorating: & one good consequence which I expect from revolutions, is that Individuals will see the necessity of individual effort; that they will act as kind neighbours & good Christians, rather than as citizens & electors; and so by degrees will purge off that error . . . of attributing to Governments a talismanic influence over our virtues & our happiness – as if Governments were not rather effects than causes. . . . Do not therefore, my Brother! consider me as an enemy to Governments & Rulers: or as one who say[s] that they are evil. I do not say so – in my opinion it were a species of blasphemy. Shall a nation of Drunkards presume to babble against sickness & the head-ach? – I regard Governments as I regard the abscesses produced by certain fevers – they are necessary consequences of the disease, & by their pain they increase the disease; but yet they are in the wisdom & goodness of Nature; & not only are they physically necessary as effects, but also as causes they are *morally* necessary in order to prevent the utter dissolution of the patient. But what should we think of the man who expected an absolute *cure* from an ulcer that only prevented his dying? – Of GUILT I say nothing; but I believe most stedfastly in original Sin; that from our mothers' wombs our understandings are darkened; and even where our understandings are in the Light, that our organization is depraved, & our volitions imperfect; and we sometimes see the good without *wishing* to attain it, and oftener *wish* it without the energy that wills & performs – And for this inherent depravity, I believe, that the *Spirit* of the Gospel is the sole cure – but permit me to add, that I look for the *spirit* of the Gospel "neither in the mountain, nor at Jerusalem" [John 4] –

You think, my Brother! that there can be but two *parties* at present, for the Government & against the Government – It may be so – I am of no party. It is true, I think the present ministry weak & perhaps unprincipled men; but I could not with a safe conscience vote for their removal; for I could point out no substitutes. I think very seldom on the subject; but as far as I have thought, I am inclined to consider the Aristocrats as the more respectable of our three factions, because they are more decorous. The Opposition & the Democrats are not only vicious – they wear the *filthy garments* of vice. . . . I am prepared to suffer without discontent the consequences of my follies & mistakes –: and unable to conceive how that which I am, of Good could have been without that which I have been of Evil, it is withheld from me to regret any thing: I therefore consent to be deemed a Democrat & a Seditionist. A man's character follows him long after he has ceased to deserve it – but I have snapped my squeaking baby-trumpet of Sedition & the fragments lie scattered in the lumber-room of Penitence. I wish to be a good man & a Christian – but I am no Whig, no Reformist, no Republican – and because of the multitude of these fiery & undisciplined spirits that lie in wait against the public Quiet under these titles, because of them I chiefly accuse the present ministers – to whose folly I attribute, in great measure, their increased & increasing numbers. . . .

In 'Recantation', *originally published in the* Morning Post *in April 1798*,[3] *Coleridge reacted strongly against the French invasion of Switzerland and regretted his previous identification of France and liberty.*

(b) "Recantation" (poem of 1798)

. . . When France in wrath her giant-limbs up-reared,
    And with that oath, which smote earth, air, and sea,
    Stamp'd her strong feet and said she would be free,
Bear witness for me, how I hoped and fear'd!
With what a joy my lofty gratulation
    Unawed I sung, amid a slavish band:
And when to whelm the disenchanted nation,
    Like fiends embattled by a wizard's wand,
      The Monarchs march'd in evil day,
      And Britain join'd the dire array;
    Though dear her shores and circling ocean,
Though many friendships, many youthful loves,
    Had swoln the patriot emotion,
And flung a magic light o'er all her hills and groves;
Yet still my voice, unalter'd, sang defeat
    To all that braved the tyrant-quelling lance,
And shame too long delay'd and vain retreat!
For ne'er, O Liberty! with partial aim
I dimm'd thy light or damp'd thy holy flame;
    But bless'd the pæans of deliver'd France,
And hung my head and wept at Britain's name. . . .

Forgive me, Freedom! O forgive those dreams!
    I hear thy voice, I hear thy loud lament,
    From bleak Helvetia's icy caverns sent –
I hear thy groans upon her blood-stain'd streams!
    Heroes, that for your peaceful country perish'd,
And ye that fleeing spot the mountain-snows
    With bleeding wounds; forgive me, that I cherish'd
One thought that ever bless'd your cruel foes!
    To scatter rage and traitorous guilt,
Where Peace her jealous home had built;
    A patriot-race to disinherit

Of all that made their stormy wilds so dear;
   And with inexpiable spirit
To taint the bloodless freedom of the mountaineer –
O France, that mockest Heaven, adulterous, blind,
   And patriot only in pernicious toils!
Was this thy boast, Champion of human kind?
   To mix with Kings in the low lust of sway,
Yell in the hunt, and share the murderous prey;
To insult the shrine of Liberty with spoils
   From freemen torn; to tempt and to betray?

*Coleridge's shifting allegiances were formulated in a series of statements identifying
the virtues of institutions which he had formerly regarded with a very jaundiced
eye. He was no longer interested in tailoring political institutions to an egalitarian
model, but claimed that they should reflect the underlying social structure and
distribution of property.*

*The following extracts are intended to chart the main steps in Coleridge's attempt
to identify how public and private freedom can be protected in situations where
property, social status and political power are very unevenly distributed. Coleridge
argues that in these circumstances institutions and practices found in countries
such as England can be beneficial. The Constitution, traditional social structures
based on landed property, and an established church all play a role in preserving
freedom; societies, such as revolutionary France, which wilfully destroy these, will
become unfree and despotic.*

*The first clear sign of Coleridge's changing perspective appeared in a series of
critical articles on the French Constitution of 1799 (the 'Constitution of the Year
VIII').*[4] *In the first of these, Coleridge's concern is with the corruption of the
electorate, but as he acquired more information on the details of the new constitution
he stressed the pernicious consequences of its failure to recognise the legitimate
interests of property. It made wealth a product of political office rather than a
prerequisite for it, but allowed the direct and corrupt intrusion of wealth into a
system in which elected and appointed office-holders were merely instruments of a
military dictator.*

(c) "On the French Constitution" (*Morning Post*, 1799)

I

. . . The prejudices of superstition, birth, and hereditary right,
have been gradually declining during the four last centuries, and
the empire of property as gradually establishing itself in their
stead. Whether or no this too will not in a distant age submit to
some more powerful principle, is, indeed, a subject fruitful in *dreams*
to poetic philosophers, who amuse themselves with reasonings on
unknown quantities; but to all present purposes it is a useless and
impertinent speculation. For the present race of men Governments
must be founded on property; that *Government is good in which
property is secure and circulates;* that *Government the best, which, in the
exactest ratio, makes each man's power proportionate to his property.* In
America, where the great mass of the people possess property,
and where, by the exertion of industry, any man may possess it
in its most permanent form, this principle may, perhaps, co-exist
with universal suffrage; but not so in old and populous countries,

in which land is of high value, and where the produce of individual labour can hardly be large enough to admit of considerable accumulation. Artificial power must be here balanced against physical power; and when the physical strength of a nation is in the poor, the Government must be in the hands of the rich.

These truths appear to have determined the present ruling faction in France, in the production of the new Constitution. In England, power is taken from the multitude by absolute exclusion and legal incompetency; in France, the statesmen are endeavouring to realise the same effect more *complaisantly*, by a system of *filtration*; for in this view only is the new Constitution intelligible. The original motion is, indeed, to be given to the people; but is modified so often by so many after impulses, that it is at last wholly swallowed up and lost. The multitude only throw in the shuttlecock; the rich men hold the battledores, and play the game, till in its due time the shuttlecock once more falls to the ground, and once again the multitude perform the same most *important* office! If this were possible, and if it had been well planned, we should have been foremost to have given it the suffrage of our approbation, as a system which stole away the artificial powers of the State from those who already possessed the physical strength, without, however, tearing from them the soothing idea of self-importance. But to us it appears that the whole merit of the new Constitution consists in its general intention; the execution is most miserable. . . .

We will subject it to a detailed examination. France, it seems, is to be divided into twenty-five prefectures, which are to be subdivided into cantons and districts. The inhabitants of these, in order to become active citizens, must pay twelve days' wages. If it were expected that the labouring poor would really, from pure patriotism, and out of their own purses, pay this purchase-money, it were, indeed, a cruel and detestable tax. But we presume that it is hoped that a multitude will be thus excluded, and the others will be paid for by richer men; and thus the people rendered either inert, or subjected to the influence of the wealthy. Had Sieyès[5] been anxious to introduce a system of corruption among his fellow-citizens, it were not easy to conceive a more happy expedient. At the moment of a general election, will the vanity of a Frenchman suffer him to remain a mere looker-on? He will give his vote for pay, rather than declare his insignificance, by not giving his vote. If for a moment we dismiss this fear of bribery and *clientism*, if the rich should not buy up the suffrages of the poor, what can be the result but turbulence and sedition? To pay the thirtieth part of their income to the privilege of giving a single vote, is an oppressive burthen; not to give their votes an intolerable exclusion; and thus the very first process of the Constitution creates a whole class of enemies to it. The power is offered to them only the more insultingly to make them feel their impotence.

This we consider as applicable only to these times of agitation, when faction, novelty, terror, and extravagant hope, suffer no part of the French community to remain purely passive. . . . In peaceable aeras it does not need the repressing influence of a contribution to preserve the mass of legal voters in their natural inertness: the sole effect were this, that the same evil would be realized in France, which England sees in its pot-boiling Boroughs. – Votes would be collected for the wealthy indeed, but only as far as they employed their wealth to the production of perjury and debauchery in the minds of those, whose morals are of more especial importance to the well-being of society.

So much for the ground work of the new Constitution. We must next suppose these active citizens met in the principal town of their canton, in order to reduce themselves to an hundred, and this hundred met once more to reduce themselves to ten. . . . Those who know some of the boroughs of England will best estimate the consequences of a contested election on the morals of the voters. If it be found that habits of intoxication and proneness to riot have adhered to such places; if aversion from regular industry have distinguished the lower classes, and hereditary feuds the higher, and all this in a dispute whether A or B, with whose persons and characters a vast majority of the voters were utterly unacquainted, should deliver in to the Minister his yea, yea, and no word beside; if this be the result with us, in a people comparatively phlegmatic, and on an occasion almost ridiculously unimportant; what may we not anticipate of a contest in France, in which all the voters *may be* and many *must be*, at once voters and candidates. . . .

The division of the Legislature into the Senate and Tribunate, the latter for the purposes of discussion, the former invested with the power of decision, seems to have a mingled tendency. A Legislature of silent listeners may probably pass laws with greater calmness, and more prospective wisdom, than a body of men perpetually heated by disputation; for every man is in some measure prejudiced in favour of arguments which he himself has adduced. And even [the circumstance] of their voting by ballot may, to a certain degree, prove preventive of faction. But, on the other hand, the individuals that compose it are too much withdrawn from that best and most salutary species of *ephorism*,[6] the opinion of the public; and the public speakers are degraded into mere advocates, the certain effect of which will be, to take all majesty from their eloquence, and thus injure and mutilate the most impressive organ of national instruction. Public speaking is far, very far, from the meanest or least important utility of a Legislature. The debates of the House of Commons have educated the people of England in the science of politics more widely and fundamentally than all the works of all our writers.

 . . . One error appears to us to pervade the whole, viz. the assumption, that checks and counter-checks can be produced in Legislative Bodies, merely by division of chambers and diversity of titles, where no real difference of interest exists in the Legislative, as individuals, except that transient one arising from their functions. . . .

II

From the article in our yesterday's paper our readers have learnt that the new Constitution will be solemnly presented to the whole French Nation, for their acceptance or rejection. . . . The whole people, without exception, are called upon to judge, and of course supposed capable of judging, upon a Constitution complex almost to entanglement; a thing of checks and counter-checks, that might almost seem intentionally formed to exhibit a metaphysical posture-master's dexterity in *balancing*. The whole people, without exception (both those who *can* sign their votes, and those who must "cause them to be signed"), are called upon to judge upon a Constitution, as momentous as it is intricate; a Constitution, . . . whose prime, leading, and fundamental principle it is, that the great mass of the nation have just virtue and wisdom enough to choose their *Constables*, and no more!

By this appeal to the universal suffrage, the sovereignty of the people is admitted in its widest extent; and the people are called upon to exercise it, as the suicide exercises his power over life, only to destroy it for ever. The indefeasible validity of *personal* rights is thus expressed as fully as the wildest Democracy could vote it; by a Constitution as Oligarchic as ever that of Venice was, and which pronounces the people at large a foul and unwholesome element, unfit to be employed in the simplest offices, without long process of filtration. But this, however, we may, perhaps, pass over, as a Courtly grimace to amuse the Half-Jacobins; an act of pure tenderness to the genius of Democracy, now on its death-bed; and it would be too rigorous to expect consistency in a mere compliment. . . .

This production of the Abbe's political science, in our humble opinion, carries with it few marks of wisdom; though it is strongly featured with cunning and personal ambition; yet it has such an imposing air of novelty, that we feel ourselves puzzled and perplexed, from what point we should first survey it. In countries where the favour of an hereditary Monarch, to whom obedience is secured by superstition, forms the predominating impulse of the State, we may expect to find a sense of honour, and all the dubious virtues that flow from pride tempered by chivalrous courtesies; in a Democracy, in which the continuance in the great public functions is short, and the elections depend immediately on the esteem and affections of the people, we might hope to meet with all that is graceful, shewy, and energetic in genius and intellect; and while we believe such a state in its nature impermanent and unadapted to man, we are compelled to admit, that while it lasted it would be a *hot-bed* for individual talent and occasional heroism; in a Government founded in property, and in a nation among whom property was the ruling spirit, we might look with confidence for active industry, attachment to law and order, and aversion from innovation. We are fortunate enough to live in a country in which, with all its defects, the national character is made up, though in different quantities, by all these three principles, the influence of a Court, the popular spirit, and the predominance of property. We find ourselves of course disposed to hail with astonishment, . . . a Constitution, in which all Legislative Functions are places of Government, Legislature itself a lucrative profession, and prefer-ment in it to be expected neither from the honorary favour of an hereditary Monarch, or from the privileges of rank, or the influence of property, or from popular favour; but, as it should seem, by secret intrigue in the palace of a military Dictator, or in the different Courts of the great all electing conservatory Senators, who are themselves that which they are by a species of organization, almost as mysterious as that of mushrooms and funguses. For who are to elect the Senate? Not the people, whose power of acquiescence we have shown to be a mere trick of French politeness – but the Committees! And who elected the Committees? Sieyès and Buon-aparte. And here we must pause – we can rise no higher in this system of causation. These are self-elected – the power and the wisdom of France impersonated in an Abbe and a Commander in Chief. . . .

III

. . . Our readers have learnt, that the candidates for all offices, national, departmental, and those of the sub-departments, are to be gradually obtained by a series of honourable *decimations*.[7] . . . We believed, and we still continue to believe, that such an arrangement must necessarily tend to exasperate those *political* agitations, so inseparable from important elections, by the super-addition of violent *personal* passions. If this has been proved to have been the case in the Primary Assemblies under the former Constitutions, if those were found to generate and diffuse the spirit of intrigue, and the disposition to innovation, the argument of course applies three fold against the present Constitution; – a Constitution, too, which makes such enormous sacrifices to the wish of producing stability and preventing innovation.

In favour of this arrangement it may be said, that it confirms and realizes two opposite advantages, and both of the highest importance. It takes from the people the all-unsettling power of acting from immediate and momentary impulses, while, at the same time, by the stimulation of hope, and the sense of personal self-importance, it impels every individual to be a *Citizen*, suffers no man to remain dead to the public interest, and thus elevates the selfish into a social principle, without detriment to social peace. And truly, if (after the process of *filtration* had been completed) the persons thus chosen by the electing assemblies to be the candidates for the different functions, were once again presented to the people, and finally appointed by their individual votes, collected *without assemblage*, we should admit this to be an important improvement on the system of universal suffrage, and perhaps the best possible form of a representative system, not expressly founded on property. But the Conservatory Senate makes the final election; a circumstance which not only alters, but absolutely reverses the effect. To have been chosen by our fellow citizens and neighbours as a good and prudent man, and again re-chosen by them as best and wisest among the good and prudent, this were indeed a noble aim for the noblest ambition! But to receive a legislative appointment from a Senate of eighty Nobles, from a body excluded equally by its *paucity* and its *privileges* from all acquaintance and fellow-feeling with the competitors or their constituents; this none but intriguers could hope for, this no honest pride, no honourable ambition would desire.

A Constitution founded on such a basis seems to possess the unfortunate prerogative of combining the injustice of the most absolute with more than the insecurity of the most popular Governments. The despotisms of the world have hitherto endeavoured to keep their subjects in inaction; they excite few hopes, and have therefore little to fear from the resentments of disappointment. In a Democracy every man may hope and struggle; but if he be disappointed, he must waste his anger on his rivals: for anger towards a populace is too ridiculous a thing to be often indulged, and, when indulged, too impotent to be dreaded; but a cabal of eighty Nobles is a fair and palpable object of hatred; a conspicuous target, to which the poorest aims may direct a successful shaft. In a nation of twenty-five millions, a nation characteristically enthusiastic and volatile, such a body must, and indeed ought to, become an object of jealousy and suspicion; and at every election may create such enemies, not only nine-tenths of the competitors (supposed the flower and pride of wealth or talent), but likewise all of the people who had wished or expected the choice to have fallen differently from the real event. The only argument, therefore, from which the justice or policy of such an order could deduce a shadow of justification, is fairly adducible against it; for from the common instincts of human nature, it militates against that permanence and security from change, to which alone it can appeal, as a sufficient reason for its existence.

A respectable Morning Paper[8] has observed, that "the present plan, by which the Representative System is consecrated, narrows excessively the exercise of the Right of Election." We should have chosen to express ourselves otherwise: we should have said – "the present plan, by which the Representative System is secretly assassinated, wholly takes away from the people the exercise of the *Power* of Election, while most absurdly, or jesuitically, it pretends to admit the *Right*." A Senate elected by Buonaparte and Sieyès can only be considered as the accomplices of Buonaparte and Sieyès. We are justified, therefore, in considering the Executive Government and the Senate as one and the same body. . . . The whole process of popular election is therefore a mere trick – a miserable masquerade domino, to throw around the nakedness of despotism.

The same respectable paper asserts, that "without providing in words, that property shall have exclusive advantages in the new *scheme*, it secures the fact". . . . Consistently with the talent and good sense, which in general pervade the opinions of our fellow-journalist, we are unable to understand this otherwise than as a trope of irony. Whom may these high-pensioned eighty nobles select, but their own creatures? For surely the writer did not assume disinterestedness and clear-sighted patriotism, as postulates and axioms – ideas involved in the very notion of a self-elected, self-perpetuating senate of eighty nobles? If indeed the legislative and judicial functions become marketable articles, the richest man will of course be the buyer, provided they will return good interest for the money; and the rich man, without talent, pride, or principle, can consent to receive his absolute creators for his unconditional masters. . . . It appears to us that the men of property will be too wise to buy, at any heavy sum, places in a silent legislature, empowered only to decide on laws proposed to them by a Commander in Chief; their very decisions too annulable by the Senate, their creators. The men of property will rather buy laws of the Government *in prospectu*, and needy men will hire themselves as the mechanic-legislators, necessary in this business of Law-making to the Government, only as the bellows-blower is to the organist. The work *must* be done; but any fellow may do it.

The whole first chapter of the Constitution we do indeed consider as the mere ornamental outworks of a military despotism. No real power is left to the people.

. . .[T]he Government of France is to be an oligarchy, supported, and only supportable, by the military, who are therefore placed entirely and absolutely under the command of the Chief Consul, Buonaparte; all which follows we regard as mere theatrical evolutions of a figure dance. . . .

IV

. . . The general detection of this gross imposture required little penetration; but in the more wearisome task of exposing the detail and minutiae, we may fairly lay claim to some degree of that patience, which we are obliged to solicit from our readers. The fourth article of the first chapter declares the right of Citizenship forfeited, by affiliation with any foreign body, which supposes distinctions of birth. The second chapter begins by constituting, in effect, such a body in France; for it constitutes eighty unremovable Senators, privileged to fill up their own vacancies[;] . . . these Nobles for life would, if the order continued long enough, become in reality, if not in name, *hereditary* Nobles. . . .

It is not here the place to discuss the advantages or disadvantages of privileged orders. Our Nobles in England, from the largeness of their landed estates, have an important stake in the immediate prosperity of their country; and, from the antiquity of their families, may be reasonably presumed likely to associate with a more deeply-rooted and partial affection. By the more delicate superstition of ancestry they counteracted in former ages, and to a certain degree still counteract, the grosser superstition of wealth.[9] Let us not forget too, that by occasion of their younger children they were the original founders of an order of Gentlemen among us, into which order a liberal education and polished manners have at length the privilege of incorporating any man, whatever his parental rank might have been: and thus, by the introduction of a greater *social* equality among us, they more than compensate to us for their *political* superiority. Meantime their Legislative capacity, which gives them dignity and public usefulness, excites no jealousy in the people, their power and *direct* influence being constitutionally less than that of the popular and representative branch. Of the Conservative Senators the number is not large enough to affect in any degree the manners of society; nor is it provided that they should be men of property; nor can the people possibly attach to their rank and origin those associations of splendid or venerable, which necessarily hang round a feudal nobility: meantime, in their political capacity, they are then only not idle when they exercise an enormous power, and that too robbed from the people, of whom exclusively it is the rightful attribute – the power of election. Still had eighty senators, so privileged, been nominated by the whole nation, if they had been selected and chosen by the free votes of their fellow-citizens, however pernicious the institution might be, yet the individuals would doubtless have possessed an origin at least as honourable, as the most adulatory herald dares attach to the most ancient nobility. But *these*, the creatures of a renegade Priest, himself the creature of a foreign mercenary – these, the stones which Buonaparte, the Deucalion of this new inundation, found beneath his feet, and flinging them behind him metamorphosed into senators – what but fear, mingled with scorn, can attach to *these*? – But if their good or kind auspices are undiscoverable, not so their evil influences. To secure to their own relatives places of honour and emolument, each Senator becomes at once an intriguer, and a centre of intrigues: he to the Government, the Government to him, and all to each other. . . .

It were wasting our readers' attention to direct it particularly to the other branches of the Legislature, the hundred Tribunes who are to talk and do nothing, and the three hundred Legislators whom the Constitution orders to be silent. What a ludicrous purgatory for three hundred Frenchmen! The shamelessness of calling that a Legislature which can neither propose nor reason, and whose acts are annullable *ad arbitrium*, can only be equalled by the exquisite absurdity involved in the very notion of splitting the intellectual faculties, and subdividing the business of Thought, almost as curiously as that of a pin manufactory. However, all these different law-manufacturers are well salaried; yet not so as to place them out of the temptation of corruption. Even the Chief Consul must find it necessary to bribe high to secure his re-election, by influence, by promises, and not improbably by taking the pay of foreign Governments. Indeed, never was a Government framed which lay so open to corruption, both in itself, and from external powers! There exists no appearance of a preventive, in a nominal Legislature, for which no property is requisite, in which no talent can be exerted, and where no popularity can be gained. The whole Constitution betrays a rooted contempt of the people, and a distrust of human virtue in general, yet leaves to none, whom it invests with power, any of those common assistants to well doing which the most virtuous man does not profess to deem useless. It has indeed divisions and sub-divisions even to superfluity; but how, under any circumstances these could be a check on each other, or on the Consulate, no where appears. It is indeed mere fraud and mockery. Checks and counterpoises can only be produced by real diversity of interests, of interests existing independent of legislative functions; but these chambers are all alike filled with the creatures of the Dictator, by him chosen, feeding on his stipends, and acting under his controul. But it cannot last: for to what body of men or species of interest can it appeal for love or protection? The property, the talent, the popular spirit, the prejudices of the Royalist, the Priest, and the Jacobin, are all injured, insulted, trodden under foot by it. And what are idle promises of individual liberty in a Constitution which recognizes in the Chief Consul the right of suspending it *ad arbitrium*, and which does not recognize in the nation that which is worth a thousand Tribunates, that without which no nation can be free or happy under the wisest Government, the LIBERTY OF THE PRESS?[10]

Coleridge's analysis of the French Constitution was complemented by a series of articles which point to the social value of property in general, and of landed property in particular. These articles compare early imperial Rome with France under the Consulate.[11] In the course of an argument showing that France's polyglot empire is a burden to both her and her subjects, Coleridge discusses the social and psychological benefits of a landed class, the role of deference in maintaining non-coercive social relationships, and the importance of ties of language, locality and history in forming the basis for social interaction.

(d) "Comparison of the Present State of France with that of Rome under Julius and Augustus Caesar" (*Morning Post*, 1802)

I

As human nature is the same in all ages, similar events will of course take place under similar circumstances; but sometimes names will run parallel, and produce the appearance of a similarity, which does not really exist. Indeed, it is generally observable that the instances in which the names run the most parallel, are not those that will best stand the tests of inspection and analysis. An examination, however, should always be instituted. We discover something well worth the trouble employed, if we do no more than detect a common source of fallacy, more especially when there is reason to suspect that this coincidence of names has been adopted by design, and for political purposes. The least attentive observer of the political world cannot but have noticed the solicitude of the French Government to represent their country as a new Roman Republic. France has its Consuls, its Tribunes, its Senate, its Proconsular Provinces, its dependent Free States and Allies, its obedient Kings. In a recent instance it has attempted to force its language upon Europe, as a general language of state, as the successor and substitute of the language of the former masters of mankind. . . . In the same spirit, too, the finest parts of Europe have been pillaged in order to convert Paris into a new Rome, a metropolis of the civilized world, of this one great European nation; and the books, statues, and pictures of Italy have undergone the same fate from the French conquerors, which those of Greece formerly experienced under the Italian.* As

---

* Even in the circumstance of *imitation*, the parallel holds good. For if the French are imitating the Romans, it is equally as certain that the Romans imitated the Greek; and that Caesar, Pompey, and their predecessors, acted on the plans of

far as the ambition and ambitious designs of the two empires are concerned, we must confess the resemblance is strict and real, the analogy in all its parts exact.

If we inquire, to what period of the Roman history the present history of France assimilates itself, the answer may prove unpleasant to the new Roman Republic; but it is not the less true. If it resemble any period at all, it must be that when Rome ceased to be a Republic, and the Government was organized into a masked and military despotism (a despotism with a frightful half-mask on its face), when the sovereign power was repeatedly and ostentatiously affirmed to reside in the people, but the right of exercising it suspended for ever, when the popular elections were transferred to a trembling Senate, and all the powers of Consul, Tribune, and Generalissimo, centered in one person. Here indeed the points of apparent resemblance are sufficiently obvious. And surely it cannot be indifferent either to Europe or to France itself, whether there be *any* real resemblance; . . . .

First, then, it cannot be denied that some resemblance does really exist. The prodigious influx of new wealth from the Asiatic conquests unsettled the balance of property in Rome, and of course the very foundations of the Roman Constitution. The same revolution was produced in France by the commercial spirit,[12] and consequent prosperity, political importance, and increased size and population of cities. In both Empires the spread of arts, sciences, eloquence, and free thinking, had been accompanied by luxury, of the most criminal kinds, corruption of domestic morals, venality, and an inordinate overgrowth of social vanity, and a general contempt of the religious creeds and establishments of their ancestors. Both in France and Rome the metaphysics and ethics of Epicurus had become the fashionable philosophy among the wealthy and powerful; a philosophy which regards man as a mere machine, a sort of living automaton, which teaches that pleasure is the sole good, and a prudent calculation of enjoyment

---

Philip and Alexander. To make one great nation of the civilised part of mankind, with one common language, and to use them as the engine of subjugating and civilising the barbarous nations, were the sanctifying pretexts of the Greek and Roman conquests. . . . If the Romans placed their deceased Emperors among the Gods, the flatterers of Bonaparte have not hesitated even in his lifetime, to style him THE PROVIDENCE of Europe; if it was said of the Roman Perpetual General First Consuls, that they were elected, not by the people, but by the active influence of the Gods (numine deorum electi), for the establishment of unity and civilisation among jarring nations, Bonaparte speaks of himself as a divine envoy for the same great purposes, as *called* by him from whom all things emanate.

the only virtue. In both States the people had been agitated by the wildest and most unprincipled demagogues, and projects of Agrarian Laws set afloat, to raise the people against the natural aristocracy of the state, and consequently to throw them into the arms of a military despot. In both countries proscriptions, and tumults, and the most shameless venality had made the very name of liberty odious, and the vices of the leaders of all parties had introduced into the minds even of good men a despair of the Republic, and a disposition to submit to the sober despotism of any individual, rather than the mad tyranny of a multitude. The distant conquests in Gaul and the Asiatic provinces had effected that in Rome, which the long and desperate war with all Europe had more rapidly brought about in France; the affections and duties of the soldiery were gradually weaned from the laws and free legislatures of their country, and transferred to their Generals. This is the common and natural course of political contests: they begin in *principles*, and end in *men*.

In France all these events followed each other more rapidly than in Rome; but the events themselves are the same. . . . The pressure of foreign enemies, from which Rome was altogether exempt, has been, in this respect at least, as fortunate for France, as it has proved luckless to England and Austria: its Republic has been changed into an empire without a civil war aᴉᴉ. .g its own generals. It has, however, been changed by the same steps as the Roman Republic was, and under the same titles and phrases: only, as before, differing in the degrees of rapidity with which the same processes have been accomplished. The reigns of the three first Caesars have been crowded into the three first years of the reign of Bonaparte. . . .

The result of the whole is plainly this: that at present the French Constitution is precisely the same with that of the Roman empire under the Caesars; and that this revolution has been brought about by similar causes. In both all effective power and patronage are in the hands of the General of the State, who has the privilege of recommending and finally appointing his own successor. In both the soldiers are to be kept, if possible, in decent awe, by the image of a civil Government, while all the powers of that Government, not included in those of the *Imperator et Consul Perpetuus*, are palsied by the dread of the soldiery. . . .

II

. . . If . . . the resemblance between the *Government* of France at present, and that of Rome under the Caesars, be both real and strict, is there *any* resemblance between the *circumstances* of the two Empires? (the circumstances, we mean, both external and internal). And if this cannot be denied, are there not likewise some important circumstances of dissimilarity, that must act as a counterpoise to the partial resemblance? And which forebode to the military despotism of France a duration as brief, as its rise has been rapid? . . .

First, . . . France has not the same justification which Rome had, either for her ambition, with regard to surrounding nations, or for the despotism of her internal government. And as all national justification must rest mainly on the existing state of mankind, what cannot be justified cannot be permanent. Rome was really an enlightener and civiliser of the world. . . . [She] spread civilisation, sciences, and the humanising comforts of social life, over amazing tracts of country, and was the cause of the facility with which that religion was propagated over Europe, Africa, and Asia, to which we ourselves owe all we enjoy, in the purity of our domestic manners, and all we dare hope for in the ultimate improvement of the species. France has no claim of this nature. . . . To all the grand purposes of civilisation and science, Europe, and European America, are already one people, beyond the most boastful dream of Roman pride. What would mankind gain, by turning this brotherhood in science and manners, into a political amalgamation? We should exchange national wars for civil wars. We should sink into barbarism from slavery, into discord from barbarism; and thus, sacrifice our close union, as men, to an appearance of alliance, as citizens. Neither has France the same excuse with Rome for the despotism of her Government. In those feudal institutions, which her shallow mock-statesmen have now made the objects of an hostile oath, she had links of social subordination, a happy intertexture of the interests and property of the state, which was in vain to be sought for in the original Constitution of Rome, in which every rich proprietor was regarded as an illegal oppressor; and that Agrarian Law was necessary for Rome, as a Republic, which would have destroyed it, as a society.[13] And though, before the usurpation of the Caesars, the City of Rome, and the free inhabitants of the Italian States, enjoyed a sort of tumultuary liberty, yet the Empire at large was miserably oppressed; every blood-stained and rapacious Pro-Consul could be brought to trial only before his accomplices; and, it is an undoubted fact, that the Emperors, while they enslaved the city, alleviated the slavery of the provinces. But these circumstances are wholly foreign to France, considered as a mighty nation composed of Frenchmen. Her *true* Empire exists in herself; it is, indeed, one and indivisible, because it is composed of men, who have the same manners, the same language; and is not like the Roman Empire, a gorgeous robe of patch-work. – The provinces were the very body and limbs of the Roman Empire, but they are only the *wens* and diseases of the French. Rome *could* not continue free, because she *consisted* of incongruous parts; the liberty of the people was sacrificed to the life of the Empire. France *is* not free, because she has wilfully *incrusted* herself with an heterogeneous compound; in all the petty States, which she has bound to herself, she has bound chains and fetters *around* herself. The soldiers, that enslaved Rome, were the natural and necessary parents of the Roman Empire; in France their power was originally *created* by the mad fear and rage of Great Britain, and her allies, at the commencement of the French Republic, and they are *continued* by the mad ambition of France itself, and at this moment rendered necessary only by reluctant and useless dependencies, by justly alarmed neighbours, and by the deep domestic discontents, of which the military despotism is itself the chief cause. Rome, in short, was *precipitated* by vice and corruptions into the slavery, which suited the nature of her empire; France by the same vices and corruptions into a slavery, which . . . will undermine her false power, and thereby bring her within the possibility of freedom.

To these considerations we must add the modern improvement in the science of politics, by the discovery of *Government by popular representation*; the great rule and law of which is, that it shall recede from universal suffrage, as the state of property in the nation to be represented recedes from the subdivisions of Agrarian equality. . . . [In ancient Greece] the republics . . . were *cities*, and at first not very large cities. Of course there was no apparent necessity for representation: they would be as little likely to fall upon, or to approve, the idea, as the inhabitants of Westminster to approve the plan of choosing electoral colleges, instead of themselves choosing their own members by their own votes. What the cities of Greece always were, Rome was for a long time. Happy it would have been for her, if the plan of representation had been suggested and adopted, at the time of the admission of the Italian States to the right of suffrage; but who could have persuaded the citizens of Rome to have abandoned their own old custom and right of exercising the supreme power in their own persons; and for the Italian States to have sent representatives, while every Roman citizen voted in person, would have been infinitely more ridiculous and disproportionate than the number of Scotch Peers in our British House of Lords.[14] Under the Empire, when the popular Assemblies ceased altogether, this objection of course no longer existed; but now the other Provinces of the Empire were more nearly on an equality, both in rights and pretensions with the Italian States. They of course would have claimed the privilege of sending Members to their Imperial Parliament; and it is highly probable, that a Parliament elected fairly from all the Provinces of the Roman Empire would have exhibited too jarring an assemblage of manners and interests, for the dignity or safety of the Empire. It is said, that this is felt in a slight degree, even in the American Congress at present, where all the difference is effected by the different climate and consequent modification of manners and opinions. None of these difficulties exist in France. Imperfect as our representation is, we still have become a great and flourishing people under its auspicious influence. In America, where the nature of the property permits, and, indeed, commands a much more extensive right of suffrage, than any wise man would wish in England or France, the result is equally in favour of a Representative Legislature. The Americans are neither very amiable nor very enlightened, as a people; yet what Government on earth has presented such continued proofs of wisdom, moderation, and love of Peace? Nothing can be conceived more violent than the contentions of the Candidates, nothing more calm, dignified, and incurable, than the conduct of the same men, as Legislators and Magistrates. France therefore cannot justify her despotism by the same necessity as Rome could; and if this be true, Frenchmen will, and do, feel it to be truth; and the despotism, which cannot be justified – cannot be permanent. . . .

Let us add to all this, as a fact least of all to be omitted in this statement of difference, that on the death of Augustus, all the power, and all the exercises of power, were wholly taken from the popular assemblies. The *people* of Rome, as distinguished from the individuals, existed only as an audience in a play-house, or as a *spectatorate* in an amphi-theatre. But France is not a city like Rome: it is a vast populous territory, and all its cities, and all its towns, feel an equal interest in the movements of government, and have been accustomed to exert almost an equal political activity with Paris. . . . So far are Frenchmen from being condemned to do nothing, that they are called forth to do a great deal – though, it must be confessed, nothing to any purpose. But to call forth large numbers of men to make fools of themselves, is a dangerous experiment; and it will require all the watchfulness of a *faithful* soldiery, and a large importation of fresh Mamelukes [note omitted], to persuade the whole people of France thus to keep their own fingers dancing to and fro before their own eyes, in order that they may not *see*, though they must *know*, that their pockets are in the act of being picked of those charters and privileges, for which many of them had bled, and all of them suffered – charters bequeathed to them in the field of battle, as the testament and dying legacy of more than a million of their best fellow-countrymen. . . .

Coleridge's move away from a reformist position is clearly apparent in his Morning Post *article, 'Once a Jacobin, Always a Jacobin'.*[15] *In part a contribution to, and an attempt to mould, current political language, the article is also of biographical interest, since the second class of Jacobins hold views that are similar to those that appeared in Coleridge's Bristol lectures. Despite the critical attitude towards Jacobinism displayed in this article, its tone and the derogatory remarks about the indiscriminate use of the epithet 'Jacobin' also involve an attack on violent, unthinking and self-serving champions of established institutions and practices. It also indicates that, although democracy may not be appropriate in inegalitarian societies, it may be suited to those where property is evenly distributed; political power must, as Coleridge argues in the first article on the French Constitution, follow the distribution of property.*

(e) "Once a Jacobin, Always a Jacobin" (*Morning Post*, 1802)

This charitable adage was at one time fashionable in the ministerial circles; and Mr Pitt himself, in one of his most powerful speeches, gave it every advantage, that is derivable from stately diction. What he thus condescended to decorate, it were well, if he had attempted to prove. But no! he found it a blank assertion, and a blank assertion he suffered it to remain. What *is* a Jacobin? Perhaps the best answer to this question would be, that it is a term of abuse, the convenient watch-word of a faction. Of course, it has either no meaning, or a very vague one: for definite terms are unmanageable things, and the passions of men do not readily gather round them. Party rage, and fanatical aversion, have their birth place, and natural abode, in floating and obscure generalities, and seldom or never burst forth, except from clouds and vapours. Thunder and lightning from a clear blue sky has been deemed a miracle in all ages. But though we should find it difficult to determine, what a Jacobin *is*, we may however easily conjecture, what the different sects of Anti-Jacobins have meant by the word.

The base and venal creatures, and the blind and furious bigots, of the late Ministry, comprehended under that word all, who from whatever cause opposed the late war, and the late Ministry, and whom they hate for this opposition with such mortal hatred, as is usual with bigots alarmed, and detected culprits. "*Once a Jacobin, always a Jacobin,*" signifies no more in the minds of these men, than "*such a one is a man, whom I shall never cease to hate.*" With other men, honest and less violent Anti-Jacobins, the word implies a man, whose affections have been warmly and deeply interested in the cause of general freedom, who has hoped all good and honourable things both *of,* and *for,* mankind. In this sense of the word, Jacobin, the adage would affirm, that no man can ever become altogether an apostate to Liberty, who has at any time been sincerely and fervently attached to it. His hopes will burn like the Greek fire, hard to be extinguished, and easily rekindling. Even when he despairs of the cause, he will yet *wish,* that it had been successful. And even when private interests have warped his public character, his convictions will remain, and his wishes often rise up in rebellion against his outward actions and public avowals. Thus interpreted, the assertion, *"Once a Jacobin, always a Jacobin",* is so favourable a representation of human nature, that we are willing, too willing perhaps, to admit it even without proof.

There is yet a third class of Anti-Jacobins, and of this class we profess ourselves to be, who use the word, *Jacobin,* as they use the word, *Whig,* and both words only for want of better; who confess, that Jacobin is too often a word of vague abuse, but believe, that there are certain definite ideas, hitherto not expressed in any single word, which may be attached to this word; and who in consequence uniformly use the word, Jacobin, with certain definite ideas attached to it, those ideas, and no other. A Jacobin, in *our* sense of the term, is one who believes, and is disposed to act on the belief, that all, or the greater part of, the happiness or misery, virtue or vice, of mankind, depends on forms of government; who admits no form of government as either good or rightful, which does not flow directly and formally from the persons governed; who – considering life, health, moral and intellectual improvement, and liberty both of person and conscience, as blessings which governments are bound as far as possible to increase and secure to every inhabitant, whether he has or has not any fixed property, and moreover as blessings of infinitely greater value to each individual, than the preservation of property can be to any individual – does consequently and consistently hold, that every inhabitant, who has attained the age of reason, has a natural and inalienable right to an *equal* share of power in the choice of the governors. In other words, the Jacobin affirms that no legislature can be rightful or good, which did not proceed from universal suffrage. In the power, and under the controul, of a legislature so chosen, he places all and every thing, with the exception of the natural rights of man, and the means appointed for the preservation and exercise of these rights, by a direct vote of the nation itself –

that is to say, by a CONSTITUTION. Finally, the Jacobin deems it both justifiable and expedient to effect these requisite changes in faulty governments, by absolute revolutions, and considers no violences as properly rebellious or criminal, which are the *means* of giving to a nation the power of declaring and enforcing its sovereign will.

In brief, therefore, a Jacobin's Creed is this: 1. A government is the organ, by which form and publicity are given to the sovereign will of the people; and by which that will is enforced and exercised. 2. A government is likewise the instrument and means of purifying and regulating the national will by its public discussions, and by direct institutions for the comforts and instruction of the people. 3. Every native of a country has an equal right to that quantity of property, which is necessary for the sustenance of his life, and health. 4. All property beyond this, not being itself a right, can confer no right. Superior wisdom, with superior virtue, would indeed confer a right of superior power; but who is to decide on the possession? Not the person himself, who makes the claim: and if the people, then the right is given, and not inherent. Votes, therefore, *cannot* be *weighed* in this way, and they *must not* be weighed in any other way, and nothing remains possible, but that they must be *numbered*. No form of electing representatives is rightful, but that of universal suffrage. Every individual has a *right* to elect, and a capability of being elected. 5. The legislature has an absolute power over all other property, but that of article 3: unless the people shall have declared otherwise in the constitution. 6. All governments not constituted on these principles are unjust Governments. 7. The people have a right to overturn them, in whatever way it is possible; and any means necessary to this end become *ipso facto*, right means. 8. It is the right and duty of each individual, living under that Government, as far as in him lies, to impel and enable the people to exercise these rights.

The man who subscribes to *all* these articles is a complete Jacobin; to many, but not to all of them, a Semi-Jacobin, and the man who subscribes to any one article (excepting the second, which the Jacobin professes only in common with every other political sect not directly an advocate of despotism), may be fairly said to have a *shade* of Jacobinism in his character. If we are not greatly deceived we could point out more than one or two celebrated Anti-Jacobins, who are not slightly infected with some of the worst symptoms of the madness against which they are raving; and one or two acts of parliament which are justifiable only upon Jacobin principles. These are the ideas which we attach to the word Jacobin; and no other single word expresses them. Not Republican; Milton was a pure Republican, and yet his notions of government were highly aristocratic; Brutus was a Republican, but he perished in consequence of having killed the Jacobin, Caesar. Neither does Demagogue express that which we have detailed; nor yet Democrat. The former word implies simply a mode of conduct, and has no reference to principles; and the latter does of *necessity* convey no more than that a man prefers in any country a form of government, without monarchy or aristocracy, which in any country he *may* do, and yet be no Jacobin, and which in some countries he can do without any impeachment of good sense or honesty; for instance, in the purely pastoral and agricultural districts of Switzerland, where there is no other property but that of land and cattle, and that property very nearly equalised.[16] Whoever builds a Government on personal and natural rights, is so far a Jacobin. Whoever builds on social rights, that is, hereditary rank, property, and long prescription, is an Anti-Jacobin, even though he should nevertheless be a Republican, or even a Democrat.

If we have been prolix, let the importance of the subject induce our readers to consider it as a venial fault. Concerning a term, which nine-tenths of the nation have been in the habit of using, either as a name of glory, or a name of reproach and abhorrence, it is not only our advantage but even our duty to have clear, correct, and definite conceptions. In the sense of the word, Jacobin, which we have here detailed (and, we dare be confident, that no other sense can be given which belongs exclusively to this word), the truth of the adage, "ONCE A JACOBIN, AND ALWAYS A JACOBIN," ought to be proved, before it can be used otherwise than wickedly and uncharitably. To prove its falsehood is rendered difficult by this circumstance alone, that there is no pretence, no shadow of an argument in support of its truth – no pretended facts, which we might invalidate – no train of reasoning, of which we might detect the sophistry. It is a blank assertion, the truth of which would be strange, inexplicable, monstrous; a fact standing by itself, without companion or analogy. An *assertion* therefore of its utter falsehood would be a complete overthrow of the assertion of its truth; and the only confutation, which it merits. It is an assertion that is consistent and pardonable only in the mouth of a thorough Jacobin, who held his principles to be of such undeniable, obvious, and eternal truth, that a man who had once understood could abandon them, no more than he could abandon the elements of geometry; and indeed we must admit, that the whole faction of Re-alarmists, from whose manufactory this precious adage proceeded, have both talked and acted precisely as if they believed in their hearts that Jacobinism presented arguments which were not answerable except by the sword, and charms, and an appearance of happiness, which were not to be withstood except by turning away our eyes from them. . . .

And why? Is it because the creed which we have stated, is dazzling at first sight to the young, the innocent, the disinterested, and to those who, judging of men in general, from their own uncorrupted hearts, judge erroneously, and expect unwisely? Is it because it deceives the mind in its purest and most flexible period? Is it because it is an error that every day's experience aids to detect? an error against which all history is full of warning examples? Or, is it because the experiment has been tried before our eyes, and the error made palpable?

From what source are we to derive this strange phaenomenon, that the young, and the inexperienced, who, we know by regular experience, are deceived in their religious antipathies, and grow wiser; in their friendships, and grow wiser; in their modes of pleasure, and grow wiser; should, if once deceived in a question of abstract politics, cling to the error for ever and ever! though, in addition to the natural growth of judgment and information with increase of years, they live in the age, in which the tenets had been unfortunately acted upon, and the consequences, deformities, at which every good man's heart sickens, and head turns giddy? We were never at any period of our life converts to the system of French politics. As far back as our memory reaches, it was an axiom in politics with us, that in every country in which property prevailed, property must be the grand basis of the government; and that that government was the best, in which the power was the most exactly proportioned to the property. Yet we do not feel the less shocked by those who would turn an error in speculative politics into a sort of sin against the Holy Ghost, which in some miraculous and inexplicable manner shuts out not only mercy but even repentance! – and who now, that religious bigotry is dying away, would substitute in its place dogmas of *election* and *reprobation* in politics. . . .

A further stage in Coleridge's move away from the political implications of his early radicalism is illustrated in the extracts of correspondence printed below.[17] *In letters discussing the 'Concordat' between the Papacy and the Napoleonic regime, Coleridge writes that he has abandoned his earlier hostility to established churches, and argues that an established church with its own property can provide a bulwark against attempts to make religion a political weapon – one that could fall into and strengthen the hands of despots such as Napoleon Buonaparte.*

(f) The Virtues of Church Establishments (letters of 1802)

. . . You have been, no doubt, interested in some measure by the French Concordat. I own, I was surprized to find it so much approved of by Clergymen of the Church/ It appeared to me a wretched Business – & first occasioned me to think accurately & with consecutive Logic on the force & meaning of the word *Established* Church/ and the result of my reflections was very greatly in favor of the Church of England maintained, as it is present is/ and those scruples, which, if I mistake not, we had in common when I last saw you, as to the effects & scriptural propriety of this (supposed) alliance of Church & State were wholly removed. – Perhaps, you will in some measure perceive the general nature of my opinions, when I say – the Church of France at present ought to be called – *a standing* Church – in the same sense as we say a *standing* Army.[18] . . .

. . . From the latter part of your Letter I fear that I must have worded my Letter to you very inacc[ur]ately in what respected the change of sentiment – in saying that I had no longer my former scruples respecting the *establishment* of the Church of England, I did not mean in any way to refer to it's peculiar Doctrines – or to the Church of England in particular. The change in my opinions applies equally to the Gallic Church, antecedent to the Revolution, and to the regular & parochial Clergy of Spain & Portugal. – The Clergy are called in a statute of Queen Elizabeth "the great, venerable third *Estate* of the Realm";[19] – that is to say, they & their property are an elementary part of our constitution, not created by any Legislature, but really & truly antecedent to any form of Government in England upon which any existing Laws can be built – They & their Property are *recognized* by the Statutes – even as the common Law frequently is – which was bona fide Law, & the most sacred Law, before the Statute/ and recognized not for the purpose of having any additional authority conferred on it, but for the removing of any ambiguities & for the increasing of it's publicity. The Church is not depend[en]t on the Government, nor can the Legislature constit[ution]ally alter it's property without consent of the Proprietor – any [more] than it constitutionally could introduce an agrarian Law. – Now this is indeed an Establishment – res stabilita – it has it's own foundations/ whereas the present church of France has no foundation of it's own – it is a House of Convenience built on the sands of a transient Legislature – & no wise differs from a *standing Army*. The colonial Soldiers under the Roman Emperors were an *established* Army, in a certain sense – & so were the Timariots under the Turks/ – but the Church of France is a *standing* church, as it's army is a *standing* army. It *stands*; and so does a Child's House of Cards – but how long it shall stand depends on the caprice of a few Individuals. – This I hold to be indeed & in sad & sober Truth an antichristian union of the Kingdom of Christ with the Kingdom of this World – & in a less degree I look upon the manner, in which the Dissenting Clergy are maintained, as objectionable on the same grounds. . . .

3

Principles and Prudence in Politics: *The Friend* (1809–10)

The extracts from The Friend[1] *printed in this chapter contain a number of arguments dealing with the relationship between morals and politics. They show that Coleridge had abandoned the unified approach that underlay his early political theory, but still maintained that the state is a moral entity, and that political obligation is a moral matter. He develops these arguments by way of critiques of Hobbes and Paley, and with the help of a Kantianised Rousseau. But, having established the moral basis of the state, he then argues that moral discourse can not be applied directly to the framing and justification of particular institutions. He contends that the sphere of morals is distinct from that of politics; the former rests upon men's possession of reason and is universal, inward and egalitarian, while the latter depends upon the exercise of the understanding (which takes account of the particular and outward), and is not possessed by all men to the same degree. Reason is the source of moral personality, but it does not provide the basis for the exercise of political rights; these depend upon the fruits of human experience, and that has shown that there should be a close connection between the possession of property and the exercise of political power.*

ESSAY IV

On the Principles of Political Philosophy

All the different philosophical Systems of political Justice, all the Theories on the rightful Origin of Government, are reducible in the end to three Classes, correspondent to the three different points of view, in which the Human Being itself may be contemplated. The first denies all truth and distinct meaning to the words, RIGHT and DUTY, and affirming that the human mind consists of nothing but manifold modifications of passive sensation, considers Men as the highest sort of Animals indeed, but at the same time the most wretched; inasmuch as their defenceless nature forces them into

Society, while such is the multiplicity of Wants engendered by the social state, that the Wishes of one are sure to be in contradiction with those of some other. The Assertors of this System consequently ascribe the Origin and continuance of Government to Fear, or the power of the Stronger, aided by the force of Custom. This is the System of Hobbes. Its Statement is its Confutation. It is, indeed, in the literal sense of the world *preposterous:*[2] for Fear pre-supposes Conquest, and Conquest a previous union and agreement between the Conquerors. A vast Empire *may* perhaps be governed by Fear; at least the idea is not absolutely inconceivable, under circumstances which prevent the consciousness of a common Strength. A million of men united by mutual Confidence and free intercourse of Thoughts, form one power, and this is as much a Real Thing as a Steam Engine; but a million of insulated Individuals is only an abstraction of the mind, and but one told so many times over without addition, as an ideot would tell the Clock at noon – one, one, one & c. But when, in the first instances, the Descendants of one Family joined together to attack those of another Family, it is impossible that their Chief or Leader should have appeared to them stronger than all the rest together: they must therefore have *chosen* him, and this as for particular purposes, so doubtless under particular Conditions, expressed or understood. . . . Therefore, even on the System of those who, in contempt of the oldest and most authentic records, consider the savage as the first and natural State of Man, Government must have *originated* in Choice and an Agreement. The apparent Exceptions in Africa and Asia are, if possible, still more subversive of this System: for they will be found to have originated in religious Imposture, and the first Chiefs to have secured a *willing* and enthusiastic Obedience to themselves, as Delegates of the Deity.

But the whole Theory is baseless. We are told by History, we learn from our Experience, we know from our own Hearts, that Fear, of itself, is utterly incapable of producing any regular, continuous and calculable effect, even on an Individual; and that the Fear, which *does* act systematically upon the mind, always presupposes a sense of Duty, as its Cause. The most cowardly of the European Nations, the Neapolitans and Sicilians, those among whom the fear of Death exercises the most tyrannous influence relatively to their own persons, are the very men who least fear to take away the Life of a Fellow-citizen by poison or assassination; while in Great Britain, a Tyrant, who has abused the Power, which a vast property has given him, to oppress a whole Neighbourhood, can walk in safety unarmed, and unattended, amid a hundred men, each of whom feels his heart burn with rage and indignation at the sight of him. . . . And yet who dare not touch a hair of his head! Whence does this arise? Is it from a cowardice of *sensibility* that makes the injured man shudder at the thought of shedding blood? Or from a cowardice of *selfishness* which makes him afraid of hazarding his own Life? Neither the one or the other! The Field of Talavara, as the most recent of an hundred equal proofs, has borne witness,

> That "bring a Briton fra his hill,
> . . . .
> Say, such is Royal George's will,
>   And there's the foe,
> He has nae thought but how to kill
>   Twa at a blow.
>
> Nae cauld, faint-hearted doubtings tease him;
> Death comes, wi' fearless eye he sees him;
> Wi' bloody hand, a welcome gies him;
>   And when he fa's
> His latest draught o' breathin leaves him
>   In faint huzzas."[3]

Whence then arises the difference of feeling in the former case? To what does the Oppressor owe his safety? To the spirit-quelling thought: the Laws of God and of my Country have made his Life sacred! I dare not touch a hair of his Head! – "'Tis Conscience that makes Cowards of us all,"[4] – but oh! it is Conscience too which makes Heroes of us all. . . .

[*Coleridge then describes Sir Alexander Ball's*[5] *success in disciplining a mutinous crew of a man-of-war by introducing a system of regulation, trial, appeal and punishment that was similar to ordinary law.*]

I have been assured, both by a gentleman who was a Lieutenant on board that Ship . . . and very recently by a grey-headed Sailor, . . . that the success of this plan was such as astonished the oldest Officers, and convinced the most incredulous. Ruffians, who like the old Buccaneers, had been used to inflict torture on themselves for sport, or in order to harden themselves beforehand, were tamed and overpowered, how or why they themselves knew not. From the fiercest Spirits were heard the most earnest entreaties for the forgiveness of their Commander: not *before* the Punishment, for it was too well known that then they would have been to no purpose, but days after it, when the bodily pain was remembered but as a dream. An *invisible* Power it was, that quelled them, a Power, which was therefore irresistible, because it took away the very Will of resisting? It was the aweful power of LAW, acting on natures pre-configured to its influences. A Faculty was appealed to in the Offender's own being; a Faculty and a Presence, of which he had not been previously made aware – but it *answered* to the appeal! its real Existence therefore could not be doubted, or its reply rendered inaudible! and the very struggle of the wilder Passions to keep uppermost counteracted its own purpose, by wasting in internal contest that Energy, which before had acted in its entireness on external resistance or provocation. Strength may be met with strength; the Power of inflicting pain may be baffled by the Pride of endurance; the eye of Rage may be answered by the stare of Defiance, or the downcast look of dark and revengeful Resolve; and with all this there is an outward and determined object to which the mind can attach its passions and purposes, and bury its own disquietudes in the full occupation of the Senses. But who dares struggle with an *invisible* Combatant? with an Enemy which exists and makes us know its existence – but *where* it is, we ask in vain. – No Space contains it – Time promises no control over it – it has no ear for my threats – it has no substance, that my hands can grasp, or my weapons find vulnerable – it commands and cannot be commanded – it acts and is insusceptible of my re-action – the more I strive to subdue it, the more am I compelled to think of it – and the more I think of it, the more do I find it to possess a reality out of myself, and not to be a phantom of my own imagination; that all, but the most abandoned men, acknowledge its authority, and that the whole strength and majesty of my Country are pledged to support it; and yet that *for me* its power is the same with that of my own permanent Self, and that all the Choice, which is permitted to me, consists in having it for my Guardian Angel or my avenging Fiend! This is the Spirit of LAW! the Lute of Amphion, the Harp of Orpheus! This is the true necessity, which compels man into the social State, now and always, by a still-beginning, never-ceasing force of moral Cohesion.

Thus is Man to be governed, and thus only can he be *governed*. For from his Creation the objects of his Senses were to become his Subjects, and the Task allotted to him was to subdue the visible World within the sphere of action circumscribed by those Senses, as far as they could act in concert. What the Eye beholds the Hand strives to reach; what it reaches, it conquers and makes the instrument of further conquest. We can be subdued by that alone which is analogous in Kind to that by which we subdue: therefore by the invisible powers of our Nature, whose immediate presence is disclosed to our inner sense, and only as the Symbols and Language of which all shapes and modifications of matter become formidable to us.

A Machine continues to move by the force which first set it in motion. If, only the smallest number in any State, properly so called, hold together through the influence of any Fear that is antecedent to the sense of Duty, it is evident that the State itself could not have commenced through animal Fear. We hear, indeed, of conquests; but how does History represent these? Almost without exception as the substitution of one set of Governors for another: and so far is the Conqueror from relying on Fear alone to secure the obedience of the Conquered, that his first step is to demand an Oath of fealty from them, by which he would impose upon them the belief, that they become *Subjects*: for who would think of administering an Oath to a Gang of Slaves? But what can make the difference between Slave and Subject, if not the existence of an implied Contract in the one case, and not in the other? And to what purpose would a Contract serve if, however it might be *entered into* through Fear, it were deemed binding only in consequence of Fear? . . . Hobbes has said, that Laws without the Sword are but bits of Parchment. How far this is true, every honest Man's heart will best tell him, if he will content himself with asking his own Heart, and not falsify the answer by his notions concerning the Hearts of other men. But were it true, still the fair answer would be – Well! but without the Laws the Sword is but a piece of Iron.[6] The wretched Tyrant, who disgraces the present Age and Human Nature itself, has exhausted the whole magazine of animal Terror, in order to consolidate his truly satanic Government. . . . The System, which I have been confuting, is indeed so inconsistent with the Facts revealed to us by our own mind, and so utterly unsupported by any Facts of History, that I should be censurable in wasting my own time and my Reader's patience by the exposure of its falsehood, but that the Arguments adduced have a value of themselves independent of their present application. Else it would have been an ample and satisfactory reply to an Assertor of this bestial Theory – Government is a thing which relates to Men, and what you say applies only to Beasts.

Before I proceed to the second of the three Systems, let me remove a possible misunderstanding that may have arisen from the use of the word Contract: as if I had asserted, that the whole Duty of Obedience to Governors is derived from, and dependent on, the *Fact* of an original Contract. I freely admit, that to make this the Cause and Origin of political Obligation, is not only a dangerous but an absurd Theory; for what could give moral force to the Contract? The same sense of Duty which binds us to keep it, must have pre-existed as impelling us to make it. . . . But in my sense, the word Contract is merely synonimous with the sense of Duty acting in a specific direction, i.e. determining our moral relations, as members of a body politic. If I have referred to a supposed *origin* of Government, it has been in courtesy to a common notion: for I myself regard the supposition as no more than a means of simplifying to our Apprehension the ever-continuing causes of social union, even as the Conservation of the World may be represented as an act of continued Creation. For, what if an original Contract had *really* been entered into, and formally recorded? Still it could do no more than bind the contracting parties to act for the general good in the best manner, that the existing relations among themselves, (state of property, religion, &c.) on the one hand, and the external circumstances on the other (ambitious or barbarous Neighbours, &c.) required or permitted. In after times it could be appealed to only for the general principle, and no more, than the ideal Contract, could it affect a question of ways and means. As each particular Age brings with it its own exigencies, so must it rely on its own prudence for the specific measures by which they are to be encountered.

Nevertheless, it assuredly cannot be denied, that an original (in reality, rather an ever-originating) Contract is a very natural and significant mode of expressing the reciprocal duties of Subject and Sovereign. . . .

. . . [H]owever speciously it may be urged, that History can scarcely produce a single example of a state dating its primary Establishment from a free and mutual Convenant, the answer is ready: if there be any difference between a Government and a band of Robbers, an act of consent must be supposed on the part of the People governed.[7] . . .

The second System corresponds to the second point of view under which the Human Being may be considered, namely, as an animal gifted with understanding, or the faculty of suiting Measures to Circumstances. According to this Theory, every Institution of national origin needs no other Justification than a proof, that under the particular circumstances it is EXPEDIENT. Having in my former Numbers expressed myself (so at least I am conscious I shall have appeared to do to many Persons) with comparative slight of the Understanding considered as the sole Guide of human Conduct, and even with something like contempt and reprobation of the maxims of Expedience, when represented as the only steady Light of the Conscience, and the absolute Foundation of all Morality; I shall perhaps seem guilty of an inconsistency, in declaring myself an Adherent of this second System, a zealous Advocate for deriving the origin of all Government from human *Prudence*, and of deeming that to be just which Experience has proved to be expedient. From this charge of inconsistency* I shall best exculpate myself by the full statement of the third System, and by the exposition of its Grounds and Consequences.

The third and last System then denies all rightful origins to Governments, except as far as they are derivable from Principles contained in the REASON of Man,[8] and judges all the relations of men in Society by the Laws of moral necessity, according to IDEAS (I here use the word in its highest and primitive sense, and as nearly synonimous with the modern word *ideal*) according to

---

* Distinct notions do not suppose different *things*. When we make a three-fold distinction in human nature, we are fully aware, that it is a distinction not a division, and that in every act of Mind the *Man* unites the properties of Sense, Understanding, and Reason. Nevertheless, it is of great practical importance, that these distinctions should be made and understood, the ignorance or perversion of them being alike injurious; as the first French Constitution has most lamentably proved. . . .

Under the term SENSE, I comprize whatever is passive in our being, without any reference to the question of Materialism or Immaterialism; all that man is in common with the animals, in *kind* at least – his sensations, and impressions, whether of his outward senses, or the inner sense. . . . By the UNDERSTANDING, I mean the faculty of thinking and forming *judgement* on the notices furnished by the Sense, according to certain rules existing in itself, which rules constitute its distinct nature. By the pure REASON, I mean the power by which we become possessed of Principle, (the eternal verities of Plato and Descartes) and of ideas, (N.B. not images) as the ideas of a point, a line, a circle, in Mathematics; and of Justice, Holiness, Free-Will, &c. in Morals. . . .

archetypal IDEAS co-essential with the Reason, and the consciousness of which is the sign and necessary product of its full
development. The following then is the fundamental Principle of
this Theory: Nothing is to be deemed rightful in civil Society, or to
be tolerated as such, but what is capable of being demonstrated
out of the original Laws of the pure Reason. Of course, as there is
but one System of Geometry, so according to this Theory there
can be but one Constitution and one System of Legislation, and
this consists in the freedom, which is the common Right of all
Men, under the controul of that moral necessity, which is the
common Duty of all men. Whatever is not *every where* necessary,
is *no where* right. On this assumption the whole Theory is built. To
state it nakedly is to confute it satisfactorily. So at least it should
seem! But in how winning and specious a manner this System
may be represented even to minds of the loftiest order, if undisciplined and unhumbled, by practical Experience, has been proved by
the general impassioned admiration and momentous effects of
Rousseau's *Du Contrat Social*, and the Writings of the French
Economists, or as they more appropriately entitled themselves,
Physiocratic Philosophers:[9] and in how tempting and dangerous a
manner it may be represented to the Populace, has been made too
evident in our own Country by the temporary effects of Paine's
Rights of Man. Relatively, however, to this latter Work it should
be observed, that it is not a *legitimate* Offspring of any one Theory,
but a confusion of the immorality of the first System with the
misapplied universal Principles of the last: and in this union, or
rather lawless alternation, consists the essence of JACOBINISM, as
far as Jacobinism is any thing but a term of abuse, or has any
meaning of its own distinct from Democracy and Sedition.[10]

A Constitution equally suited to China and America, or to Russia
and Great Britain, must surely be equally unfit for both, and
deserves as little respect in political, as a Quack's panacaea in
medical, Practice. Yet there are three weighty motives for a
distinct exposition of this Theory, and of the ground on which its
pretensions are bottomed: and I dare affirm, that for the same
reasons there are few subjects which in the present state of
the World have a fairer claim to the attention of every serious
Englishman, who is likely, directly or indirectly, as Partizan or as
Opponent, to interest himself in schemes of Reform. The first
motive is derived from the propensity of mankind to mistake the
feelings of disappointment, disgust, and abhorrence occasioned
by the unhappy effects or accompaniments of a particular System

for an insight into the falsehood of its Principles which alone can secure its permanent rejection. For by a wise ordinance of Nature our feelings have no abiding-place in our memory, nay the more vivid they are in the moment of their existence the more dim and difficult to be remembered do they make the thoughts which accompanied them. . . . [H]uman experience, like the Stern lights of a Ship at Sea, illumines only the path which we have passed over. The horror of the Peasants' War in Germany, and the direful effects of the Anabaptist Tenets, which were only nominally different from those of Jacobinism by the substitution of religious for philosophical jargon, struck all Europe for a time with affright. Yet little more than a Century was sufficient to obliterate all effective memory of those events: the same Principles budded forth anew and produced the same fruits from the imprisonment of Charles the First to the Restoration of his Son. . . .

That erroneous political notions (they having become general and a part of the popular creed), have practical consequences, and these, of course, of a most fearful nature, is a Truth as certain as historic evidence can make it: and that when the feelings excited by these Calamities have passed away, and the interest in them has been displaced by more recent events, the same Errors are likely to be started afresh, pregnant with the same Calamities, is an evil rooted in Human Nature in the present state of general information, for which we have hitherto found no *adequate* remedy. . . . But if there be any means, if not of preventing, yet of palliating the disease and, in the more favoured nations, of checking its progress at the first symptoms; and if these means are to be at all compatible with the civil and intellectual Freedom of Mankind; they are to be found only in an intelligible and thorough exposure of the error, and, through that discovery, of the source, from which it derives its speciousness and powers of influence, on the human mind. This therefore is my first motive for undertaking the disquisition.

The second is, that though the French Code of revolutionary Principles is now generally rejected as a *System*, yet every where in the speeches and writings of the English Reformers, nay, not seldom in those of their Opponents, I find certain maxims asserted or appealed to, which are not tenable, except as constituent parts of that System. Many of the most specious arguments in proof of the imperfection and injustice of the present Constitution of our Legislature will be found, on closer examination, to pre-suppose the truth of certain Principles, from which the Adducers of these arguments loudly profess their dissent. But in political changes no permanence can be hoped for in the edifice, without consistency in the Foundation. The third motive is, that by detecting the true source of the influence of these Principles, we shall at the same time discover their natural place and object: and that in themselves they are not only Truths, but most important and sublime Truths, and that their falsehood and their danger consist altogether in their misapplication. Thus the dignity of Human Nature will be secured, and at the same time a lesson of Humility taught to each Individual, when we are made to see that the universal necessary Laws, and pure IDEAS of Reason, were given us, not for the purpose of flattering our Pride and enabling us to become national Legislators; but that by an energy of continued self-conquest, we might establish a free and yet absolute Government in our own Spirits.

ESSAY VI

On the Grounds of Government as Laid Exclusively in Pure Reason; . . .

. . . I return to . . . my promise of developing from its' embryo Principles the Tree of French Liberty, of which the Declaration of the Rights of Man, and the Constitution of 1791 were the Leaves, and the succeeding and present State of France the Fruits. . . .

The System commences with an undeniable Truth, and an important deduction there from equally undeniable.[11] All voluntary Actions, say they, having for their Objects, Good or Evil, are *moral* actions. But all morality is grounded in the Reason. Every Man is born with the faculty of Reason: and whatever is without it, be the Shape what it may, is not a Man or PERSON, but a THING. Hence the sacred Principle, recognized by all Laws, human and divine, the Principle indeed, which is the *ground-work* of all Law and Justice, that a Person can never become a Thing, nor be treated as such without wrong. But the distinction between Person and Thing consists herein, that the latter may rightfully be used, altogether and merely, as a *Means*; but the former must always be included in the *End*, and form a part of the final Cause. We plant the Tree and we cut it down, we breed the Sheep and we kill it, wholly as *means* to our own *ends*. The Wood-cutter and the Hind are likewise employed as *Means*, but on an agreement of reciprocal advantage, which includes them as well as their Employer in the *end*. Again: as the faculty of Reason implies Free-agency, Morality (i.e. the dictate of Reason) gives to every rational Being the right of acting as a free agent, and of finally determining his conduct by his own Will, according to his own Conscience: and this right is inalienable except by guilt, which is an act of Self-forfeiture, and the Consequences therefore to be considered as the Criminal's own moral election. In respect of their Reason all Men are equal. The measure of the Understanding and of all other Faculties of Man, is different in different Persons: but Reason is not susceptible of degree. For since it merely decides whether any given thought or action is or is not in contradiction with the rest, there can be no reason better, or more *reason*, than another.[12]

REASON! best and holiest gift of Heaven and bond of union with the Giver! The high title by which the Majesty of Man claims precedence above all other living Creatures! Mysterious Faculty, the Mother of Conscience, of Language, of Tears, and of Smiles! Calm and incorruptible legislator of the Soul, without whom all its' other Powers would "meet in mere oppugnancy." Sole Principle of Permanence amid endless Change! in a World of discordant Appetites and imagined Self-interests the one only common Measure! which taken away,

> "Force should be right; or, rather right and wrong
> (Between whose endless jar justice resides)
> Should lose their names and so should justice too.
> Then every thing includes itself in power,
> Power into will, will into appetite;
> And appetite, an universal wolf,
> So doubly seconded with will and power,
> Must make perforce an universal prey!"[13]

Thrice blessed faculty of Reason! all other Gifts, though goodly and of celestial origin, Health, Strength, Talents, all the powers and all the means of enjoyment, seem dispensed by Chance or sullen Caprice – thou alone, more than even the Sunshine, more than the common Air, art given to all Men, and to every Man alike! To thee, who being one art the same in all, we owe the privilege, that of all we can become one, a living *whole*! that we have a COUNTRY! Who then shall dare prescribe a Law of moral Action for any rational Being, which does not flow immediately from that

Reason, which is the Fountain of all Morality? Or how without breach of Conscience can we limit or coerce the Powers of a Free-Agent, except by coincidence with that Law in his own Mind, which is at once the Cause, the Condition, and the Measure, of his Free-agency? Man must be *free* or to what purpose was he made a Spirit of Reason, and not a Machine of Instinct? Man must *obey*; or wherefore has he a Conscience? The Powers, which create this difficulty, contain its solution likewise: for *their* Service is perfect Freedom. And whatever Law or System of law compels any other service, disennobles our Nature, leagues itself with the Animal against the Godlike, kills in us the very Principle of joyous Well-doing, and fights against Humanity.

By the Application of these Principles to the social State there arises the following System, which as far as respects its first grounds is developed the most fully by J. J. Rousseau in his Work *Du contrat social*. If then no Individual possesses the Right of prescribing any thing to another Individual, the rule of which is not contained in their common Reason, Society, which is but an aggregate of Individuals, can communicate this Right to no one. It cannot possibly make that rightful which the higher and inviolable Law of Human Nature declares contradictory and unjust. But concerning Right and Wrong, the Reason of each and every Man is the competent Judge: for how else could he be an amenable Being, or the proper Subject of *any* Law? This Reason, therefore, in any Man, cannot even in the social state be rightfully subjugated to the Reason of any other. Neither an Individual, nor yet the whole Multitude which constitutes the State, can possess the Right of compelling him to do any thing, of which it cannot be demonstrated that his own Reason must join in prescribing it. If therefore Society is to be under a *rightful* constitution of Government, and one that can impose on rational Beings a true and moral Obligation to obey it, it must be framed on such Principles that every Individual follows his own Reason while he obeys the Laws of the Constitution, and performs the Will of the State while he follows the Dictate of his own Reason. This is expressly asserted by Rousseau, who states the problem of a perfect Constitution of Government in the following words: ". . . To find a form of Society according to which each one uniting with the whole shall yet obey himself only and remain as free as before."[14] This right of the Individual to retain his whole natural Independence, even in the social State, is absolutely inalienable. He cannot possibly concede or compromise it: for this very Right is one of his most sacred Duties. He would sin against himself, and commit high treason against the Reason which the Almighty Creator has given him, if he dared abandon its' exclusive right to govern his actions.

Laws obligatory on the Conscience, can only therefore proceed from that Reason which remains always one and the same, whether it speaks through this or that Person: like the voice of an external Ventriloquist, it is indifferent from whose lips it appears to come, if only it be audible. The Individuals indeed are subject to Errors and Passions, and each Man has his own defects. But when Men are assembled in Person or by real Representatives, the actions and re-actions of individual Self-love balance each other; errors are neutralized by opposite errors; and the Winds rushing from all quarters at once with equal force, produce for the time a deep calm, during which the general will arising from the general Reason displays itself. . . .

This, however, as my Readers will have already detected, is no longer a demonstrable deduction from Reason. It is a mere *probability*, against which other probabilities may be weighed: as the lust of Authority, the contagious nature of Enthusiasm, and other of the acute or chronic diseases of deliberative Assemblies. But which of these results is the more probable, the correction or the contagion of Evil, must depend on Circumstances and grounds of Expediency: and thus we already find ourselves beyond the magic Circle of the pure Reason, and within the Sphere of the Understanding and the Prudence. Of this important fact Rousseau was by no means unaware in his Theory, though with gross inconsistency he takes no notice of it in his Application of the Theory to Practice. He admits the possibility, he is compelled by History to allow even the *probability*, that the most numerous popular Assemblies, nay even whole Nations, may at times be hurried away by the same Passions, and under the dominion of a common Error. This Will of all is *then* of no more value, than the Humours of any one Individual: and must therefore be sacredly distinguished from the pure Will which flows from universal Reason. To this point then I entreat the Readers' particular attention: for in this distinction, established by Rousseau himself, between the *Volonté de Tous* and the *Volonté generale*,[15] (i.e. between the collective Will, and a casual over-balance of Wills) the Falsehood or Nothingness of the whole System becomes manifest. For hence it follows, as an inevitable Consequence, that all which is said in the *Contrat social* of that sovereign Will, to which the right of universal Legislation appertains, applies to no one Human Being, to no Society or Assemblage of Human Beings, and least of all to the mixed Multitude that makes up the PEOPLE; but entirely and exclusively to REASON itself, which, it is true, dwells in every Man *potentially*, but actually and in perfect purity is found in no Man and in no body of Men. This distinction the latter Disciples of Rousseau chose completely to forget and, (a far more melancholy case!) the Constituent Legislators of France forgot it likewise. . . .

. . . In his [Rousseau's] whole System there is beyond controversy much that is true and well reasoned, if only its application be not extended farther than the nature of the case permits. But then we shall find that little or nothing is won by it for the institutions of Society; and least of all for the constitution of Governments, the Theory of which it was his wish to ground on it. Apply his Principles to any case, in which the sacred and inviolable Laws of Morality are immediately interested, all becomes just and pertinent. No Power on Earth can oblige me to act against my Conscience. No Magistrate, no Monarch, no Legislature, can without Tyranny compel me to do any thing which the acknowledged Laws of God have forbidden me to do. So act that thou mayest be able, without involving any contradiction, to will that the Maxim of thy Conduct should be the Law of all intelligent Beings – is the one universal and sufficient Principle and Guide of Morality. And why? Because the *object* of Morality is not the outward act, but the internal Maxim of our Actions.[16] And so far it is infallible. But with what shew of Reason can we pretend, from a Principle by which we are to determine the purity of our motives, to deduce the form and matter of a rightful Government, the main office of which is to regulate the outward Actions of particular Bodies of men, according to their particular Circumstances? Can we hope better of Constitutions framed by ourselves than of that which was given by Almighty Wisdom itself? The Laws of the Hebrew Commonwealth, which flowed from the pure Reason, remain and are immutable; but the Regulations dictated by Prudence, though by the *Divine* Prudence, and though given in thunder from the Mount, have passed away; and while they lasted, were binding only for that one State, whose particular Circumstances rendered them expedient.

Rousseau indeed asserts, that there is an inalienable sovereignty inherent in every human being possessed of Reason: and from this the Framers of the Constitution of 1791 deduce, that the People itself is it's own sole rightful Legislator, and at most dare only recede so far from its right as to delegate to chosen Deputies the Power of representing and declaring the general Will. But this is wholly without proof; for it has already been fully shewn, that according to the Principle out of which this consequence is attempted to be drawn, it is not the actual Man, but the abstract Reason alone, that is the sovereign and rightful Lawgiver. The confusion of two things so different is so gross an Error, that the Constituent Assembly could scarce proceed a step in their Declaration of Rights, without some glaring inconsistency. Children are excluded from all political Power – are they not human beings in whom the faculty of Reason resides? Yes? but in them the faculty is not yet adequately developed. But are not gross Ignorance, inveterate Superstition, and the habitual Tyranny of Passion and Sensuality, equal Preventives of the developement, equal impediments to the rightful exercise of the Reason, as Childhood and early Youth? Who would not rely on the judgement of a well-educated English Lad, bred in a virtuous and enlightened Family, in preference to that of a brutal Russian, who believes that he can scourge his wooden Idol into good humour, or attributes to himself the merit of perpetual Prayer, when he has fastened the Petitions, which his Priest has written for him, on the wings of a Windmill? Again: Women are likewise excluded – full half, and that assuredly the most innocent, the most amiable half, of the whole human Race, is excluded, and this too by a Constitution which boasts to have no other foundations but those of universal Reason! Is Reason then an affair of Sex? No! But Women are commonly in a state of *dependence*, and are not likely to exercise their Reason with freedom. Well! and does not this ground of exclusion apply with equal or greater force to the Poor, to the Infirm, to Men in embarrassed Circumstances, to all in short whose maintenance, be it scanty or be it ample, depends on the Will of others? How far are we to go? Where must we stop? What Classes should we admit? Whom must we disfranchise? The objects, concerning whom we are to determine these Questions, are all Human Beings and differenced from each other by *degrees* only, these degrees too oftentimes changing. Yet the Principle on which the whole System rests is, that Reason is not susceptible of degree. Nothing therefore, which subsists wholly in degrees, the changes of which do not obey any necessary Law, can be Subjects of pure Science, or determinable by mere Reason.

For these things we must rely on our *Understandings* enlightened by past experience and immediate Observation, and determining our choice by comparisons of Expediency. . . .

The chief object, for which Men first formed themselves into a State was not the protection of their Lives but of their Property. For where the nature of the Soil and Climate precludes all Property but personal, and permits that only in its simplest forms, as in Greenland, men remain in the domestic State and form Neighbourhood, but not Governments. And in North America, the Chiefs appear to exercise Government in those Tribes only which possess individual landed Property: among the rest the Chief is their General only; and Government is exercised only in Families by the Fathers of Families. But where individual landed Property exists, there must be inequality of Property: the nature of the Earth and the nature of the Mind unite to make the contrary impossible. But to suppose the Land the Property of the State, and the Labour and the Produce to be equally divided among all the Members of the State, involves more than one contradiction: for it could not subsist without gross injustice, except where the Reason of all and of each was absolute Master of the selfish passions of Sloth, Envy, &c.; and yet the same State would preclude the greater part of the means by which the Reason of man is developed. In whatever state of Society you would place it, from the most savage to the most refined, it would be found equally unjust and impossible; and were there a race of Men, a Country, and a Climate, that permitted such an order of things, the same Causes would render all Government superfluous. To Property, therefore, and to its inequalities, all human Laws directly or indirectly relate, which would not be equally Laws in the state of Nature. Now it is impossible to deduce the Right of Property from pure Reason.[17] The utmost which Reason could give would be a property in the *forms* of things, as far as the forms were produced by individual Power. In the *matter* it could give no Property. We regard Angels and glorified Spirits as Beings of pure Reason: and whoever thought of Property in Heaven? Even the simplest and most moral form of it, namely, Marriage, (we know from the highest authority) is excluded from the state of pure Reason. Rousseau himself expressly admits, that Property cannot be deduced from the Laws of Reason and Nature; and he ought therefore to have admitted at the same time, that his whole Theory was a thing of Air. In the most respectable point of view he could regard his System as analogous only to Geometry. (If indeed it be purely scientific, how could it be otherwise?) Geometry holds forth an *ideal* which can never be fully realised in Nature, even because it is Nature: because Bodies are more than Extension, and to pure extension of space only the mathematical Theorems wholly correspond. In the same manner the moral Laws of the intellectual World, as far as they are deducible from pure Intellect, are never perfectly applicable to our mixed and sensitive Nature, because Man is something besides Reason; because his Reason never acts by itself, but must cloath itself in the Substance of individual Understanding and specific Inclination, in order to become a Reality and an Object of Consciousness and Experience. It will be seen hereafter that together with this, the Key-stone of the Arch, the greater part and the most specious of the popular Arguments in favour of universal Suffrage fall in and are crushed. I will mention one only at present. Major Cartwright,[18] in his deduction of the Rights of the Subject from Principles "not susceptible of proof, being self-evident – if one of which be violated all are shaken," affirms (Principle 98th; though the greater part indeed are moral Aphorisms, or blank Assertions, not scientific Principles) "that a Power which ought never to be used ought never to exist." Again he affirms that "Laws to bind all must be assented to by all, and consequently every Man, even the poorest, has an equal Right to Suffrage:" and this for an additional reason, because "all without exception are capable of feeling Happiness or Misery, accordingly as they are well or ill governed." But are they not then capable of feeling Happiness or Misery, according as they do or do not possess the means of a comfortable Subsistence? and who is the Judge, what is a comfortable Subsistence, but the Man himself? Might not then, on the same or equivalent Principles a Leveller construct a Right to equal Property?[19] The Inhabitants of this Country without Property form, doubtless, a great majority: each of these has a Right to a Suffrage, and the richest Man to no more: and the object of this Suffrage is, that each Individual may secure himself a true efficient Representative of his Will. Here then is a legal power of abolishing or equalising Property: and according to himself, *a Power which ought never to be used ought not to exist.*

Therefore, unless he carries his System to the whole length of common Labour and common Possession, a Right to universal Suffrage cannot exist; but if not to universal Suffrage, there can exist no *natural right* to Suffrage at all. In whatever way he would obviate this objection, he must admit *Expedience* founded on *Experience* and particular Circumstances, which will vary in every different Nation, and in the same Nation at different times, as the Maxim of all Legislation and the Ground of all legislative Power. For his universal Principles, as far as they are Principles and universal, necessarily suppose uniform and perfect Subjects, which are to be found in the *Ideas* of pure Geometry and (I trust) in the *Realities* of Heaven, but never, never, in Creatures of Flesh and Blood.

4

Property and Responsibility: *A Lay Sermon* (1817)

In the second 'Lay Sermon'[1] Coleridge analyses the causes of the post-war crisis in Britain and assesses the qualifications of those who advance solutions to it. He is critical of radical arguments that focus on the system of taxation and the political institutions of the country, and condemns the motives and conduct of radical political agitators. He also rejects the view (associated with proponents of 'political economy') that hardship is an unavoidable result of the play of market forces. Coleridge argues that the end of the war was bound to be followed by a period of painful readjustment, but claims that this has been exacerbated by the sophisms of radicals and political economists, and also by the upper classes' irresponsible attitude towards commercial values. The root cause of present difficulties is the 'overbalance' of the commercial spirit, and its permeation of areas of human life that should have provided a counterbalance to it. In A Lay Sermon, Coleridge seeks to encourage the upper classes to restore the balance by attaching themselves to the humanising values found in philosophy and intellectualised religion, and performing those ameliorating functions traditionally associated with the possession of landed property. Although Coleridge defends commerce against the attacks of radicals and claims that it has produced significant additions to the opportunities for free action, he claims that these opportunities should be additional to, not substitutes for, the recognition of moral personality that is central to the justification of the state, and closely connected with those fixed, landed-proprietorial interests that are integral to it. In A Lay Sermon the moral view of the state that Coleridge had advanced in The Friend *is combined with a social analysis of landed property which builds upon that which had appeared in his turn-of-the-century articles on French affairs.*

If ye do not hope, ye will not find: for in despairing ye block up the mine at its mouth! ye extinguish the torch, even when ye are already in the shaft.

> God and the world we worship still together,
> Draw not our laws to Him, but His to ours;
> Untrue to both, so prosperous in neither,

The Imperfect will brings forth but barren flowers!
Unwise as all distracted interests be,
Strangers to God, fools in humanity:
Too good for great things and too great for good,
While still *"I dare not"* waits upon *"I wou'd."*[2]

INTRODUCTION

Fellow-Countrymen! You I mean, who fill the higher and middle stations of society! The comforts, perchance the splendors, that surround you, designate your rank, but cannot constitute your moral and personal fitness for it. Be it enough for others to know, that you are its *legal* – but by what mark shall you stand accredited to your own consciences, as its *worthy* – possessors? Not by common sense or common honesty; for these are equally demanded of all classes, and therefore mere negative qualifications in *your* rank of life, or characteristic only by the aggravated ignominy consequent on their absence. Not by genius or splendid talent: for these, as being gifts of Nature, are objects of moral interest for those alone, to whom they have been allotted. Nor yet by eminence in learning; for this supposes such a devotion of time and thought, as would in many cases be incompatible with the claims of active life. Erudition is, doubtless, an *ornament*, that especially beseemes a high station: but it is *professional* rank only that renders its attainment a duty.

The mark in question must be so far *common*, that we may be entitled to look for it in *you* from the mere circumstance of your situation, and so far distinctive, that it must be such as cannot be expected generally from the inferior classes. Now either there is no such criterion in existence, or the Desideratum is to be found in *an habitual consciousness of the ultimate principles, to which your opinions are traceable.* The least, that can be demanded of the least favored among you, is an earnest *endeavour* to walk in the Light of your own knowledge; and not, as the *mass* of mankind, by laying hold on the skirts of Custom. Blind followers of a blind and capricious guide, forced likewise (though oftener, I fear, by their own improvidence,*³ than by the lowness of their estate) to consume Life in the means of living, the multitude may make the sad confession

> Tempora mutantur: nos et mutamur in illis
> [Times change and we change with them]

unabashed.⁴ But to English Protestants in the enjoyment of a present competency, much more to such as are defended against the anxious Future, it must needs be a grievous dishonor (and not the less grievous, though perhaps less striking, from its frequency) to change with the times, and thus to debase their motives and maxims, the sacred household of conscience, into slaves and creatures of fashion. *Thou therefore art inexcusable,* O man! if thou dost not give to thyself *a reason for the faith that is in thee:* if thou dost not thereby learn the safety and the blessedness of that other apostolic precept, *Whatsoever ye do, do it in* Faith.⁵ Your habits of reflection should at least be equal to your opportunities of leisure: and to that which is itself a *species* of leisure – your immunity from bodily labour, from the voice and lash of the imperious ever-recurring This Day! Your attention to the objects, that stretch away below you in the living landscape of good and evil, and your researches into their existing or practicable bearings on each other, should be proportional to the elevation that extends and diversifies your prospect. If you possess more than is necessary for your own wants, more than your own wants ought to be felt by you as your own interests. You are pacing on a smooth terrace, which you owe to the happy institutions of your country, – a terrace on the mountain's breast. To what purpose, by what *moral* right, if you continue to gaze only on the sod beneath your feet? Or if converting means into ends and with all your thoughts and efforts

---

* [Coleridge added a note at this point, the last section of which is included below as an indication of the argument of *The Statesman's Manual*.] We judge harshly because we expect irrationally. But on the other hand, this disproportion of the power to the wish, will sooner or later, end in that tame acquiescence in things as they are, which is the sad symptom of a moral *necrosis* commencing. And commence it will, if its causes are not counteracted by the philosophy of history, that is, by history read in the spirit of prophecy! if they are not overcome by the faith which, still re-kindling hope, still re-enlivens charity. Without the knowledge of Man, the knowledge of Men is a hazardous acquisition. What insight might not our statesmen acquire from the study of the Bible merely as history, if only they had been previously accustomed to study history in the same spirit, as that in which good men read the Bible!

absorbed in selfish schemes of climbing cloudward, you turn your back on the wide landscape, and stoop the lower, the higher you ascend.

The remedial and prospective advantages, that may be rationally anticipated from the habit of contemplating particulars in their universal laws; its tendency at once to fix and to liberalize the morality of private life, at once to produce and enlighten the spirit of public zeal; and let me add, its especial utility in recalling the origin and primary purport of the term, GENEROSITY,* to the heart and thoughts of a populace tampered with by sophists and incendiaries of the revolutionary school; these advantages I have felt it my duty and have made it my main object to press on your serious attention during the whole period of my literary labors from earliest manhood to the present hour. Whatever may have been the specific theme of my communications, and whether they related to criticism, politics, or religion, still PRINCIPLES, their subordination, their connection, and their application, in all the divisions of our tastes, duties, rules of conduct and schemes of belief, have constituted my chapter of contents.

It is an unsafe partition, that divides opinions without principle from unprincipled opinions. If the latter are not followed by correspondent actions, we are indebted for the escape, not to the agent himself, but to his habits of education, to the sympathies of superior rank, to the necessity of character, often, perhaps, to the absence of temptation from providential circumstances or the accident of a gracious Nature. These, indeed, are truths of all times and places; but I seemed to see especial reason for insisting on them in our own times. A long and attentive observation had convinced me, that formerly MEN WERE WORSE THAN THEIR PRIN- CIPLES, but that at present the PRINCIPLES ARE WORSE THAN THE MEN.[6]

Few are sufficiently aware how much reason most of us have, even as common moral livers, to thank God for being ENGLISHMEN. It would furnish grounds both for humility towards Providence and for increased attachment to our country, if each individual could but see and feel, how large a part of his innocence he owes to his birth, breeding, and residence in Great Britain. The

---

* A *genre*: the qualities either supposed natural and instinctive to men of noble race, or such as their rank is calculated to inspire, as disinterestedness, devotion to the service of their friends, and clients, &c. frankness, &c.

administration of the laws; the almost continual preaching of moral prudence; the number and respectability of our sects; the pressure of our ranks on each other, with the consequent reserve and watchfulness of demeanor in the superior ranks, and the emulation in the subordinate; the vast depth, expansion and systematic movements of our trade; and the consequent inter-dependence, the arterial or nerve-like *net-work* of property, which make every deviation from outward integrity a calculable loss to the offending individual himself from its mere effects, as obstruction and irregularity; and lastly, the naturalness of doing as others do: – these and the like influences, peculiar, some in the kind and all in the degree, to this privileged island, are the buttresses, on which our foundationless well-doing is upheld, even as a house of cards, the architecture of our infancy, in which each is supported by all.

Well then may we pray, give us peace in our time, O Lord! Well for us, if no revolution, or other general visitation, betray the *true* state of our national morality! But above all, well will it be for us if *even now* we dare disclose the secret of our own souls! Well will it be for as many of us as have duly reflected on the Prophet's assurance, *that we must take root downwards if we would bear fruit upwards,*[7] if we would bear fruit, and *continue* to bear fruit, when the foodful plants that stand straight, only because they grow in company; or whose slender surface-roots owe their whole stedfastness to their intertanglement; have been beaten down by the continued rains, or whirled aloft by the sudden hurricane! Nor have we far to seek for whatever it is most important that we should find. The wisdom from above has not ceased for us! "*The principles of the oracles of God*"[8] are still uttered from before the altar! ORACLES, which we may consult without cost! Before an ALTAR, where no sacrifice is required, but of the vices which unman us! no victims demanded, but the unclean and animal passions, which we may have suffered to house within us, forgetful of our baptismal dedication – no victim, but the spiritual sloth, or goat, or fox, or hog, which lay waste the vineyard that the Lord had fenced and planted for himself.

I have endeavored in a previous discourse to persuade the more highly gifted and educated part of my friend and fellow-christians, that as the *New* Testament sets forth the means and conditions of spiritual convalescence, with all the laws of conscience relative to our future state and permanent Being; so does the *Bible* present to us the elements of *public* prudence, instructing us in the true causes, the surest preventives, and the only cures, of public evils.[9] The authorities of Raleigh, Clarendon and Milton must at least exempt me from the blame of singularity, if undeterred by the contradictory charges of paradoxy from one party and of adherence to vulgar and old-fashioned prejudices from the other, I persist in avowing my conviction, that the inspired poets, historians and sententiaries of the Jews, are the clearest teachers of political economy: in short, that their writings [note omitted] are the STATESMAN'S BEST MANUAL, not only as containing the first principles and ultimate grounds of state-policy whether in prosperous times or in those of danger and distress, but as supplying likewise the details of their *application*, and as being a full and spacious repository of precedents and facts in proof.

Well therefore (again and again I repeat to you,) well will it be for us if we have provided ourselves from this armory while "yet the day of trouble and of treading down and of perplexity" appears at far distance and only "in the valley of Vision:" if we have humbled ourselves and have confessed our thin and unsound state, even while "from the uttermost parts of the earth we were hearing songs of praise and glory to the upright nation."[10]

But if indeed the day of treading down is present, it is still in our power to convert it into a time of substantial discipline for ourselves, and of enduring benefit to the present generation and to posterity. The splendor of our exploits, during the late war, is less honorable to us than the magnanimity of our views, and our generous confidence in the victory of the better cause. Accordingly, we have obtained a good name, so that the nations around us have displayed a disposition to follow our example and imitate our institutions – too often I fear even in parts where from the difference of our relative circumstances the imitation had little chance of proving more than mimickry. But it will be far more glorious, and to our neighbours incomparably more instructive, if in distresses to which all countries are liable we bestir ourselves in remedial and preventive arrangements which all nations may more or less adopt; inasmuch as they are grounded on principles intelligible to all rational and obligatory on all moral beings; inasmuch as, having been taught by God's word, exampled by God's providence, commanded by God's law, and recommended by promises of God's grace, they alone can form the foundations of a christian community. Do we love our country? These are the principles, by which the true friend of the people is contradistinguished from the factious demagogue. They are at once the rock and the quarry. On these alone and with these alone is the solid welfare of a people to be built. Do we love our own souls? These are the principles, the neglect of which writes hypocrite and suicide on the brow of the professing christian. For these are the keystone of that arch on which alone we can cross the torrent of life and death with safety on the passage; with peace in the retrospect; and with hope shining upon us from through the cloud, toward which we are travelling. Not, my christian friends! by all the lamps of worldly wisdom clustered in one blaze, can we guide our paths so securely as by fixing our eyes on this inevitable cloud, through which all must pass, which at every step becomes darker and more threatening to the children of this world, but to the children of faith and obedience still thins away as they approach, to melt at length and dissolve into that glorious light, from which as so many gleams and reflections of the same falling on us during our mortal pilgrimage, we derive all principles of true and lively knowledge, alike in science and in morals, alike in communities and in individuals.[11] . . .

A LAY SERMON, &c.

ISAIAH, xxxii 20
Blessed are ye that sow beside all waters.

. . . Peace has come without the advantages expected from Peace, and on the contrary, with many of the severest inconveniences usually attributable to War. "We looked for peace, but no good came: for a time of health and behold trouble. The harvest is past, the summer is ended, and we are not saved." The inference therefore contained in the preceding verse is unavoidable. Where war has produced no repentance, and the cessation of war has brought neither concord or tranquillity, we may safely cry aloud with the Prophet: "They have healed the hurt of the daughter of my people slightly, saying peace, peace, when there is no peace." The whole remaining subject therefore may be comprised in the three questions implied in the last of the verses, recited to you; in three questions, and in the answers to the same.[12] First, who are they who have hitherto prescribed for the case, and are still tampering with it? What are their qualifications? What has been their conduct? Second, What is the true seat and source of the complaint, – the ultimate causes as well as the immediate occasions? And lastly, What are the appropriate medicines? Who and where are the true physicians?

And first then of those who have been ever loud and foremost in their pretensions to a knowledge both of the disease and the remedy. In a preceding part of the same chapter from which I extracted the line prefixed, the Prophet Isaiah enumerates the conditions of a nation's recovery from a state of depression and peril, and among these one condition which he describes in words that may be without any forced or over-refined interpretation unfolded into an answer to the present question. "A vile person," he tell us, "must no more be called liberal, nor the churl be said to be bountiful. For the vile person shall speak villainy, and his heart will work iniquity to practice hypocrisy and to utter error against the Lord; to make empty the soul of the needy, and he will cause the drink of the thirsty to fail. The instruments also of the churl are evil: he deviseth wicked devices to destroy the poor with lying words, even when the needy speaketh aright. But the Liberal deviseth liberal things, and by liberal things shall he stand."[13]

Such are the political empirics mischievous in proportion to their effrontery, and ignorant in proportion to their presumption, the detection and exposure of whose true characters the inspired statesman and patriot represents as indispensable to the re-establishment of the general welfare, while his own portrait of these imposters whom in a former chapter (ix. 15. 16.) he calls, *the tail of the Nation*, and in the following verse, *Demagogues that cause the people to err*, affords to the intelligent believer of all ages and countries the means of detecting them, and of undeceiving all whose own malignant passions have not rendered them blind and deaf and brutish. For these noisy and calumnious zealots, whom (with an especial reference indeed to the factious leaders of the populace who under this name exercised a tumultuary despotism in Jerusalem, at once a sign and a cause of its approaching downfall) St. John beheld in the Apocalyptic vision[14] as a compound of Locust and Scorpion, are not of one place or of one season. They are the perennials of history: and though they may disappear for a time, they exist always in the egg and need only a distempered atmosphere and an accidental ferment to start up into life and activity.

. . . Worthless persons of little or no estimation for rank, learning, or integrity, not seldom profligates, with whom debauchery has outwrestled rapacity, easy because unprincipled and generous because dishonest, are suddenly cried up as men of enlarged views and liberal sentiments, our only genuine patriots and philanthropists: and churls, that is, men of sullen tempers and surly demeanor; men tyrannical in their families, oppressive and troublesome to their dependents and neighbours, and hard in their private dealings between man and man; men who clench with one hand what they have grasped with the other; these are extolled as public benefactors, the friends, guardians, and advocates of the poor! Here and there indeed we may notice an individual of birth and fortune

(For great estates enlarge not narrow minds)[15]

who has been duped into the ranks of incendiaries and mob-sycophants by an insane restlessness, and the wretched ambition of figuring as the triton of the minows. Or we may find perhaps a professional man of shewy accomplishments but of a vulgar taste, and shallow acquirements, who in part from vanity, and in part as a means of introduction to practice, will seek notoriety by an eloquence well calculated to set the multitude agape, and excite *gratis* to overt-acts of sedition or treason which he may afterwards be fee'd to defend! These however are but exceptions to the general rule. Such as the Prophet has described, such is the *sort* of men; and in point of historic fact it has been from men of this sort, *that profaneness is gone forth into all the land.*[16]

In harmony with the general character of these false prophets, are the particular qualities assigned to them. First, a passion for vague and violent invective, an habitual and inveterate predilection for the language of hate, and rage and contumely, an ungoverned appetite for abuse and defamation! THE VILE WILL TALK VILLAINY.

But the fetid flower will ripen into the poisonous berry, and the fruits of the hand follow the blossoms of the slanderous lips. HIS HEART WILL WORK INIQUITY. That is, he will plan evil, and do his utmost to carry his plans into execution. The guilt exists already; and there wants nothing but power and opportunity to condense it into crime and overt-act. *He that hateth his brother is a murderer!* says St. John:[17] and of many and various sorts are the brother-haters, in whom this truth may be exemplified. Most appropriately for our purpose, Isaiah has selected the fratricide of sedition, and with the eagle eye and practised touch of an intuitive demonstrator he unfolds the composition of the character, part by part, in the secret history of the agent's wishes, designs and attempts, of his ways, his means, and his ends. The agent himself, the incendiary and his kindling combustibles, had been already sketched by Solomon, with the rapid yet faithful outline of a master in the art: *"The beginning of the words of his mouth is foolishness and the end of his talk mischievous madness."*[18] If in the spirit of Prophecy [note omitted], the wise Ruler had been present to our own times, and their procedures; if while he sojourned *in the valley of vision* he had actually heard the very harangues of our reigning demagogues to the convened populace; could he have more faithfully characterised either the speakers or the speeches? Whether in spoken or in printed Addresses, whether in periodical Journals or in yet cheaper implements of irritation, the ends are the same, the process is the same, and the same is their general line of conduct. On all occasions, but most of all and with a more bustling malignity, whenever any public distress inclines the lower classes to turbulence, and renders them more apt to be alienated from the government of their country – in all places and at every opportunity pleading *to* the Poor and Ignorant, no where and at no time are they found actually pleading *for* them.[19] Nor is this the worst. They even plead against them. Yes! Sycophants to the *crowd*, enemies of the *individuals*, and well-wishers only to the continuance of their miseries, they plead *against* the poor and afflicted, under the weak and wicked pretence, that we are to do nothing of what we can, because we cannot do all, that we would wish. Or if this sophistry of sloth (*sophisma pigri*) should fail to check the bounty of the rich, there is still the sophistry of slander in reserve to chill the gratitude of the poor. If they cannot dissuade *the Liberal from devising liberal things*, they will at least blacken the motives of his beneficence. If they cannot close the hand of the giver, they will at least embitter the gift in the mouth of the receivers. Is it not as if they had said within their hearts: the sacrifice of charity has been offered indeed in despite of us; *but with bitter herbs shall it be eaten!*[20] Imagined Wrongs shall make it distasteful. We will infuse vindictive and discontented fancies into minds, already irritable and suspicious from distress: till the fever of the heart shall coat the tongue with gall and spread wormwood on the palate?

However angrily our demagogues may disclaim all intentions of this kind, such has been their procedure, and it is susceptible of no other interpretation. We all know, that the shares must be scanty, where the dividend bears no proportion to the number of the claimants. Yet He, who satisfied the multitude in the wilderness with a few loaves and fishes, is still present to his church. Small as the portions are, if they are both given and taken in the spirit of his commands, a Blessing will go with each; and *the handful of meal shall not fail, until the day when the Lord bringeth back plenty on the land.*[21] But no Blessing can enter where Envy and Hatred are already in possession; and small good will the poor man have of the food prepared for him by his more favored Brother, if he have been previously taught to regard it as a mess of pottage given to defraud him of his Birth-right.

If then to promise medicine and to administer poison; if to flatter in order to deprave; if to affect love to all and shew pity to none; if to exaggerate and misderive the distress of the labouring classes in order to make them turbulent, and to discourage every plan for their relief in order to keep them so; if to skulk from private infamy in the mask of public spirit, and make the flaming patriot privilege the gamester, swindler or adulterer; if to seek amnesty for a continued violation of the laws of God by an equal pertinacity in outraging the laws of the land; if these characterize the hypocrite, we need not look far back or far round for faces, wherein to recognize the third striking feature of this prophetic portrait! When therefore the verifying facts press upon us in real life; when we hear persons, the tyranny of whose will is the only law in their families, denouncing all law as tyranny in public – persons, whose hatred of power in others is in exact proportion to their love of it for themselves; when we behold men of sunk and irretrievable characters, to whom no man would entrust his wife, his sister, or his purse, have the effrontery to propose that we should entrust to them our religion and our country; when we meet with *Patriots*, who aim at an enlargement of the rights and liberties of the people by inflaming the populace to acts of madness that necessitate fetters – pretended heralds of freedom and actual pioneers of military despotism; we will call to mind the words of the prophet Isaiah, and say to ourselves: this is no new thing under the Sun! We have heard it with our own ears, and it was declared to our fathers, and in the old time before them, that one of the main characteristics of demagogues in all ages is, TO PRACTISE HYPO-CRISY.[22]

Such, I assert, has been the general line of conduct pursued by the political Empirics of the day: and your own recent experience will attest the truth of the assertion. It was affirmed likewise at the same time, that as the conduct, such was the *process*: and I will seek no other support of this charge, I need no better test both of the men and their works, than the plain question: is there one good feeling, to which they do – is there a single bad passion, to which they do not appeal? If they are the enemies of liberty in general, inasmuch as they tend to make it appear incompatible with public quiet and personal safety, still more emphatically are they the enemies of the liberty of the PRESS in particular; and therein of all the truths human and divine which a free press is the most efficient and only commensurate means of protecting, extending and perpetuating. The strongest, indeed the only plausible, arguments against the education of the lower classes, are derived from the writings of these incendiaries; and if for our neglect of the light that hath been vouchsafed to us beyond measure, the land should be visited with a spiritual dearth, it will have been in no small degree occasioned by the erroneous and wicked principles which it is the trade of these men to propagate. . . . Alas! it is a hard and a mournful thing, that the Press should be constrained to call out for the harsh curb of the law against the Press! . . . And yet will we avoid this seeming injustice, we throw down all fence and bulwark of public decency and public opinion. Already has political calumny joined hands with private slander, and every principle, every feeling, that binds the citizen to his country, the spirit to its Creator, is in danger of being undermined. – Not by reasoning, for from that there is no danger; but – by the mere habit of hearing them reviled and scoffed at with impunity. Were we to contemplate the evils of a rank and unweeded Press only in its effects on the manners of a people, and on the general tone of thought and conversation, the greater love we bore to literature, and to all the means and instruments of human improvement, the more anxiously should we wish for some Ithuriel spear that might remove from the ear of the ignorant and half-learned, and expose in their own fiendish shape, those reptiles, which *inspiring venom and forging illusions as they list,*

―――thence raise,
At least distemper'd discontented thoughts,
Vain hopes, vain aims, inordinate desires.[23]

. . . This is the Pharmacopoeia of political empirics, here and everywhere, now and at all times! These are the drugs administered, and the tricks played off by the Mountebanks and Zanies of Patriotism; drugs that will continue to poison as long as Irreligion secures a predisposition to their influence; and artifices, that like stratagems in war, are never the less successful for having succeeded a hundred times before. "They *bend their tongues as a bow: they shoot out deceits as arrows: they are prophets of the deceit of their own hearts: they cause the people to err by their dreams and their lightness: they make the people vain, they feed them with wormwood, they give them the water of gall for drink; and the people love to have it so. And what is the end thereof?*"[24]

The Prophet answers for me in the concluding words of the description – To DESTROY THE POOR EVEN WHEN THE NEEDY SPEAKETH ARIGHT – that is, to impel them to acts that must end in their ruin by inflammatory falsehoods and by working on their passions till they lead them to reject the prior convictions of their own sober and unsophisticated understandings. As in all the preceding features so in this, with which the prophetic portrait is compleated, our own experience supplies both proof and example. The ultimate causes of the present distress and stagnation are in the Writer's opinion complex and deeply seated; but the immediate occasion is too obvious to be over-looked but by eyes at once red and dim through the intoxication of factious prejudice, that maddening spirit which pre-eminently deserves the title of vinum daemonum [devil's wine] applied by an ancient Father of the Church to a far more innocent phrenzy.[25] It is demonstrable that taxes, the product of which is circulated in the Country from which they are raised, can never injure a Country *directly* by the mere amount; but either from the time or circumstances under which they are raised, or from the injudicious mode in which they are levied, or from the improper objects to which they are applied. The Sun may draw up the moisture from the river, the morass, and the ocean, to be given back in genial showers to the garden, the pasture and the cornfield; but it may likewise force upward the moisture from the fields of industry to drop it on the stagnant pool, the saturated swamp, or the unprofitable sand-waste. The corruptions of a system can be duly appreciated by those only who have contemplated the system in that ideal state of perfection exhibited by the reason: the nearest possible approximation to which under existing circumstances it is the business of the prudential understanding to realize. Those on the other hand, who commence the examination of a system by identifying it with its abuses or imperfections, degrade their understanding into the pander of their passions, and are sure to prescribe remedies more dangerous than the disease. Alas! there are so many real evils, so many just causes of complaint in the constitutions and administration of all governments, our own not excepted, that it becomes the imperious duty of the true patriot to prevent, as much as in him lies, the feelings and efforts of his fellow country-men from losing themselves on a wrong scent.

If then we are to master the *Ideal* of a beneficent and judicious system of Finance as the preliminary to all profitable insight into the defects of any particular system in actual existence, we could not perhaps find an apter illustration than the gardens of southern Europe would supply. The tanks or reservoirs would represent the capital of a nation: while the hundred rills hourly varying their channels and directions, under the gardener's spade, would give a pleasing image of the dispersion of that capital through the whole population by the joint effect of taxation and trade. For taxation itself is a part of commerce, and the Government may be fairly considered as a great manufacturing-house, carrying on in different places, by means of its partners and overseers, the trades of the ship-builder, the clothier, the iron-founder, &c. &c. As long as a balance is preserved between the receipts and the returns of Government in their amount, quickness, and degree of dispersion; as long as the due proportion obtains in the sums levied to the mass in productive circulation, so long does the wealth and circumstantial prosperity of the nation, (its wealth, I say, not its real welfare; its outward prosperity, but not necessarily its happiness) remain unaffected, or rather they will appear to increase in consequence of the additional stimulus given to the circulation itself by the reproductive action of all large capitals, and through the check which taxation, in its own nature, gives to the indolence of the wealthy in its continual transfer of property to the industrious and enterprizing. If different periods be taken, and if the comparative weight of the taxes at each be calculated, as it ought to be, not by the sum *levied on* each individual, but by the sum *left in his possession*, the settlement of the account will be in favor of the national wealth, to the amount of all the additional productive labor sustained or excited by the taxes during the intervals between their efflux and their re-absorption.

But on the other hand, in a direct ratio to this increase will be the distress produced by the disturbance of this balance, by the loss of this proportion; and the operation of the distress will be at least equal to the total amount of the difference between the taxes still levied, and the quantum of aid withdrawn from individuals by the abandonment of others, and of that which the taxes, that still remain, have ceased to give by the altered mode of their re-dispersion. But to this we must add the number of persons raised and reared in consequence of the demand created by the preceding state of things, and now discharged from their occupations: whether the latter belong exclusively to the Executive Power, as that of soldiers, &c. or from those in which the labourers for the nation in general are already sufficiently numerous. Both these classes are thrown back on the Public, and sent to a table where every seat is pre-occupied.[26] The employment lessens as the number of men to be employed is increased; and not merely in the same, but from additional causes and from the indirect consequences of those already stated, in a far greater ratio. For it may easily happen, that the very same change, which had produced this depression at home, may from equivalent causes have embarrassed the countries in commercial connection with us. At one and the same time the great customer at home wants less, and our customers abroad are able to buy less. The conjoint action of these circumstances will furnish, for a mind capable of combining them, a sufficient solution of the melancholy fact. They cannot but occasion much distress, much obstruction, and these again in their re-action are sure to be more than doubled by the still greater and universal alarm, and by the consequent check of confidence and enterprize, which they never fail to produce.

Now it is a notorious fact, that these causes did all exist to a very extraordinary degree, and that they all worked with united strength, in the late sudden transition from War to Peace. It was one among the many anomalies of the late War, that it acted, after a few years, as a universal stimulant. We almost monopolized the commerce of the world. The high wages of our artisans and the high prices of agricultural produce intercirculated. Leases of no unusual length not seldom enabled the provident and thrifty farmer to purchase the estate he had rented. Every where might be seen roads, rail-ways, docks, canals, made, making, and projected; villages swelling into towns, while the metropolis surrounded itself, and became (as it were) *set* with new cities. Finally, in spite of all the waste and havock of a twenty years' war, the population of the empire was increased by more than two millions! The efforts and war-expenditure of the nation, and the yearly revenue, were augmented in the same proportion: and to all this we must add a fact of the utmost importance in the present question, that the war did not, as was usually the case in former wars, die away into a long expected peace by gradual exhaustion and weariness on both sides, but *plunged* to its conclusion by a concentration, we might almost say, by a *spasm* of energy, and consequently by an *anticipation* of our resources. We conquered by compelling *reversionary* power into alliance with our existing and natural strength. The first intoxication of triumph having passed over, this our "agony of glory," was succeeded, of course, by a general stiffness and relaxation. The antagonist passions came into play; financial solicitude was blended with constitutional and political jealousies, and both, alas! were exacerbated by personal imprudences, the chief injury of which consisted in their own tendency to disgust and alienate the public feeling. And with all this, the financial errors and prejudices even of the more educated classes, in short, the general want or imperfection of clear views and a scientific insight into the true effects and influences of Taxation, and the mode of its operation, became now a real misfortune, and opened an additional source of temporary embarrassment. Retrenchment could no longer proceed by cautious and calculated steps; but was compelled to hurry forward, like one who crossing the sands at too late an hour finds himself threatened by the inrush of the tide. Nevertheless, it was a truth susceptible of little less than mathematical demonstration, that the more, and the more suddenly, the Revenue was diminished by the abandonment of the war-taxes, the greater would be the disturbance of the Balance*: so that the agriculturalist, the manufacturer,

---

* The disturbance of this balance may be illustrated thus: – Suppose a great Capitalist to have founded, in a large market-town, a factory that gradually increasing employed at length from five to six hundred workmen; and that he had likewise a second factory at a distance from the former . . . employing half that number, all the latter having been drafted from and still belonging to the first Parish. After some years we may further suppose, that a large proportion of the housekeepers and trades-people might have a running account with the Capitalist,

or the tradesman, (all in short but annuitants and fixed stipendiaries) who during the war having paid as Five had Fifteen left behind, would shortly have less than Ten after having paid but Two and a Half.[27]

But there is yet another circumstance, which we dare not pass by unnoticed. In the best of times – or what the world calls such – the spirit of commerce will occasion great fluctuations, some falling while others rise, and therefore in all times there will be a large sum of individual distress. Trades likewise have their seasons, and at all times there is a very considerable number of artificers who are not employed on the average more than seven or eight months in the year: and the distress from this cause is great or small in proportion to the greater or less degree of dissipation and improvidence prevailing among them. But besides this, that artificial life and vigor of Trade and Agriculture, which was produced or occasioned by the direct or indirect influences of the late War, proved by no means innoxious in its effects. Habit and the familiarity with outward advantages, which takes off their *dazzle*; sense of character; and above all, the counterpoise of intellectual pursuits and resources; are all necessary preventives and antidotes to the dangerous properties of wealth and power with the great majority of mankind. It is a painful subject: and I leave to your own experience and recollection the assemblage of folly, presumption, and extravagance, that followed in the procession of our late unprecedented prosperity; the blind practices and blending

---

many with him, as being their landlord, and still more for their stock. The workmen would in a like manner be for the greater part on the books of the tradesfolks. As long as this state of things continued, all would go on well; – nay, the town would be more prosperous with every increase of the factory. THE BALANCE IS PRESERVED. The circulations counterpoise each other, or rather they are neutralized by interfluence. But some sudden event leads or compels the Capitalist to put down both factories at once and with little or no warning; and to call in the moneys owing to him, and which by law had the preference to all other debts. – What would be the consequence? The workmen are no longer employed, and cannot at once pay up their arrears to the tradesmen; and though the Capitalist should furnish the latter with goods at half price, and make the same abatement in their rent, these deductions would afford little present relief; while, in the meantime the discharged workmen from the distant factory would fall back on the Parish, and increase the general distress. THE BALANCE IS DISTURBED. – Put the Country at large for the parishioners, and the Government in all departments of expenditure for the Capitalist and his factories: and nearly such is the situation in which we are placed by the transition from the late War to the present Peace. But the difference is this. The Town may never recover its temporary prosperity, and the Capitalist may spend his remaining fortune in another county; but a nation, of which the Government is an organic part with perfect interdependence of interests, can never remain in a state of depression thus produced, but by its own fault: that is, from moral causes.

passions of speculation in the commercial world, with the shoal of ostentatious fooleries and sensual vices which the sudden influx of wealth let in on our farmers and yeomanry. Now though the whole mass of calamity consequent on these aberrations from prudence should in all fairness be attributed to the sufferer's own conduct; yet when there supervenes some one common cause or occasion of distress which pressing hard on many furnishes a pretext to all, this too will pass muster among its actual effects, and assume the semblance and dignity of national calamity. Each unfortunate individual shares during *the hard times* in the immunities of a privileged order, as the most tottering and ruinous houses equally with those in best repair are included in the same brief after an extensive fire. The change of the moon will not produce a change of weather, except in places where the atmosphere has from local and particular causes been predisposed to its influence. But the former is one, placed aloft and conspicuous to all men; the latter are many and intricate, and known to few. Of course it is the moon that must bear the entire blame of wet summers and scanty crops. All these, however, whether they are distresses common to all times alike, or though *occasioned* by the general revolution and stagnation, yet really *caused* by personal improvidence or misconduct, combine with its peculiar and inevitable effects in making the cup overflow. The latter class especially, as being in such cases always the most clamorous sufferers, increase the evil by swelling the alarm.

The *principal* parts of the preceding explication, the *main* causes of the present exigencies are so obvious, and lay so open to the common sense of mankind, that the labouring classes saw the connection of the change in the times with the suddenness of the peace, as clearly as their superiors, and being less heated with speculation, were in the first instance less surprized at the results. To a public event of universal concern there will often be more attributed than belongs to it; but never in the natural course of human feelings will there be less. That the depression began *with* the Peace would have been of itself a sufficient proof with the Màny, that it arose *from* the Peace. But this opinion suited ill with the purposes of sedition. The truth, that could not be precluded, must be removed; and *"when the needy speaketh aright"* the more urgent occasion is there for the *"wicked device"* and the *"lying words."* Where distress is felt, tales of wrong and oppression are readily believed, to the sufferer's own disquiet. Rage and Revenge make the cheek pale and the hand tremble, worse than even want itself: and the cup of sorrow overflows by being held unsteadily. On the other hand nothing calms the mind in the hour of bitterness so efficaciously as the conviction that it was not within the means of those above us, or around us, to have prevented it. An influence, mightier than fascination, dwells in the stern eye of Necessity, when it is fixed steadily on a man: for together with the *power* of resistance it takes away its agitations likewise. This is one mercy that always accompanies the visitations of the Almighty when they are received *as* such. If therefore the sufferings of the lower classes are to supply air and fuel to their passions, and are to be perverted into instruments of mischief, they must be attributed to causes that can be represented as removeable; either to individuals who had been previously rendered unpopular, or to whole classes of men, according as the immediate object of their seducers may require. What, though nothing should be more remote from the true cause? What though the invidious charge should be not only without proof, but in the face of strong proof to the contrary? What though the pretended remedy should have no possible end but that of exasperating the disease? All will be of little or no avail, if these truths have not been administered beforehand. When *the wrath is gone forth, the plague is already begun. . . . Wrath is cruel*, and where is there a deafness like that of an outrageous multitude? *For as the matter of the fire is, so it burneth.* Let the demagogue but succeed in maddening the crowd, he may bid defiance to demonstration, and direct the madness against whom it pleaseth him. *A slanderous tongue has disquieted many, and driven them from nation to nation; strong cities hath it pulled down and overthrown the houses of great men.*[28] . . .

We see in every promiscuous public meeting the effect produced by the bold assertion that the present hardships of all classes are owing to the number and amount of PENSIONS and SINE-CURES. Yet from the unprecedented zeal and activity in the education [note omitted] of the poor, of the thousands that are inflamed by, and therefore give credit to, these statements, there are few without a child at home, who could prove their impossibility by the first and simplest rules of arithmetic; there is not one, perhaps, who taken by himself and in a cooler mood, would stand out against the simple question: whether it was not folly to suppose that the lowness of his wages, or his want of employment could be occasioned by the circumstance, that a sum (the whole of which, as far as it is raised by taxation, cannot take a yearly penny from him) was dispersed and returned into the general circulation by Annuitants of the Treasury instead of Annuitants of the Bank, by John instead of Peter: however blameable the regulation might be in other respects? What then? the hypothesis allows of a continual reference to *persons*, and to all the uneasy and malignant passions which personalities are of all means the best fitted to awaken. The *grief* itself, however grinding it may be, is of no avail to this end; it must first be converted into a *grievance*. Were the audience composed chiefly of the lower Farmers and the Peasantry, the same circumstance would for the same reason have been attributed wholly to the Clergy and the system of TYTHES; as if the corn would be more plentiful if the Farmers paid their whole rent to one man, instead of paying nine parts to the Landlords and the tenth to the Tythe-owners! But let the meeting be composed of the Manufacturing Poor, and then it is the MACHINERY of their Employers that is devoted to destruction: though it would not exceed the truth if I affirmed, that to the use and perfection of this very Machinery the majority of the poor deluded destroyers owe their very *existence*, owe to it that they ever beheld the light of heaven!

Even so it is with the Capitalists and Storekeepers, who by spreading the dearness of provisions over a larger space and time prevent scarcity from becoming real famine, the frightful lot at certain and not distant intervals of our less commercial forefathers. These men by the mere instinct of self-interest are not alone birds of warning, that prevent waste; but as the raven of Elijah, they bring supplies from afar. But let the incendiary spirit have rendered them birds of ill omen: and it is well if the deluded Malcontents can be restrained from levelling at them missiles more alarming than the curse of the unwise that alighteth not. . . . Wretches! they would without remorse detract the hope that is the subliming and expanding warmth of public credit,[29] destroy the public credit that is the vital air of national industry, convert obstruction into stagnation, and make grass grow in the exchange and the market-place; if so they might but goad ignorance into riot, and fanaticism into rebellion! They would snatch the last morsel from the poor man's lips to make him curse the Government in his heart – alas! to fall at length, either ignominiously beneath the *strength* of the outraged Law, of (if God in his anger, and for the punishment of general depravity should require a severer and more extensive retribution) to perish still more lamentably among the victims of its *weakness*.

Thus then, I have answered at large to the first of the three questions proposed as the heads and divisions of this Address. I am well aware that our demagogues are not the only empirics who have tampered with the case. But I felt unwilling to put the mistakes of sciolism, or even those of vanity and self-interest, in the same section with crime and guilt. What is omitted here will find its place elsewhere; the more readily, that having been tempted by the foulness of the ways to turn for a short space out of my direct path, I have encroached already on the second question; that, namely, which respects the ultimate causes and immediate occasions of the complaint.

The latter part of this problem I appear to myself to have solved fully and satisfactorily. To those who deem any further or deeper research superfluous, I must content myself with observing, that I have never heard it denied, that there is more than a sufficiency of food in existence. I have, at least, met with no proof, that there is, or has been any scarcity, either in the materials of all necessary comforts, or any lack of strength, skill and industry to prepare them. If we saw a man in health pining at a full table because there was not "the savory meat there which he loved," and had expected, the wanton delay or negligence of the messenger would be a compleat answer to our enquiries after the *occasion* of this sullenness or inappetence; but the *cause* of it we should be tempted to seek in the man's own undisciplined temper, or habits of self-indulgence. So far from agreeing therefore with those who find the causes in the occasions, I think the half of the question already solved of very unequal importance with that which yet remains for solution.

The immediate occasions of the existing distress may be correctly given with no greater difficulty than would attend any other series of known historic facts; but toward the discovery of its true seat and sources, I can but offer a humble contribution. They appear to me, however, resolvable into the OVERBALANCE* OF THE COMMER-

* I entreat attention to the word, *over*-balance. My opinions would be greatly misinterpreted if I were supposed to think hostilely of the spirit of commerce to which I attribute the largest proportion of our actual freedom (i.e. as *Englishmen*, and not merely as *Landowners*) and at least as large a share of our virtues as of our vices. Still more anxiously would I guard against the suspicion of a design to inculpate any number or class of individuals. It is not in the power of a minister or of a cabinet to say to the current of national tendency, stay here! or, flow there! The excess can only be remedied by the slow progress of intellect, the influences of religion, and irresistible events guided by Providence. In the points even, which

CIAL SPIRIT IN CONSEQUENCE OF THE ABSENCE OR WEAKNESS OF THE
COUNTER-WEIGHTS; this overbalance considered as displaying itself,
1. In the COMMERCIAL WORLD itself: 2. In the Agricultural: 3. In
the Government: and, 4. In the combined Influence of all three on
the more numerous and labouring Classes.

Of the natural counter-forces to the impetus of trade the first,
that presents itself to my mind, is the ancient feeling of rank and
ancestry, compared with our present self-complacent triumph over
these supposed prejudices.[30] Not that titles and the rights of
precedence are pursued by us with less eagerness than by our
Forefathers. The contrary is the case; and for this very cause,
because they inspire less reverence. In the old times they were
valued by the possessors and revered by the people as distinctions
of *Nature*, which the crown itself could only ornament, but not
give. Like the stars in Heaven, their influence was wider and more
general, because for the mass of mankind there was no hope of
reaching, and therefore no desire to appropriate, them. That many
evils as well as advantages accompanied this state of things I am
well aware: and likewise that many of the latter have become
incompatible with far more important blessings. It would therefore
be sickly affectation to suspend the thankfulness due for our
immunity from the one in an idle regret for the loss of the other.
But however true this may be, and whether the good or the evil
preponderated, still it acted as a counterpoise to the grosser
superstition for wealth. Of the efficiency of this counter-influence
we can offer negative proof only: and for this we need only look
back on the deplorable state of Holland in respect of patriotism
and public spirit at and before the commencement of the French
revolution.

The limits and proportions of this address allow little more than
a bare reference to this point. The same restraint I must impose
on myself in the following. For under this head I include the
general neglect of all the austerer studies; the long and ominous
eclipse of Philosophy; the usurpation of that venerable name by
physical and psychological Empiricism; and the non-existence of a
learned and philosophic Public, which is perhaps the only innoxious form of an imperium in imperio [empire within an empire],

---

I have presumed to blame, by the word Government I intend all the directors of
political power, that is, the great estates of the Realm, temporal and spiritual, and
not only the Parliament, but all the elements of Parliament.

but at the same time the only form which is not directly or indirectly encouraged.[31] So great a risk do I incur of malignant interpretation, and the assertion itself is so likely to appear paradoxical even to men of candid minds, that I should have passed over this point, most important as I know it to be; but that it will be found stated more at large, with all its proofs, in a work on the point of publication. The fact is simply this. We have – *Lovers*, shall I entitle them? Or must I not rather hazard the introduction of their own phrases, and say, *Amateurs* or *Dillettanti*, as Musicians, Botanists, Florists, Mineralogists, and Antiquarians. Nor is it denied that these are ingenuous pursuits, and such as become men of rank and fortune. Neither in these or in any other points do I complain of any excess in the pursuits themselves; but of that which arises from the deficiency of the counterpoise. The effect is the same. Every work, which can be made use of either to immediate profit or immediate pleasure, every work which falls in with the desire of acquiring wealth suddenly, or which can gratify the senses, or pamper the still more degrading appetite for scandal and personal defamation, is sure of an appropriate circulation. But neither Philosophy or Theology in the strictest sense of the words, can be said to have even a public *existence* among us. . . . As to that which passes with us under the name of metaphysics, philosophic elements, and the like, I refer every man of reflection to the contrast between the present times and those shortly after the restoration of ancient literature. In the latter we find the greatest men of the age, Statesmen, Warriors, Monarchs, Architects, in closest intercourse with philosophy. I need only mention the names of Lorenzo the magnificent; Picus, Count Mirandula, Ficinus and Politian; the abstruse subjects of their discussion, and the importance attached to them, as the requisite qualifications of men placed by Providence as guides and governors of their fellow-creatures. If this be undeniable, equally notorious is it that at present the more effective a man's talents are, and the more likely he is to be useful and distinguished in the highest situations of public life, the earlier does he shew his aversion to the metaphysics and the books of metaphysical speculation, which are placed before him: though they come with the recommendation of being so many triumphs of modern good sense over the schools of ancient philosophy. Dante, Petrarch, Spencer, Sir Philip Sidney, Algernon Sidney, Milton and Barrow were Platonists. But all the men of genius, with whom it has been my fortune to converse, either profess to know nothing of the present systems, or to despise them. It would be equally unjust and irrational to seek the solution of this difference in the men; and if not, it can be found only in the philosophic systems themselves. And so in truth it is. The *Living* of former ages communed gladly with a life-breathing philosophy. The *Living* of the present age wisely leave the dead to take care of the dead.

But whatever the causes may be, the result is before our eyes. An excess in our attachment to temporal and personal objects can be counteracted only by a pre-occupation of the intellect and the affections with permanent, universal, and eternal truths. Let no man enter, said Plato, who has not previously disciplined his mind by Geometry.[32] He considered this science as the first purification of the soul, by abstracting the attention from the accidents of the senses. We too teach Geometry; but that there may be no danger of the pupil's becoming too *abstract* in his conceptions, it has been not only proposed, but the proposal has been adopted, that it should be taught by *wooden* diagrams! . . .

There is a third influence, alternately our spur and our curb, without which all the pursuits and desires of man must either exceed or fall short of their just measure. Need I add, that I mean the influence of Religion? I speak of that sincere, that entire interest, in the undivided faith of Christ which demands the first-fruits of the whole man, his affections no less than his outward acts, his understanding equally with his feelings. For be assured, never yet did there exist a full faith in the divine Word, (by whom not Immortality alone, but *Light* and Immortality were brought into the world) which did not expand the intellect while it purified the heart; which did not multiply the aims and objects of the mind, while it fixed and simplified those of the desires and passions. If acquiescence without insight; if warmth without light; if an immunity from doubt given and guaranteed by a resolute ignorance; if the habit of taking for granted the words of a catechism, remembered or forgotten; if a sensation of *positiveness* substituted – I will not say, for certainty; but – for that calm assurance, the very means and conditions of which it supersedes; if a belief that seeks the darkness, and yet strikes no root, immovable as the limpet from its rock, and like the limpet fixed there by mere force of adhesion; if these suffice to make us Christians, in what intelligible sense could our Lord have announced it as the height and consummation of the signs and *miracles* which attested his Divinity, that the Gospel was preached to the POOR? . . . Is it not especially significant, that in the divine oeconomy, as revealed to us in the New Testament, the peculiar office of Redemption is attributed to the WORD, that is, to the *intelligential* wisdom which from all eternity is with God, and is God? that in *him* is life, and the life is the *light* of men?

In the present day we hear much, and from men of various creeds, of the *plainness* and *simplicity* of the Christian religion: and a strange abuse has been made of these words, often indeed with no ill intention, but still oftener by men who would fain transform the necessity of believing *in* Christ into a recommendation to believe him. The advocates of the latter scheme grew out of a sect that were called Socinians, but having succeeded in disbelieving far beyond the last foot-marks of the Socini, have chosen to designate themselves by the name of *Unitarians*. . . . Their true designation, which simply expresses a fact admitted on all sides, would be that of *Psilanthropists*,* or assertors of the *mere* humanity of Christ. It is the interest of these men to speak of the Christian religion as comprized in a few plain doctrines, and containing nothing not intelligible, at the first hearing, to men of the narrowest capacities.[33] Well then, (it might be replied) we are disposed to place a full reliance on the veracity of the great Founder of the Christian Religion, and likewise – which is more than you yourselves are on all occasions willing to admit – on the accuracy and competence of the Writers, who first recorded his acts and sayings. We have learned from you, *whom*, – and we now wish to hear from you – *what* we are to believe. The answer is: – the actual occurrence of an extraordinary event, as recorded by the biographers of Jesus, in confirmation of doctrines, without the *previous* belief of which, no man would, or rather, according to St. Paul's declaration, *could* become a convert to Christianity; doctrines, which it is certain, that Christ's immediate disciples believed, not less confidently before they had acknowledged his mission, than they did afterwards. Religion and politics, they tell us, require but the application of a common sense, which every man possesses, to a subject in which every man is concerned. "To be a musician, an orator, a painter, or even a good mechanician, presupposes *genius*; to be an excellent artizan or mechanic requires more than

* New things justify new terms. . . . We never speak of the *unity* of Attraction, or of the unity of Repulsion; but of the unity of Attraction and Repulsion in each one corpuscle. The essential diversity of the ideas, unity and sameness, was among the elementary principles of the old Logicians. . . .

an average degree of *talent*; but to be a legislator or a theologian, or both at once, demands nothing but common sense."³⁴ Now we willingly admit that nothing can be necessary to the salvation of a Christian which is not in his power. For such, therefore, as have neither the opportunity or the capacity of learning more, sufficient, doubtless, will be the belief of those plain truths, and the fulfilment of those commands, which to be incapable of understanding, is to be a man in appearance only. But even to this scanty creed the *disposition* of faith must be added: and let it not be forgotten, that though nothing can be easier than to understand a code of belief, four-fifths of which consists in avowals of disbelief, and the remainder in truths, concerning which (in this country at least) a man must have *taken pains to learn* to have any doubt; yet it is by no means easy to reconcile this code of negatives with the declarations of the Christian Scripture. On the contrary, it requires all the resources of verbal criticism, and all the perverse subtlety of special pleading, to work out a plausible semblance of correspondency between them. It must, however, be conceded, that a man may consistently spare himself the trouble of the attempt, and leave the New Testament unread, after he has once thoroughly persuaded himself that it can teach him nothing of any real importance that he does not already know. St. Paul indeed thought otherwise. For though he too teaches us, that in the religion of Christ there is milk for babes; yet he informs us at the same time, that there is meat for strong men!³⁵ and to the like purpose one of the Fathers has observed, that in the New Testament there are shallows where the lamb may ford, and depths where the elephant must swim. The Apostle exhorts the followers of Christ to the continual study of the new religion, on the ground that in the mystery of Christ, which in other ages was not made known to the sons of men, and in the riches of Christ which no research could exhaust, there were contained all the treasures of knowledge and wisdom. Accordingly, in that earnestness of spirit, which his own personal experience of the truth inspired, he prays with a solemn and a ceremonious fervor, that being "strengthened with might in the inner man, they may be able to comprehend with all saints what is the breadth and length and depth and height," of that living Principle, at once the Giver and the Gift! of that anointing Faith, which in endless evolution *"teaches us of all things, and is truth!"*³⁶ For all things are but parts and forms of its progressive manifestation, and every new knowledge but a new organ of sense and insight into this one all-inclusive **Verity**, which, still filling the vessel of the understanding, still dilates it to a capacity of yet other and yet greater Truths, and thus makes the soul feel its poverty by the very amplitude of its present, and the immensity of its reversionary, wealth. All truth indeed is simple, and needs no extrinsic ornament. And the more profound the truth is, the more simple: for the whole labour and building-up of knowledge is but one continued process of simplification. But I cannot comprehend, in what ordinary sense of the words the properties of *plainness* and *simplicity* can be applied to the Prophets, or to the Writings of St. John, or to the Epistles of St. Paul; . . . I can well understand, however, what is and has been the practical consequence of this notion. It is this very consequence, indeed, that occasioned the preceding remarks, makes them pertinent to my present subject, and gives them a place in the train of argument requisite for its illustration. For what need of any after-recurrence to the sources of information concerning a religion, the whole contents of which can be thoroughly acquired at once, and in a few hours? An occasional *remembrancing* may, perhaps, be expedient; but what object of *study* can a man propose to himself in a matter of which he knows all that can be known, all at least, that it is of use to know? Like the first rules of arithmetic, its few plain and obvious truths may hourly serve the man's purposes, yet never once occupy his thoughts. But it is impossible that the affections should be kept constant to an object which gives no employment to the understanding. The energies of the intellect, increase of insight, and enlarging views, are necessary to keep alive the substantial faith in the heart. They are the appointed fuel to the sacred fire. In the state of *Perfection* all other faculties may, perhaps, be swallowed up in love; but it is on the wings of the *Cherubim*, which the ancient Hebrew Doctors interpreted as meaning the powers and efforts of the Intellect, that we must first be borne up to the "pure Empyrean": and it must be Seraphs and not the hearts of poor Mortals, that can burn unfuelled and self-fed. "Give me *understanding* (exclaimed the royal Psalmist) and I shall observe thy law with my whole heart. Teach me *knowledge* and good *judgment*. Thy commandment is exceeding *broad*: O how I love thy law! it is my *meditation* all the day. The entrance of thy words giveth *light*, it giveth *understanding* to the simple. I prevented the dawning of the morning: mine eyes prevent the nightwatches, that I might meditate upon thy word."[37] Now where the very contrary of this is the opinion of many, and the practice of most, what results can be expected but those which are actually presented to us in our daily experience?

There is one class of men* who read the Scriptures, when they do read them, in order to pick and choose their faith; or (to speak more accurately) for the purpose of plucking away *live-asunder*, as it were, from the divine organism of the Bible, textuary morsels and fragments for the support of doctrines which they had learned beforehand from the higher oracle *of their own natural Common-Sense. Sanctas Scripturas frustant ut frustrent* [They rend the Holy Scriptures asunder in order to render them vain].[38] Through the gracious dispensations of Providence a complexity of circumstances may co-operate as antidotes to a noxious principle, and realize the paradox of a very good man under a very evil faith. It is not denied, that a Socinian may be as honest, useful and benevolent a character as any of his neighbours; and if he *thinks* more and derives a larger portion of his pleasures from intellectual sources, he is likely to be more so. But in such instances, and I am most willing to bear witness from my own experience, that they are not infrequent, the fruit is from the grafts not from the tree. The native produce is, or would be, an intriguing, overbearing, scornful and worldly disposition; and in point of fact, it is the only scheme of Religion that inspires in its adherents a contempt for the understandings of all who differ from them. But be this as it may, and whatever be its effects, it is not probable that Christianity will have any *direct* influence on men who pay it no other compliment than that of calling by its name the previous dictates and decisions of their own mother-wit.

But the more numerous class is of those who do not trouble themselves at all with religious matters, which they resign to the clergyman of the parish. But while not a few among these men consent to pray and hear by proxy; and while others, more attentive

---

* Whether it be on the increase, as a Sect, is doubtful. But it is admitted by all – nay, strange as it may seem, made a matter of boast, – that the number of its secret adherents, outwardly of other denominations, is tenfold greater than that of its avowed and incorporated Followers. And truly in our cities and great manufacturing and commercial towns, among Lawyers and such of the Tradesfolk as are the ruling members in Bookclubs, I am inclined to fear that this has not been asserted without good ground. For, Socinianism in its present form, consisting almost wholly in attack and imagined detection, has a particular charm for what are called *shrewd, knowing* men. . . . [Coleridge then lists the main features of the Unitarian faith in support of a claim that its 'main success . . . is owing to the small proportion which the affirmative articles of their Faith . . . bear to the negative'.]

to the prudential advantages of a decorous character, yield the customary evidence of their church-membership; but, this performed, are at peace with themselves, and

——think their Sunday's task
As much as God or Man can fairly ask,[39]

there exists amongst the most respectable Laity of our cities and great towns, an active, powerful, and enlarging minority, whose industry, while it enriches their families, is at the same time a support to the revenue, and not seldom enlivens their whole neighbourhood: men whose lives are free from all disreputable infirmities, and of whose activity in the origination, patronage, and management both of charitable and of religious associations, who must not have read or heard? and who that has, will dare deny to be most exemplary? After the custom of our forefathers, and their pure household religion [note omitted], these, in so many respects estimable persons, are for the greater part in the habit of having family-prayer, and a portion of Scripture read every morning and evening. In this class, with such changes or substitutions as the peculiar tenets of the sect require, we must include the sensible, orderly and beneficent Society of the FRIENDS, more commonly called Quakers. Here then, if any where, (that is, in any *class* of men; for the present argument is not concerned with individuals) we may expect to find Christianity tempering commercial avidity and sprinkling its holy damps on the passion of accumulation. This, I say, we might expect to find, if an undoubting belief in the threats and promises of Revelation, and a consequent regularity of personal, domestic, and social demeanor, sufficed to constitute that Christianity, the power and privilege of which is so to renew and irradiate the whole intelligential and moral life of man, as to overcome the *spirit of the world*. If this, the appointed test, were found wanting, should we not be forced to apprehend, nay, are we not compelled to infer, that the spirit of prudential motive, however ennobled by the magnitude and awfulness of its objects [note omitted], and though as the termination of a lower, it may be the commencement (and not seldom the *occasion*) of an higher state, is not, even in respect of *morality* itself, that abiding and continuous principle of action, which is either *one* with the faith spoken of by St. Paul, or its immediate offspring. It cannot be that *spirit* of obedience to the commands of Christ, by which the soul dwelleth in him, and he in it: . . . and which our Saviour himself announces as a *being born again*. And this indispensable act, or influence, or impregnation, of which, as of a divine tradition, the eldest philosophy is not silent; which flashed through the darkness of the pagan mysteries; and which it was therefore a reproach to a Master in Israel, that he had not already known; – this is else-where explained, as a seed which, though of gradual development, did yet *potentially* contain the essential form not merely of a better, but of an *other* life: amidst all the frailties and transient eclipses of mortality making, I repeat, the subjects of this regeneration not so properly better as *other* men, whom therefore the world could not but hate, as aliens. Its own native growth, however, improved by cultivation (whether thro' the agency of blind sympathies, or of an intelligent self-interest, the utmost heights to which the *worldly life* can ascend) the World has always been ready and willing to acknowledge and admire. *They are of the world: therefore speak they out of the heart of the world* (ἐκ τοῦ κόσμου) *and the world heareth them.*[40]

To abstain from acts of wrong and violence, to be moreover industrious, useful, and of seemly bearing, are qualities presup-posed in the gospel code, as the preliminary conditions, rather than the proper and peculiar effects, of Christianity. But they are likewise qualities so palpably indispensable to the temporal interests of mankind that, if we except the brief frenzies of revolutionary Riot, there never was a time, in which the World did not profess to reverence them: nor can we state any period, in which a more than ordinary character for assiduity, regularity, and charitableness did not secure the World's praise and favor, and were not calculated to advance the individual's own worldly interests: provided only, that his manners and professed tenets were those of some known and allowed body of men.

I ask then, what is the fact? We are – and, till its good purposes, which are many, have been all achieved, and we can become something better, long may we continue such! – a busy, enterpri-zing, and commercial nation. The habits attached to this character must, if there exist no adequate counterpoise, inevitably lead us, under the specious names of utility, practical knowledge, and so forth, to look at all things thro' the medium of the market, and to estimate the Worth of all pursuits and attainments by their marketable value. In this does the Spirit of Trade consist. Now would the general experience bear us out in the assertion, that amid the absence or declension of all other antagonist Forces, there is found in the very circle of the trading and opulent themselves, in the increase, namely, of religious professors among them, a spring of resistance to the excess of the commercial impetus, from the impressive example of *their* unworldly feelings evidenced by *their* moderation in worldly pursuits? I fear, that we may anticipate the answer wherever the religious zeal of such professors does not likewise manifest itself by the glad devotion of as large a portion of their Time and Industry, as the duty of providing a fair competence for themselves and their families leaves at their own disposal, to the comprehension of those inspired writings and the evolution of those pregnant truths, which are proposed for our earnest, sedulous research, in order that by occupying our understandings they may more and more assimilate our affections? I fear, that the inquiring traveller would more often hear of zealous Religionists who have read (and as a duty too and with all due acquiescence) the prophetic, "Wo to them that join house to house and lay field to field, that they may be alone in the land!"[41] and yet find no object deform the beauty of the prospect from their window or even from their castle turrets so annoyingly, as a meadow not their own, or a field under ploughing with the beam-end of the plough in the hands of its humble owner! I fear, that he must too often make report of men lawful in their dealings, scriptural in their language, alms-givers, and patrons of Sunday schools, who are yet resistless and overawing Bidders at all Land Auctions in their neighbourhood, who live in the center of farms without leases, and tenants without attachments! Or if his way should lie through our great towns and manufacturing districts, instances would grow cheap with him of wealthy religious practitioners, who never travel for orders without cards of edification in prose and verse, and small tracts of admonition and instruction, all "plain and easy, and suited to the meanest capacities;" who pray daily, as the first act of the morning and as the last of the evening, Lead us not into temptation! but deliver us from evil![42] and employ all the interval with an edge of appetite keen as the scythe of Death in the pursuit of yet more and yet more of a temptation so perilous, that (as they have full often read, and heard read, without the least questioning, or whisper of doubt) no power short of Omnipotence could make their deliverance from it credible or conceivable. Of all denominations of Christians, there is not one in existence or on record whose whole scheme of faith and worship was so expressly framed for the one purpose of spiritualizing the mind and of abstracting it from the vanities of the world, as the Society of Friends! not one, in which the church members are connected, and their professed principles enforced, by so effective and wonderful a form of discipline. But in the zeal of their Founders and first Proselytes for perfect Spirituality they excluded from their system all ministers specially trained and educated for the ministry, with all Professional Theologians: and they omitted to provide for the raising up among themselves any other established class of learned men, as teachers and schoolmasters for instance, in their stead. Even at this day, though the Quakers are in general remarkably shrewd and intelligent in all worldly concerns, yet learning, and more particularly theological learning, is more rare among them in proportion to their wealth and rank in life, and held in less value, than among any other known sect of Christians. What has been the result? If the occasion permitted, I could dilate with pleasure on their decent manners and decorous morals, as individuals, and their exemplary and truly illustrious philanthropic efforts as a Body. From all the gayer and tinsel vanities of the world their discipline has preserved them, and the English character owes to their example some part of its manly plainness in externals. But my argument is confined to the question, whether Religion in its present state and under the present conceptions of its demands and purposes does, even among the most religious, exert any efficient force of controul over the commercial spirit, the excess of which we have attributed not to the extent and magnitude of the commerce itself, but to the absence or imperfection of its appointed checks and counteragents. Now as the system of the Friends in its first intention is of all others most hostile to worldly-mindedness on the one hand; and as, on the other, the adherents of this system both in confession and *practice* confine Christianity to feelings and motives; they may be selected as representatives of the strict, but unstudied and uninquiring, Religionists of every denomination. Their characteristic propensities will supply, therefore, no unfair test for the degree of resistance, which our present Christianity is capable of opposing to the cupidity of a trading people. That species of Christianity I mean, which, as far as knowledge and the faculties of thought are concerned, – which, as far as the growth and grandeur of the *intellectual* man is in question – is to be learnt ex tempore! A Christianity poured in on the Catechumen all and all at once, as from a shower-bath: and which, whatever it may be in the heart, yet for the understanding and reason is from boyhood onward a thing past and perfected! If the almost universal opinion be tolerably correct, the question is answered. But I by no means *appropriate* the remark to the wealthy Quakers, or even apply it to them in any particular or eminent sense, when I say, that often as the motley reflexes of my experience move in long procession of manifold groups before me, the distinguished and world-honored company of Christian Mammonists appear to the eye of my imagination as a drove of camels heavily laden, yet all at full speed, and each in the confident expectation of passing through the EYE OF THE NEEDLE, without stop or halt, both beast and baggage.

Not without an uneasy reluctance have I ventured to tell the truth on this subject, lest I should be charged with the indulgence of a satirical mood and an uncharitable spleen. But my conscience bears me witness, and I know myself too near the grave to trifle with its name, that I am solely actuated by a sense of the *exceeding* importance of the subject at the present moment. I feel it an awful duty to exercise the honest liberty of free utterance in so dear a concernment as that of preparing my country for a change in its external relations, which must come sooner or later; which I believe to have already commenced; and that it will depend on the presence or absence of a corresponding change in the *mind* of the nation, and above all in the aims and ruling opinions of our gentry and moneyed men whether it is to cast down our strength and prosperity, or to fix them on a firmer and more august basis. "Surely to every good and peaceable man it must in nature needs be a hateful thing to be the displeaser and molester of thousands; but when God commands to take the trumpet and blow a dolorous or a jarring blast, it lies not in man's will what he shall say and what he shall conceal."[43] . . .

Thus then, of the three most approved antagonists to the Spirit of Barter, and the accompanying disposition to overvalue Riches with all the Means and Tokens thereof – of the three fittest and most likely checks to this tendency, namely, the feeling of ancient birth and the respect paid to it by the community at large; a genuine intellectual Philosophy with an accredited, learned, and philosophic *Class*; and lastly, Religion; we have found the first declining, the second not existing, and the third efficient, indeed, in many respects and to many excellent purposes, only not in this particular direction: the Religion here spoken of, having long since parted company with that inquisitive and bookish Theology which tends to defraud the student of his worldly wisdom, inasmuch as it diverts his mind from the accumulation of wealth by pre-occupying his thoughts in the acquisition of knowledge. For the Religion of best repute among us holds all the truths of Scripture and all the doctrines of Christianity so very transcendent, or so very easy, as to make study and research either vain or needless. It professes, therefore, to hunger and thirst after Righteousness alone, and the rewards of the Righteous; and thus habitually *taking for granted* all truths of spiritual import leaves the understanding vacant and at leisure for a thorough insight into present and temporal interests: which, doubtless, is the true reason why its followers are in general such shrewd, knowing, wary, well-informed, thrifty and thriving men of business. But this is likewise the reason, why it neither does or can check or circumscribe the Spirit of Barter; and to the consequent *monopoly* which this commercial Spirit possesses, must its over-balance be attributed, not to the extent or magnitude of the Commerce itself.

Before I enter on the result assigned by me as the chief ultimate *cause* of the present state of the country, and as the main *ground* on which the immediate occasions of the general distress have worked, I must entreat my Readers to reflect that the spirit of Trade has been a thing of insensible growth; that whether it be enough, or more or less than enough, is a matter of relative, rather than of positive determination; that it depends on the degree in which it is aided or resisted by all the other tendencies that co-exist with it; and that in the best of times this spirit may be said to live on a narrow isthmus between a sterile desert and a stormy sea, still threatened and encroached on either by the Too Much or the Too Little. As the argument does not depend on any precise accuracy in the dates, I shall assume it to have commenced, as an influencing part of the national character, with the institution of the Funds in the reign of William the Third,[44] and from the peace of Aix-la-Chapelle in 1748, to have been hurrying onward to its maximum, which it seems to have attained during the late war. The short interruptions may be well represented as a few steps backwards, that it might leap forward with an additional momen-tum. The words, old and modern, now and then, are applied by me, the latter to the whole period since the Revolution,[45] and the former to the interval between this epoch and the Reformation; the one from 1460 to 1680, the other from 1680 to the present time.

Having premised this explanation, I can now return an intelligible answer to a question, that will have risen in the Reader's mind during his perusal of the last three or four pages. How, it will be objected, does all this apply to the present times in particular? When was the industrious part of mankind *not* attached to the pursuits most likely to reward their industry? Was the wish to make a fortune or, if you prefer an invidious phrase, the lust of lucre, less natural to our forefathers than to their descendants? If you say, that though a not less frequent, or less powerful passion with them than with us, it yet met with a more frequent and more powerful check, a stronger and more advanced boundary-line, in the Religion of old times, and in the faith, fashion, habits, and authority of the Religious: in what did this difference consist? and in what way did these points of difference act? If indeed the antidote in question once possessed virtues which it no longer possesses, or not in the same degree, what is the ingredient, either added, omitted, or diminished since that time, which can have rendered it less efficacious now than then?

Well! (I might reply) grant all this: and let both the profession and the professors of a spiritual principle, as a counterpoise to the worldly weights at the other end of the Balance, be supposed much the same in the one period as in the other! Assume for a moment, that I can establish neither the fact of its lesser efficiency, nor any points of difference capable of accounting for it! Yet it might still be a sufficient answer to this objection, that as the commerce of the country, and with it the spirit of commerce, has increased fifty-fold since the commencement of the latter period, it is not enough that the counterweight should be as great as it was in the former period: to remain the same in its effect, it ought to have become very much greater. But though this be a consideration not less important than it is obvious, yet I do not purpose to rest in it. I affirm, that a difference may be shewn, and of no trifling importance as to that one point, to which my present argument is confined. For let it be remembered, that it is not to any extraordinary influences of the religious principle that I am referring, not to voluntary poverty, or sequestration from social and active life, or schemes of mortification. I speak of Religion merely as I should of any worldly object, which, as far as it employs and interests a man, leaves less room in his mind for other pursuits: except that this must be more especially the case in the instance of Religion, because beyond all other Interests it is calculated to occupy the whole mind, and employ successively all the faculties of man; and because the objects which it presents to the Imagination as well as to the Intellect cannot be actually contemplated, much less can they be the subject of frequent meditation, without dimming the lustre and blunting the rays of all rival attractions. It is well known, and has been observed of old, that Poetry tends to render its devotees [note omitted] careless of money and outward appearances, while Philosophy inspires a contempt of both as objects of Desire or Admiration. But Religion is the Poetry and Philosophy of all mankind; unites in itself whatever is most excellent in either, and while it at one and the same time calls into action and supplies with the noblest materials both the imaginative and the intellective faculties, superadds the interests of the most substantial and home-felt reality to both, to the poetic vision and the philosophic idea. But in order to produce a similar effect it must act in a similar way: it must reign in the thoughts of a man and in the powers akin to thought, as well as exercise an admitted influence over his hopes and fears, and through these on his deliberate and individual acts.

Now as my first presumptive proof of a difference (I might almost have said, of a contrast) between the religious character of the period since the Revolution, and that of the period from the accession of Edward the Sixth to the abdication of the second James,[46] I refer to the Sermons and to the theological Works generally, of the latter period. It is my full conviction, that in any half dozen Sermons of Dr. Donne, or Jeremy Taylor,[47] there are more thoughts, more facts and images, more excitements to inquiry and intellectual effort, than are presented to the congregations of the present day in as many churches or meetings during twice as many months. Yet both these were the most popular preachers of their times, were heard with enthusiasm by crowded and promiscuous Audiences, and the effect produced by their eloquence was held in reverential and affectionate remembrance by many attendants on their ministry, who, like the pious Isaac Walton,[48] were not themselves men of learning or education. In addition to this fact, think likewise on the large and numerous editions of massy, closely printed folios: the impressions so large and the editions so numerous, that all the industry of destruction for the last hundred years has but of late sufficed to make them rare. From the long list select those works alone, which we know to have been the most current and favorite works of their day: and of these again no more than may well be supposed to have had a place in the scantiest libraries, or perhaps with the Bible and Common Prayer Book to have *formed* the library of their owner. Yet on the single shelf so filled we should find almost every possible question, that could interest or instruct a reader whose whole heart was in his religion, discussed with a command of intellect that seems to exhaust all the learning and logic, all the historical and moral relations, of each several subject. The very length of the discourses, with which these "rich souls of wit and knowledge" fixed the eyes, ears, and hearts of their crowded congregations, are a source of wonder now-a-days, and (we may add) of self-congratulation, to many a sober christian, who forgets with what delight he himself has listened to a two hours' harangue on a Loan or Tax, or at the trial of some remarkable cause or culprit. The transfer of the interest makes and explains the whole difference. For though much may be fairly charged on the revolution in the *mode* of preaching as well as in the matter, since the fresh morning and fervent noon of the Reformation, when there was no need to visit the conventicles of fanaticism in order to

> See God's ambassador in the pulpit stand,
> Where they could take notes from his Look and Hand;
> And from his speaking *action* bear away
> More sermon than our preachers use to *say*;[49]

yet this too must be referred to the same change in the habits of men's minds, a change that involves both the shepherd and the flock: though like many other *Effects*, it tends to reproduce and strengthen its own cause.

The last point, to which I shall appeal, is the warmth and frequency of the religious controversies during the former of the two periods; the deep interest excited by them among all but the lowest and most ignorant classes; the importance attached to them by the very highest; the number, and in many instances the transcendent merit, of the controversial publications – in short, the rank and value assigned to *polemic divinity*. The subjects of the controversies may or may not have been trifling; the warmth, with which they were conducted, may have been disproportionate and indecorous; and we may have reason to congratulate ourselves that the age, in which we live, is grown more indulgent and less captious. The fact is introduced not for its own sake, but as a *symptom* of the general state of men's feelings, as an evidence of the direction and main channel, in which the thoughts and interests of men were then flowing. We all know, that lovers are apt to take offence and wrangle with each other on occasions that perhaps are but trifles, and which assuredly would appear such to those who had never been under the influence of a similar passion. These quarrels may be no proofs of wisdom; but still in the imperfect state of our nature the entire absence of the same, and this too on far more serious provocations, would excite a strong suspicion of a comparative *indifference* in the feelings of the parties towards each other, who can love so coolly where they profess to love so well. I shall believe our present religious tolerancy to proceed from the abundance of our charity and good sense, when I can see proofs that we are equally cool and forbearing, as Litigators and political Partizans. And I must again intreat my reader to recollect, that the present argument is exclusively concerned with the requisite correctives of the commercial spirit, and with Religion therefore no otherwise, than as a counter-charm to the sorcery of wealth: and my main position is, that neither by reasons drawn from the nature of the human mind, or by facts of actual experience, are we justified in expecting this from a religion which does not employ and actuate the understandings of men, and combine their affections with it as a system of Truth gradually and progressively manifesting itself to the intellect; no less than as a system of motives and moral commands learnt as soon as heard, and containing nothing but what is plain and easy to the lowest capacities. Hence it is, that Objects, the ostensible principle of which I have felt it my duty to oppose . . . and objects, the which and the measures for the attainment of which possess my good wishes and have had the humble tribute of my public advocation and applause – I am here alluding to the British and Foreign Bible Society[50] – may yet converge, as to the point now in question. They may, both alike, be symptoms of the same predominant disposition to that Coalition-system in Christianity, for the expression of which Theologians have invented or appropriated the term, *Syncretism* [note omitted][51]: although the former may be an ominous, the latter an auspicious symptom, though the one may be worse from Bad, while the other is an instance of Good educed from Evil. . . .

Though an overbalance of the commercial spirit is involved in the deficiency of its counterweights; yet the facts, that exemplify the mode and extent of its operation, will afford a more direct and satisfactory kind of proof. And first I am to speak of this overbalance as displayed in the commercial world itself. But as this is the first, so is it for my present purpose the least important point of view. A portion of the facts belonging to this division of the subject I have already noticed, . . . and for the remainder let the following suffice as the substitute or representative. The moral of the tale I leave to the Reader's own reflections. Within the last sixty years or perhaps a somewhat larger period, (for I do not pretend to any nicety of dates, and the documents are of easy access) there have occurred at intervals of about 12 or 13 years each, certain periodical Revolutions of Credit. Yet Revolution is not the precise word. To state the thing that it is, I ought to have said, certain gradual expansions of credit ending in sudden contractions, or, with equal propriety, ascensions to a certain utmost possible height, which has been different in each successive instance; but in every instance the attainment of this, its ne plus ultra, has been instantly announced by a rapid series of explosions (in mercantile language, a *Crash*) and a consequent precipitation of the general system. For a short time this Icarian Credit, or rather this illegitimate offspring of Confidence, to which it stands in the same relation as Phäethon to his parent god in the old fable, seems to lie stunned by the fall; but soon recovering, again it strives upward, and having once more regained its mid region,

> ——thence many a league,
> As in a cloudy chair, ascending rides
> Audacious!

till at the destined zenith of its vaporous exaltation, *"all unawares, fluttering its pennons vain, plumb down it drops!"*[52] Or that I may descend myself to the "cool element of prose," Alarm and suspicion gradually diminish into a judicious circumspectness; but by little and little, circumspection gives way to the desire and emulous ambition of *doing business*; till Impatience and Incaution on one side, tempting and encouraging headlong Adventure, Want of principle, and Confederacies of false credit on the other, the movements of Trade become yearly gayer and giddier, and end at length in a vortex of hopes and hazards, of blinding passions and blind practices, which should have been left where alone they ought ever to have been found, among the wicked lunacies of the Gaming Table.

I am not ignorant that the power and circumstantial prosperity of the Nation has been increasing during the same period, with an accelerated force unprecedented in any country, the population of which bore the same proportion to its productive soil: and partly, perhaps, even in consequence of this system. By facilitating the *means* of enterprize it must have called into activity a multitude of enterprizing Individuals and a variety of Talent that would otherwise have lain dormant: while by the same ready supply of excitements to Labor, together with its materials and instruments, even an unsound credit has been able within a short time to [note omitted] substantiate itself. We shall perhaps be told too, that the very Evils of this System, even the periodical *crash* itself, are to be regarded but as so much superfluous steam ejected by the Escape Pipes and Safety Valves of a self-regulating Machine: and lastly, that in a free and trading country *all things find their level.*[53]

I have as little disposition as motive to recant the principles, which in many forms and through various channels I have labored to propagate; but there is surely no inconsistency in yielding all due honor to the spirit of Trade, and yet charging sundry evils, that weaken or reverse its blessings, on the over-balance of that spirit, taken as the paramount principle of action in the Nation at large. Much I still concede to the arguments for the present scheme of Things, as adduced in the preceding paragraph: but I likewise see, and always have seen, much that needs winnowing. Thus instead of the position, that all things *find*, it would be less equivocal and far more descriptive of the fact to say, that Things are always *finding*, their level: which might be taken as the paraphrase or ironical definition of a storm, but would be still more appropriate to the Mosaic Chaos, ere its brute tendencies had been enlightened by the WORD (i.e. the communicative Intelligence) and before the Spirit of Wisdom [note omitted] moved on the *level-finding* Waters. But Persons are not *Things* – but Man does not find his level. Neither in body nor in soul does the Man find his level! After a hard and calamitous season, during which the thousand Wheels of some vast manufactory had remained silent as a frozen water-fall, be it that plenty has returned and that Trade has once more become brisk and stirring: go, ask the overseer, and question the parish doctor, whether the workman's health and temperance with the staid and respectful Manners best taught by the inward dignity of conscious self-support, have found *their* level again! Alas! I have more than once seen a group of children in Dorsetshire, during the heat of the dog-days, each with its little shoulders up to its ears, and its chest pinched inward, the very habit and *fixtures*, as it were, that had been impressed on their frames by the former ill-fed, ill-clothed, and unfuelled winters. But as with the Body, so or still worse with the Mind. Nor is the effect confined to the laboring classes, whom by an ominous but too appropriate a change in our phraseology we are now accustomed to call the Laboring Poor. I cannot persuade myself, that the frequency of Failures with all the disgraceful secrets of Fraud and Folly, of unprincipled Vanity in expending and desperate Speculation in retrieving, can be familiarized to the thoughts and experience of Men, as matters of daily occurrence, without serious injury to the Moral Sense: more especially in times when Bankruptcies spread, like a fever, at once contagious and epidemic; swift too as the travel of an Earthquake, that with one and the same chain of Shocks opens the ruinous chasm in cities that have an ocean between them! – in times, when the Fate flies swifter than the Fear, and yet the report, that follows the flash, has a ruin of its own and arrives but to multiply the Blow! – when princely capitals are often but the Telegraphs of distant calamity: and still worse, when no man's treasure is safe who had adopted the ordinary means of safety, neither the high or the humble; when the Lord's rents and the Farmer's store, entrusted perhaps but as yesterday, are asked after at closed doors! – but worse of all, in its moral influences as well as in the cruelty of suffering, when the old Laborers' Savings, the precious robberies of self-denial from every day's comfort; when the Orphan's Funds; the Widow's Livelihood; the fond confiding Sister's humble Fortune; are found among the victims to the remorseless mania of dishonest Speculation, or to the desperate cowardice of Embarrassment, and the drunken stupor of a usurious Selfishness that for a few months respite dares incur a debt of guilt and infamy, for which the grave itself can plead no statute of limitation. Name to me any Revolution recorded in History, that was not followed by a depravation of the national Morals. The Roman character during the Triumvirate, and under Tiberius; the reign of Charles the Second; and Paris at the present moment; are obvious instances. What is the main cause? The sense of Insecurity. On what ground then dare we hope, that with the same accompaniment Commercial Revolutions should not produce the same effect, in proportion to the extent of their sphere?

But these Blessings – with all the specific terms, into which this most comprehensive Phrase is to be resolved? Dare we unpack the bales and cases so marked, and look at the articles, one by one? Increase of human Life and increase of the means of Life are, it is true, reciprocally cause and effect: and the Genius of Commerce and Manufactory has been the cause of both to a degree that may well excite our *wonder*. But do the last results justify our exultation likewise? Human Life, alas! is but the malleable Metal, out of which the thievish Picklock, the Slave's Collar, and the Assassin's Stiletto are formed as well as the clearing Axe, the feeding Plough-share, the defensive Sword, and the mechanic Tool. But the subject is a painful one: and fortunately the labors of others, with the communications of medical men concerning the state of the manufacturing Poor, have rendered it unnecessary. I will rather (though in strict method it should, perhaps, be reserved for the following Head) relate a speech made to me near Fort Augustus, as I was travelling on foot through the Highlands of Scotland. The Speaker was an elderly and respectable widow, who expressed herself with that simple eloquence, which strong feeling seldom fails to call forth in humble life, but especially in women. She spoke English, as indeed most Highlanders do who speak it at all, with a propriety of phrase and a discrimination of tone and emphasis that more than compensated for the scantiness of her vocabulary. After an affecting account of her own wrongs and ejectment, (which however, she said, bore with comparative lightness on her, who had had saved up for her a wherewithal to live, and was blessed with a son well to do in the world), she made a movement with her hand in a circle, directing my eye meanwhile to various objects as marking its outline: and then observed, with a deep sigh and a suppressed and slow voice which she suddenly raised and quickened after the first drop or cadence – Within this space – how short a time back! there lived a hundred and seventy-three persons: and now there is only a shepherd, and an underling or two. Yes, Sir! One hundred and seventy-three Christian souls, man, woman, boy, girl, and babe; and in almost every home an old man by the fire-side, who would tell you of the troubles, before our roads were made; and many a brave youth among them who loved the birth-place of his forefathers, yet would swing about his broad-sword and want but a word to march off to the battles over sea; aye Sir, and many a good lass, who had a respect for herself! Well! but they are gone, and with them the bristled bear [note omitted], and the pink haver [note omitted], and the potatoe plot that looked as gay as any flower garden with its blossoms![54] I sometimes fancy, that the very birds are gone, all but the crows and the gleads! Well, and what then? Instead of us all, there is one shepherd man, and it may be a pair of small lads – and a many, many sheep! And do you think, Sir! that God allows of such proceedings?

Some days before this conversation, and while I was on the shores of the Loch Kathern [note omitted], I had heard of a sad counterpart to the widow's tale, and told with a far fiercer indignation, of a "Laird who had raised a company from the country round about, for the love that was borne to his name, and who gained high preferment in consequence: and that it was but a small part of those that he took away whom he brought back again. And what were the thanks which the folks had both for those that came back with him, some blind and more in danger of blindness; and for those that had perished in the hospitals, and for those that fell in battle, fighting before or beside him? Why, that their fathers were all turned out of their farms before the year was over, and sent to wander like so many gipsies, unless they would consent to shed their gray hairs, at ten-pence a day, over the new canals. Had there been a price set upon his head, and his enemies had been coming upon him, he needed but have whistled, and a hundred brave lads would have made a wall of flame round about him with the flash of their broad-swords! Now if the——— should come among us, as (it is said) they will, let him whistle to his sheep and see if *they* will fight for him!" The frequency with which I heard, during my solitary walk from the end of Loch-Lomond to Inverness, confident expectations of the kind expressed in his concluding words—nay, far too often eager hopes mingled with vindictive resolves—I spoke of with complaint and regret to an elderly man, whom by his dress and way of speaking, I took to be a schoolmaster. Long shall I recollect his reply: "O, Sir, it kills a man's love for his country, the hardships of life coming by change and with injustice!" I was sometime afterwards told by a very sensible person who had studied the mysteries of political oeconomy, and was therefore entitled to be listened to, that more food was produced in consequence of this revolution, that the mutton must be eat somewhere, and what difference where? If three were fed at Manchester instead of two at Glencoe or the Trossacs, the balance of human enjoyment was in favor of the former. I have passed through many a manufacturing town since then, and have watched many a group of old and young, male and female, going to, or returning from, many a factory, but I could never yet persuade myself to be of his opinion. Men, I still think, ought to be weighed not counted. Their *worth* ought to be the final estimate of their value.

Among the occasions and minor causes of this change in the views and measures of our Land-owners, and as being itself a consequent on that system of credit, the outline of which was given in a preceding page, the universal practice of enhancing the sale price of every article on the presumption of Bad Debts, is not the least noticeable. Nor, if we reflect that this additional per centage is repeated at each intermediate stage of its elaboration and distribution from the Grower or Importer to the last Retailer *inclusively*, will it appear the least operative. Necessary, and therefore justifiable, as this plan of reprisal by anticipation may be in the case of each individual dealer, yet taken collectively and without reference to persons, the plan itself would, I suspect, startle an unfamiliarized conscience, as a sort of non-descript Piracy, not promiscuous in its exactions only because by a curious anomaly it grants a free pass to the offending party. Or if the Law maxim, *volentibus nulla fit injuria* [no injury is done to a consenting party], is applicable in this case, it may perhaps be described more courteously as a *Benefit Society* of all the careful and honest men in the kingdom to pay the debts of the dishonest or improvident. It is mentioned here, however, as one of the appendages to the twin paramount causes, the Paper Currency and the National Debt, and for the sake of the conjoint results. Would we learn what these results are? What they have been in the higher, and what in the most numerous, class of society? Alas! that some of the intermediate rounds in the social ladder have been broken and not replaced, is itself one of these results. Retrace the progress of things from 1792 to 1813, when the tide was at its height, and then, as far as its rapidity will permit, the ebb from its first turn to the dead low-water mark of the last quarter. Then see whether the remainder may not be generalized under the following heads. Fluctuation in the wages of labor, alternate privation and excess (not in all at the same time, but successively in each) consequent improvidence, and over all discontent and a system of factious confederacy – these form the history of the mechanics and lower ranks of our cities and towns. In the country, a peasantry sinking into pauperism, step for step with the rise of the farmer's profits and indulgencies. On the side of the landlord and his compeers, we shall find the presence of the same causes attested by answerable effects. Great as "their almost magical effects"—[note omitted] on the increase of prices were in the necessaries of life, they were still greater, disproportionally greater, in all articles of shew and luxury. With few exceptions, it soon became difficult, and at length impracticable, for the gentry of the land, for the possessors of fixed property to retain the rank of their ancestors, or their own former establishments, without joining in the general competition under the influence of the same trading spirit. Their dependents were of course either selected from, or driven into, the same eddy; while the temptation of obtaining more than the legal interest for their principal became more and more strong with all persons who, neither trading nor farming, had lived on the interest of their fortunes. It was in this latter class that the rash, and too frequently, the unprincipled projector found his readiest dupes. Had we but the secret history of the *building* speculations only in the vicinity of the metropolis, too many of its pages would supply an afflicting but instructive comment. That both here, and in all other departments, this increased momentum in the spirit of trade has been followed by results of the most desirable nature, I have myself [note omitted], exerted my best powers to evince, at a period when to present the fairest and most animating features of the system, and to prove their vast and charm-like influence on the power and resources of the nation appeared a duty of patriotism. Nothing, however, was advanced incompatible with the position, which even then I did not conceal, and which from the same sense of duty I am now attempting to display; namely, that the extension of the commercial spirit into our agricultural system, *added* to the over-balance of the same spirit, even within its own sphere; *aggravated* by the operation of our Revenue Laws; and finally *reflected* in the habits, and tendencies of the Laboring Classes; is the ground-work of our calamity, and the main predisposing cause, without which the late *occasions* would (some of them not have existed, and the remainder) not have produced the present distresses.

That Agriculture requires principles essentially different from those of Trade, – that a gentleman ought not to regard his estate as a merchant his cargo, or a shopkeeper his stock, – admits of an easy proof from the different tenure of Landed Property,* and from the purposes of Agriculture itself, which ultimately are the same as those of the State of which it is the offspring.[55] (For we do not include in the name of Agriculture the cultivation of a few vegetables by the women of the less savage Hunter Tribes.) If the continuance and independence of the State be its object, the final causes of the State must be its final causes. We suppose the negative ends of a State already attained, viz. its own safety by means of its own strength, and the protection of person and property for all its members. There will then remain its positive ends: – 1. To make the means of subsistence more easy to each individual. 2. To secure to each of its members THE HOPE† of bettering his own condition or that of his children. 3. The development of those faculties which are essential to his Humanity, i.e. to his rational and moral Being. Under the last head we do not mean those degrees of intellectual cultivation which distinguish man from man in the same civilized society, but those only that raise the civilized man above the Barbarian, the Savage, and the Animal. We require, however, on the part of the State, in behalf of all its members, not only the outward means of *knowing* their essential

---

* The very idea of *individual* or private property, in our present acceptation of the term, and according to the current notion of the *right* to it, was originally confined to moveable things: and the more moveable, the more susceptible of the nature of property. Proceeding from the more to the less perfect *right*; we may bring all the objects of an independent ownership under five heads: – viz., 1. Precious stones, and other jewels of as easy transfer: 2. The precious metals, and foreign coin taken as weight of metal; 3. Merchandize, by virtue of the contract between the importer and the sovereign in whose person the unity and integrity of the *common* wealth were represented; i.e. after the settled price had been paid by the former for the permission to import, and received by the latter under the further obligation of protecting the same: – 4. The coin of the Country in the possession of the natural subject; and last of all, and in *certain* cases, the live stock, the *peculium a pecus* [property in cattle]. Hence, the minds of men were most familiar with the idea in the case of Jews and Aliens: till gradually, the privileges attached to the vicinity of the Bishops and mitred Abbots prepared an asylum for the fugitive Vassal and the oppressed Frankling, and thus laid the first foundations of a fourth class of freeman, that of Citizens and Burghers. To the Feudal system we owe the *forms*, to the Church the *substance* of our liberty. As comment take, first, the origin of towns and cities; next, the holy war waged against slavery and villenage, and with such success that the law had barely to sanction an opus jam consummatum [work already completed] at the Restoration.

† The civilized man gives up those stimulants of Hope and Fear; the mixture or alternation of which constitutes the chief charm of the savage life: and yet his Maker has distinguished him from the Brute that perishes, by making Hope an instinct of his nature and an indispensable condition of his moral and intellectual progression. But a natural instinct constitutes a natural right, as far as its gratification is compatible with the equal rights of others. Hence our ancestors classed those who were incapable of altering their condition from that of their parents, as Bondsmen or Villains, however advantageously they might otherwise be situated.

duties and dignities as men and free men, but likewise, and more especially, the discouragement of all such Tenures and Relations as must in the very nature of things render this knowledge inert, and cause the good seed to perish as it falls. Such at least is the appointed Aim of a State: and at whatever distance from the ideal Mark the existing circumstances of a nation may unhappily place the actual statesman, still every movement ought to be in this direction. But the negative merit of not forwarding – but the exemption from the crime of necessitating – the debasement and virtual disfranchisement of any class of the community, may be demanded of every State under all circumstances: and the Government, that pleads difficulties in repulse or demur of this claim, impeaches its own wisdom and fortitude. But as the *specific* ends of Agriculture are the maintenance, strength, and security of the State, so (we repeat) must its *ultimate* ends be the same as those of the State: even as the ultimate end of the spring and wheels of a watch must be the same as that of the watch. Yet least of all things dare we overlook or conceal, that morally and with respect to the character and conscience of the Individuals, the Blame of unfaithful Stewardship is aggravated, in proportion as the Difficulties are less, and the consequences, lying within a narrower field of vision, are more evident and affecting. An injurious system, the connivance at which we scarcely dare more than regret in the Cabinet or Senate of an Empire, may justify an earnest reprobation in the management of private Estates: provided always, that the System only be denounced, and the pleadings confined to the Court of Conscience. For from this court only can the redress be awarded. All Reform or Innovation, not won from the free Agent by the presentation of juster Views and nobler Interests, and that does not leave the merit of having effected it sacred to the individual proprietor, it were folly to propose, and worse than folly to attempt. Madmen only would dream of digging or blowing up the foundation of a House in order to employ the materials in repairing the walls.[56] Nothing more dare be asked of the State, no other duty is imposed on it, than to withhold or retract all extrinsic and artificial aids to an injurious system; or at the utmost to invalidate in extreme cases such claims as have arisen indirectly from the letter or unforeseen operations of particular Statutes: claims that instead of being contained in the Rights of its proprietary Trustees are incroachments on its own Rights, and a destructive Trespass on a part of its own inalienable and untransferable Property – I mean the health, strength, honesty, and filial love of its children.

It would border on an affront to the understandings of our Landed Interest, were I to explain in detail what the plan and conduct would be of a gentleman;* if, as the result of his own free conviction the *marketable* produce of his Estates were made a subordinate consideration to the living and moral growth that is to remain on the land. I mean a healthful, callous-handed but high-and-warm-hearted Tenantry, twice the number of the present landless, parish-paid Laborers, and ready to march off at the first call of their country with a SON OF THE HOUSE at their head, because under no apprehension of being (forgive the lowness of the expression) *marched off* at the whisper of a Land-taster! If the admitted rule, the paramount *Self*-commandment, were comprized in the fixed resolve – I will improve my *Estate* to the utmost; and my *rent-roll* I will raise as much as, but no more than, is compatible with the three great ends (before enumerated) which being those of my country must be mine inclusively! This, I repeat, it would be more than superfluous to particularize. It is a problem, the solution of which may be safely entrusted to the common sense of every one who has the hardihood to ask himself the question. But how encouraging even the approximations to such a system, of what fair promise the few fragmentary samples are, may be seen in the Report of the Board of Agriculture for 1816, p. 11, from the Earl of Winchelsea's communication, in every paragraph of which Wisdom seems to address us in behalf of Goodness.[57]

But the plan of my argument requires the reverse of this picture. I am to ask what the results would be, on the supposition, that Agriculture is carried on in the spirit of Trade; and if the necessary answer coincide with the known general practice, to shew the connection of the consequences with the present state of distress and uneasiness. In Trade, from its most innocent form to the abomination of the African commerce nominally abolished after a hard-fought battle of twenty years, no distinction is or can be

---

* Or, (to put the question more justly as well as more candidly) of the Land-owners collectively: – for who is not aware of the facilities that accompany a conformity with the general practice, or of the numerous hindrances that retard, and in the final imperfection that commonly awaits, a deviation from it? On the distinction . . . between Things and Persons, all law human and divine is grounded. It consists in this: that the former may be *used* as *mere* means; but the latter *dare* not be employed as the means to an end without directly or indirectly sharing in that end. . . .

acknowledged between Things and Persons. If the latter are part of the concern, they come under the denomination of the former. Two objects only can be proposed in the management of an Estate, considered as a *Stock* in Trade – first, that the Returns should be the largest, quickest, and securest possible; and secondly, with the least out-goings in the providing, over-looking, and collecting the same – whether it be expenditure of money paid for other men's time and attention, or of the tradesman's own, which are to him *money's worth*, makes no difference in the argument. Am I disposing of a bale of goods? The man whom I most love and esteem must yield to the stranger that outbids him; or if it be sold on credit, the highest price, with equal security, must have the preference. I may fill up the deficiency of my friend's offer by a private gift, or loan; but as a tradesman, I am bound to regard honesty and established character themselves, as *things*, as *securities*, for which the known unprincipled dealer may offer an unexceptionable substitute. Add to this, that the security being equal, I shall prefer, even at a considerable abatement of price, the man who will take a thousand chests or bales at once, to twenty who can pledge themselves only for fifty each. For I do not seek trouble for its own sake; but among other advantages I seek wealth for the sake of freeing myself more and more from the necessity of taking trouble in order to attain it. The personal worth of those, whom I benefit in the course of the Process, or whether the persons are really benefited or no, is no concern of mine. The Market and the Shop are open to all. To introduce any other principle in Trade, but that of obtaining the highest price with adequate security for Articles fairly described, would be tantamount to the position, that Trade ought not to exist. If this be admitted, then what as a Tradesman I cannot do, it cannot be my Duty, as a Tradesman, to attempt: and the only remaining question in reason or morality is – what are the proper objects of Trade. If my Estate be such, my plan must be to make the most of it, as I would of any other mode of Capital. As my Rents will ultimately depend on the quantity and value of the Produce raised and brought into the best market from my Land, I will entrust the latter to those who bidding the most have the largest Capital to employ on it: and this I cannot effect but by dividing it into the fewest Tenures, as none but extensive Farms will be an object to men of extensive capital and enterprizing minds. I must prefer this system likewise for my own ease and security. The Farmer is of course actuated by the same motives, as the Landlord: and, provided they are both faithful to their engagements, the objects of both will be: 1. the utmost Produce that can be raised without injuring the estate; 2. with the least possible consumption of the Produce on the Estate itself; 3. at the lowest wages; and 4. with the substitution of machinery for human labor where ever the former will cost less and do the same work. What are the modest remedies proposed by the majority of correspondents in the last Report of the Board of Agriculture? Let measures be taken, that rents, taxes, and wages be lowered, and the Markets raised! A great calamity has befallen us, from importation, the lessened purchases of Government, and *"the evil of a superabundant Harvest"*—of which we deem ourselves the more entitled to complain, because *"we had been long making* 112 *shillings per quarter of our Corn,"* and of all other articles in proportion. As the best remedies for this calamity, we propose that we should pay less to our Landlords, less to our Laborers, nothing to our Clergyman, and either nothing or very little to the maintenance of the Government and of the Poor; but that we should sell at our former prices to the Consumer! – In almost every page we find deprecations of the Poor Laws: and I hold it impossible to exaggerate their pernicious tendency and consequences. But let it not be forgotten, that in agricultural districts three-fourths of the Poors' Rates are paid to healthy, robust, and (O sorrow and shame!) *industrious, hard-working* Paupers in lieu of Wages – (for men cannot at once work and starve:) and therefore if there are twenty Housekeepers in the Parish, who are not holders of Land, their contributions are so much Bounty Money to the latter. But the Poor Laws form a subject, which I should not undertake without trembling, had I the space of a whole volume to allot to it. Suffice, that this enormous mischief is *undeniably* the offspring of the Commercial System. In the only plausible Work, that I have seen, in favor of our Poor Laws on the present plan, the Defence is grounded: first, on the expediency of having Labor cheap, and Estates let out in the fewest possible portions – in other words, of large Farms and low Wages – each as indispensable to the other, and both conjointly as the only means of drawing Capital to the Land, by which alone the largest Surplus is attainable for the *State*: that is, for the Market, or in order that the smallest possible proportion of the largest possible Produce may be consumed by the Raisers and their families! Secondly, on the impossibility of supplying, as we have supplied, all the countries of the civilized

World (India perhaps and China excepted) and of underselling them even in their own markets, if our *working* Manufacturers were not secured by the State against the worst consequences of those failures, stagnations, and transfers, to which the different branches of Trade are exposed, in a greater or less degree, beyond all human prevention; or if the *Master* Manufacturers were compelled to give previous security for the maintenance of those whom they had, by the known Law of human Increase, virtually called into existence.

Let me not be misunderstood. I do not myself admit this impossibility. I have already denied, and I now repeat the denial, that these are *necessary* consequences of our extended Commerce. On the contrary, I feel assured that the Spirit of Commerce is itself capable of being at once counteracted and enlightened by the Spirit of the State, to the advantage of both. But I *do* assert, that they are necessary consequences of the Commercial Spirit *un*-counteracted and *un*-enlightened, wherever Trade has been carried to so vast an extent as it has in England. I assert too, historically and as matter of fact, that they *have been* the consequence of our commercial system. The laws of Lycurgus, like those of the inspired Hebrew Legislator, were anti-commercial: those of Solon and Numa were at least uncommercial. Now I ask myself, what the impression would have been on the Senate of the Roman or of the Athenian Republic, if the following proposal had been made to them and introduced by the following preamble. "Conscript Fathers, (or Senators of Athens!) it is well known to you, that circumstances being the same and the time allowed proportional, the human animal may be made to multiply as easily, and at as small an expence, as your sheep or swine: which is meant, perhaps, in the fiction of our Philosophers, that Souls are out of all proportion more numerous than the Bodies, in which they can subsist and be manifested. It is likewise known to you, Fathers! that though in various States various checks have been ordained to prevent this increase of births from becoming such as should frustrate or greatly endanger the ends for which freemen are born; yet the most efficient limit must be sought for in the moral and intellectual prerogatives of men, in their foresight, in their habituation to the comforts and decencies of society, in the pride of independence; but above all in THE HOPE that enables men to withstand the tyranny of the present impulse, and in their expectation of honor or discredit from the rank, character, and condition of their children. Now there are proposed to us the speedy means of at once increasing the number of the rich, the wealth of those that are already such, and the revenues of the State: and the latter, Fathers! to so vast an amount, that we shall be able to pay not only your own soldiers but those of the monarchs whom we may thus induce to become our Allies. But for this it will be requisite and indispensable that all men of enterprize and sufficiency among us should be permitted, without restraint, to encourage, and virtually to occasion, the birth of many myriads of free citizens, who from their childhood are to be amassed in clusters and employed as parts of a mighty system of machinery. While all things prove answerable to the schemes and wishes of these enterprisers, the Citizens thus raised and thus employed by them will find an ample maintenance, except in such instances where the individual may have rendered himself useless by the effects of his own vices. It dare not, however, be disguised from you, that the nature of the employments and the circumstances to which these citizens will be exposed, will often greatly tend to render them intemperate, diseased, and restless. Nor has it been yet made a part of the proposal, that the employers should be under any bond to counteract such injurious circumstances by education, discipline, or other efficient regulations. Still less may it be withheld from your knowledge, O Fathers of the State, that should events hereafter prove hostile to all or to any branch of these speculations, to many or to any one of the number that shall have devoted their wealth to the realization of the same – and the light, in which alone they can thrive, is confessedly subject to partial and even to total eclipses, which there are no means of precisely foretelling! the guardian planets, to whose conjunction their success is fatally linked, will at uncertain periods, for a longer or shorter time, act in malignant oppositions! – Then, Fathers, the Principals are to shift for themselves, and leave the disposal of the calamitous, and therefore too probably turbulent, multitude, now unemployed and useless, to the mercy of the community, and the solicitude of the State: or else to famine, violence, and the vengeance of the Laws!"

If, on the maxims of ancient prudence, on the one hand not enlightened, on the other not dazzled by the principles of Trade, the immediate answer would have been: – "We should deem it danger and detriment, were we to permit so indefinite and improvident increase even of our Slaves and Helots: in the case of free Citizens, our countrymen, who are to swear to the same laws, and worship at the same altars, it were profanation! May the Gods avert the Omen!" – If this, I say, would have been their rescript, it may be safely concluded, that the connivance at the same scheme, much more than the direct encouragement of it, must be attributed to that spirit which the ancients did not recognize, namely, the Spirit of Commerce.

But we have shewn, that the same system has gradually taken possession of our agriculture. What have been the results? For him who is either unable or unwilling to deduce the whole truth from the portion of it revealed in the following extract from Lord Winchelsea's Report, whatever I could have added would have been equally in vain.[58] His Lordship speaking of the causes which oppose all attempts to better the Laborers' condition, mentions, as one great cause, the dislike the generality of Farmers have to seeing the Laborers rent any land. Perhaps, (he continues) "one of the reasons for their disliking this is, that the land, if not occupied by the laborers, would fall to their own share; and another I am afraid is, that they rather wish to have the laborers more dependent upon them; for which reasons they are always desirous of hiring the house and land occupied by a laborer, under pretence, that by that means the landlord will be secure of his rent, and that they will keep the house in repair. This the agents of estates are too apt to give into, as they find it much less trouble to meet six than sixty tenants at a rent-day, and by this means avoid the being sometimes obliged to hear the wants and complaints of the poor. All parties therefore join in persuading the landlord, who it is natural to suppose (unless he has time and inclination to investigate the matter very closely) will agree to this their plan, from the manner in which it comes recommended to him: and it is in this manner that the laborers have been dispossessed of their cow-pastures in various parts of the midland counties. The moment the farmer obtains his wish, he takes every particle of the land to himself, and re-lets the house to the laborer, who by this means is rendered miserable; the Poor Rate increased; the value of the Estate to the Land-owner diminished; and the house suffered to go to decay; which once fallen the tenant will never rebuild, but the landlord must, at a considerable expence. Whoever travels through the midland counties, and will take the trouble of enquiring, will generally receive for answer, that formerly there were a great many cottagers who kept cows, but that the land is now thrown to the farmers; and if he enquires still farther, he will find that in those parishes the poors' rates have increased in an amazing degree, more than according to the average rise throughout England." – In confirmation of his Lordship's statement I find in the Agricultural Reports, that the county, in which I read of nothing but farms of 1000, 1500, 2000, and 2500 acres, is likewise that in which the poor rates are most numerous, the distresses of the poor most grievous, and the prevalence of revolutionary principles the most alarming. But if we consider the subject on the largest scale and nationally, the consequences are, that the most important rounds in the social ladder are broken, and the Hope, which above all other things distinguishes the free man from the slave, is extinguished. The peasantry therefore are eager to have their children add as early as possible to their wretched pittances, by letting them out to manufactories; while the youths take every opportunity of escaping to towns and cities. And if I were questioned, as to my opinion, respecting the ultimate cause of our liability to distresses like the present, the cause of what has been called a vicious (i.e. excessive) population with all the furies that follow in its train – in short, of a state of things so remote from the simplicity of nature, that we have almost deprived Heaven itself of the power of blessing us; a state in which, without absurdity, a superabundant Harvest can be complained of as an evil, and the recurrence of the same a ruinous calamity – I should not hesitate to answer – *the vast and disproportionate number of men who are to be fed from the produce of the fields, on which they do not labor.*

What then is the remedy? Who the physicians? The reply may be anticipated. An evil, which has come on gradually, and in the growth of which all men have more or less conspired, cannot be removed otherwise than gradually, and by the joint efforts of all. If we are a christian nation, we must learn to act nationally as well as individually, as Christians. We must remove the half-truths, the most dangerous of errors (as those of the poor visionaries called SPENCEANS) by the whole Truth. The Government is employed already in retrenchments; but he who expects immediate relief from these, or who does not even know that if they do any thing at all, they must for the time tend to aggravate the distress, cannot have studied the operation of public expenditure.

I am persuaded that more good would be done, not only ultimate and permanent, but immediate, good, by the abolition of the Lotteries accompanied with a public and parliamentary declaration of the moral and religious grounds that had determined the

Legislature to this act; of their humble confidence in the blessing of God on the measure; and of their hopes that this sacrifice to principle, as being more exemplary from the present pressure on the Revenue of the State, would be the more effective in restoring confidence between man and man – I am deeply convinced, that more sterling and visible benefits would be derived from this one solemn proof and pledge of moral fortitude and national faith, than from retrenchments to a tenfold greater amount. Still more, if our Legislators should pledge themselves at the same time, that they would hereafter take council for the gradual removal or counteraction of all similar encouragements and temptations to Vice and Folly, that had alas! been tolerated hitherto, as the easiest way of supplying the exchequer. And truly, the financial motives would be strong indeed, if the Revenue Laws in question were but half as productive of money to the State as they are of guilt and wretchedness to the people.

Our manufacturers must consent to regulations; our gentry must concern themselves in the *education* as well as in the *instruction* of their natural clients and dependents, must regard their estates as secured indeed from all human interference by every principle of law, and policy, but yet as offices of trust, with duties to be performed, in the sight of God and their Country. Let us become a better people, and the reform of all the public (real or supposed) grievances, which we use as pegs whereon to hang our own errors and defects, will follow of itself. In short, let every man measure his efforts by his power and his sphere of action, and do all he can do! Let him contribute money where he cannot act personally; *but let him act personally and in detail* wherever it is practicable. Let us palliate where we cannot cure, comfort where we cannot relieve; and for the rest rely upon the promise of the King of Kings by the mouth of his Prophet, "BLESSED ARE YE THAT SOW BESIDE ALL WATERS."

5

The Idea of the Constitution: *On the Constitution of the Church and State, According to the Idea of Each* (1829)

On the Constitution of the Church and State[1] *is Coleridge's last and most important contribution to political theory. In this work he analyses the constitutional requirements of a state that would facilitate an advance towards the ends specified in* A Lay Sermon *and in* The Friend. *The principle of balance, which plays an important role in* A Lay Sermon, *is here applied to the organisation of political and constitutional, rather than social, forces, although these are seen as reflecting the social and economic power associated with the ownership of property. Coleridge focuses on both a narrow and a wide conception of the Constitution. The 'constitution of the state' (narrow conception) is concerned with the organisation of government, and the representation of interests; it balances differing proprietorial interests and different sorts of social powers. The 'constitution of the nation', however, is broader, and necessarily includes the National Church. This institution counterbalances the interests and powers included in the narrow idea of the Constitution by providing an institutionalised and independent focus for an educated and educational elite who preserve, convey and enrich the 'culture' of the community, or its particular expression of those distinctly human values that reflect men's status as creatures who are marked off from the rest of God's creation.*

Coleridge's account of the balance of forces within the 'constitution of the state' is in many respects similar to that which had appeared in his Morning Post *articles on French affairs. However, the argument of* Church and State *makes it clear that such a balance will only allow the state to pursue its proper ends if it is integrated with an institution based on values that are independent of proprietorial interests and the power of the masses.*

There Is A Mystery In The Soul Of State,
Which Hath An Operation More Divine
Than Our Mere Chroniclers Dare Meddle With.[2]

CHAPTER I

Prefatory Remarks on the true import of the word, IDEA; *and what the author means by "according to the Idea"*

THE Bill lately passed for the admission of Roman Catholics into the Legislature[3] comes so near the mark to which my convictions and wishes have through my whole life, since earliest manhood, unwaveringly pointed, and has so agreeably disappointed my fears, that my first impulse was to suppress the pages, which I had written while the particulars of the Bill were yet unknown, in compliance with the request of an absent friend, who had expressed an anxiety "to learn from myself the nature and grounds of my apprehension, that the measure would fail to effect the object immediately intended by its authors."

In answer to this, I reply, that the main ground of that apprehension is certainly much narrowed; but as certainly not altogether removed. I refer to the securities.[4] And, let it be understood, that in calling a certain provision hereafter specified, a *security*, I use the word *comparatively*, and mean no more, than that it has at least an equal claim to be so called, as any of those that have been hitherto proposed as such. Whether either one or the other deserve the name; whether the thing itself is possible; I leave undetermined. This premised, I resume my subject, and repeat, that the main objection, from which my fears as to the practical results of the supposed Bill were derived, applies with nearly the same force to the actual Bill; though the fears themselves have, by the spirit and general character of the clauses, been considerably mitigated. The principle, the solemn recognition of which I deemed indispensable as a security, and should be willing to receive as the only security – superseding the necessity, though possibly not the expediency of any other, but itself by no other superseded – this principle is not formally recognized. It may perhaps be *implied* in one of the clauses (that which forbids the assumption of local titles by the Romish bishops); but this implication, even if really contained in the clause, and actually intended by its framers, is not calculated to answer the ends, and utterly inadequate to supply the place, of the solemn and formal declaration which I had required, and which, with my motives and reasons for the same, it will be the object of the following pages to set forth.

But to enable you fully to understand, and fairly to appreciate, my arguments, I must previously state (what I at least judge to be) the true Idea of A CONSTITUTION; and, likewise, of a NATIONAL CHURCH. And in giving the essential character of the latter, I shall briefly specify its distinction from the Church of Christ, and its contra-distinction from a third form, which is neither national nor Christian, but irreconcileable with, and subversive of, both. By an *idea*, I mean, (in this instance) that conception of a thing, which is not abstracted from any particular state, form, or mode, in which the thing may happen to exist at this or at that time; nor yet generalized from any number or succession of such forms or modes; but which is given by the knowledge of *its ultimate aim*.

Only one observation I must be allowed to add, that this knowledge, or sense, may very well exist, aye, and powerfully influence a man's thoughts and actions, without his being distinctly conscious of the same, much more without his being competent to express it in definite words. This, indeed, is one of the points which distinguish *ideas* from *conceptions*, both terms being used in their strict and proper significations. The latter, *i.e.* a conception, *consists* in a conscious act of the understanding, bringing any given object or impression into the same class with any number of other objects, or impressions, by means of some character or characters common to them all. *Concipimus*, id est, capimus hoc *cum* illo [*We conceive*, that is, we take this *with* that], – we take hold of both at once, we *comprehend* a thing, when we have learnt to comprise it in a known *class*. On the other hand, it is the privilege of the few to possess an idea: of the generality of men, it might be more truly affirmed, that they are possessed by it.

What is here said, will, I hope, suffice as a popular explanation. For some of my readers, however, the following definition may not, perhaps, be useless or unacceptable. That which, contemplated *objectively* (*i.e.* as existing *externally* to the mind), we call a LAW; the same contemplated *subjectively* (*i.e.* as existing in a subject or mind), is an idea. Hence Plato often names ideas laws; and Lord Bacon, the British Plato, describes the Laws of the material universe as the Ideas in nature. Quod in naturâ *naturatâ* LEX, in naturâ *naturante* IDEA dicitur [What is called LAW in *created* nature is called IDEA in *creative* nature].[5] By way of illustration take the following. Every reader of Rousseau, or of Hume's Essays, will understand me when I refer to the Original Social Contract, assumed by Rousseau, and by other and wiser men before him, as the basis of all legitimate government.[6] Now, if this be taken as the assertion of an historical fact, or as the application of a conception, generalized from ordinary compacts between man and man, or nation and nation, to an actual occurrence in the first ages of the world; namely, the formation of the first contract, in which men covenanted with each other to associate, or in which a multitude entered into a compact with a few, the one to be governed and the other to govern, under certain declared conditions; I shall run little hazard at this time of day, in declaring the pretended fact a pure fiction, and the conception of such a fact an idle fancy. It is at once false and foolish [note omitted]. For what if an original contract had actually been entered into, and formally recorded? Still I cannot see what addition of moral force would be gained by the fact. The same sense of moral obligation which binds us to keep it, must have pre-existed in the same force and in relation to the same duties, impelling our ancestors to make it. For what could it do more than bind the contracting parties to act for the general good, according to their best lights and opportunities? It is evident, that no specific scheme or constitution can derive any other claim to our reverence, than that which the presumption of its necessity or fitness for the general good shall give it; and which claim of course ceases, or rather is reversed, as soon as this general presumption of its utility has given place to as general a conviction of the contrary. It is true, indeed, that from duties anterior to the formation of the contract, because they arise out of the very constitution of our humanity, which supposes the social state – it is true, that in order to a rightful removal of the institution, or law, thus agreed on, it is required that the conviction of its inexpediency shall be as general, as the presumption of its fitness was at the time of its establishment. This, the first of the two great paramount interests of the social state demands, namely, that of permanence; but to attribute more than this to any fundamental articles, passed into law by any assemblage of individuals, is an injustice to their successors, and a high offence against the other great interest of the social state, namely, – its progressive improvement. The conception, therefore, of an original contract, is, we repeat, incapable of historic proof as a fact, and it is senseless as a theory.

But if instead of the *conception* or *theory* of an original social contract, you say the *idea* of an ever-originating social contract, this is so certain and so indispensable, that it constitutes the whole ground of the difference between subject and serf, between a commonwealth and a slave-plantation. And this, again, is evolved

out of the yet higher idea of *person*, in contra-distinction from *thing* –
all social law and justice being grounded on the principle, that a
person can never, but by his own fault, become a thing, or, without
grievous wrong, be treated as such: and the distinction consisting
in this, that a thing may be used altogether and merely as the *means*
to an end; but the person must always be included in the *end*: his
interest must form a part of the object, a *means* to which, he, by
consent, *i.e.* by his own act, makes himself.[7] We plant a tree, and
we fell it; we breed the sheep, and we shear or we kill it; in both
cases wholly as means to *our* ends. For trees and animals are *things*.
The wood-cutter and the hind are likewise employed as *means*, but
on agreement, and that too an agreement of reciprocal advantage,
which includes them as well as their employer in the *end*. For they
are *persons*. And the government, under which the contrary takes
place, is not worthy to be called a STATE, if, as in the kingdom of
Dahomy, it be unprogressive; or only by anticipation, where, as in
Russia, it is in advance to a better and more *man-worthy* order of
things. Now, notwithstanding the late wonderful spread of learning
through the community, and though the schoolmaster and the
lecturer are abroad, the hind and the woodman may, very con-
ceivably, pass from cradle to coffin, without having once contemplated this idea, so as to be conscious of the same. And there would
be even an improbability in the supposition that they possessed the
power of presenting this Idea to the minds of others, or even to
their own thoughts, verbally as a distinct proposition. But no man,
who has ever listened to laborers of this rank, in any alehouse, over
the Saturday night's jug of beer, discussing the injustice of the
present rate of wages, and the iniquity of their being paid in part
out of the parish poor-rates, will doubt for a moment that they are
fully possessed by the idea.

In close, though not perhaps obvious connection, with this, is
the idea of moral freedom, as the ground of our proper responsibility. Speak to a young Liberal, fresh from Edinburgh or Hackney[8]
or the Hospitals, of Free-will, as implied in Free-agency, he will
perhaps confess to you with a smile, that he is a Necessitarian, –
proceed to assure you that the liberty of the will is an impossible
conception, *a contradiction in terms* [note omitted], and finish by
recommending you to read Jonathan Edwards, or Dr. Crombie: or
as it may happen, he may declare the will itself a mere delusion, a
non-entity, and ask you if you have read Mr. Lawrence's Lecture.
Converse on the same subject with a plain, single-minded, yet

reflecting neighbour, and he may probably say (as St. Augustin
had said long before him, in reply to the question, What is Time?)
I know it well enough when you do not ask me.[9] But alike with
both the supposed parties, the self-complacent student, just as
certainly as with your less positive neighbour – attend to their
actions, their feelings, and even to their words: and you will be in
ill luck, if ten minutes pass without affording you full and
satisfactory proof, that the *idea* of man's moral freedom possesses
and modifies their whole practical being, in all they say, in all they
feel, in all they do and are done to: even as the spirit of life, which
is contained in no vessel, because it permeates all.

Just so is it with the *constitution. Ask any of our politicians
what is meant by the constitution, and it is ten to one that he will
give you a false explanation, *ex. gr.* that it is the body of our laws,
or that it is the Bill of Rights; or perhaps, if he have read Tom
Payne,[10] he may tell you, that we have not yet got one; and yet
not an hour may have elapsed, since you heard the same individual
denouncing, and possibly with good reason, this or that code of
laws, the excise and revenue laws, or those for including pheasants,
or those for excluding Catholics, as altogether unconstitutional:
and such and such acts of parliament as gross outrages on the
constitution. Mr. Peel, who is rather remarkable for groundless
and unlucky concessions, owned that the present Bill breaks in on
the constitution of 1688: and, A. D. 1689, a very imposing minority
of the then House of Lords, with a decisive majority in the Lower
House of Convocation, denounced the constitution of 1688, as
breaking in on the English Constitution.[11]

But a Constitution is an idea arising out of the idea of a state;
and because our whole history from Alfred onward demonstrates
the continued influence of such an idea, or ultimate aim, on the
minds of our fore-fathers, in their characters and functions as
public men; alike in what they resisted and in what they claimed;
in the institutions and forms of polity which they established, and
with regard to those, against which they more or less successfully
contended; and because the result has been progressive, though
not always a direct, or equable advance in the gradual realization
of the idea; and that it is actually, though even because it is an *idea*

* I do not say, with the idea: for the constitution itself is an IDEA. This will sound
like a parodox or a sneer to those with whom an Idea is but another word for *a
fancy*, a something unreal; but not to those who in the ideas contemplate the most
real of all realities, and of all operative powers the most *actual*.

it cannot be *adequately*, represented in a correspondent scheme of means really existing; we speak, and have a right to speak, of the idea itself, as actually existing, *i.e.*, as a *principle*, existing in the only way in which a principle can exist – in the minds and consciences of the persons, whose duties it prescribes, and whose rights it determines. In the same sense that the sciences of arithmetic and of geometry, that mind, that life itself, have reality; the constitution has real existence, and does not the less exist in reality, because it both *is*, and *exists as*, an IDEA.

There is yet another ground for the affirmation of its reality; that, as the fundamental idea, it is at the same time, the final criterion by which all particular frames of government must be tried: for here only can we find the great constructive principles of our representative system (I use the term in its widest sense, in which the crown itself is included as representing the unity of the people, the true and primary sense of the word majesty); those principles, I say, in the light of which it can alone be ascertained what are excrescences, symptoms of distemperature and marks of degeneration; and what are native growths, or changes naturally attendant on the progressive development of the original germ, symptoms of immaturity perhaps, but not of disease; or at worst, modifications of the growth by the defective or faulty, but remedi- less, or only gradually remediable, qualities of the soil and sur- rounding elements.

There are two other characters, distinguishing the class of substantive truths, or truth-powers here spoken of, that will, I trust, indemnify the reader for the delay of the two or three short sentences required for their explanation. The first is, that in distinction from the *conception* of a thing, which being abstracted or generalized from one or more particular states, or modes, is necessarily posterior in order of thought to the thing thus conceived, – an idea, on the contrary, is in order of thought always and of necessity contemplated as antecedent. In the idea or principle, Life, for instance – the vital *functions* are the result of the organization; but this organization supposes and pre-supposes the vital *principle*. The bearings of the planets on the sun are determined by the ponderable matter of which they consist; but the *principle* of gravity, the *law* in the material creation, the *idea* of the Creator, is pre-supposed in order to the existence, yea, to the very concep- tion of the existence, of matter itself.

This is the first. The other distinctive mark may be most

conveniently given in the form of a caution. We should be made aware, namely, that the particular form, construction, or model, that may be best fitted to render the idea intelligible, and most effectually serve the purpose of an instructive *diagram*, is not necessarily the mode or form in which it actually arrives at realization. In the works both of man and of nature – in the one by the imperfection of the means and materials, in the other by the multitude and complexity of simultaneous purposes – the fact is most often otherwise. A naturalist, (in the infancy of physiology, we will suppose, and before the first attempts at comparative anatomy) whose knowledge had been confined exclusively to the human frame, or that of animals similarly organized; and who, by this experience had been led inductively to the idea of respiration, as the copula and mediator of the vascular and the nervous systems, – might, very probably, have regarded the lungs, with their appurtenants, as the only form in which this idea, or ultimate aim, was realizable. Ignorant of the functions of the spiracula in the insects, and of the gills of the fish, he would, perhaps, with great confidence degrade both to the class of non-respirants. But alike in the works of nature and the institutions of man, there is no more effectual preservative against pedantry, and the positiveness of sciolism, than to meditate on the law of compensation, and the principle of compromise; and to be fully impressed with the wide extent of the one, the necessity of the other, and the frequent occurrence of both.

Having (more than sufficiently, I fear), exercised your patience with these preparatory remarks, for which the anxiety to be fully understood by you is my best excuse, though in a moment of less excitement they might not have been without some claim to your attention for their own sake, I return to the idea, which forms the present subject – the English Constitution, which an old writer calls, "Lex Sacra, Mater Legum [Sacred Law, Mother of Laws], than which (says he), nothing can be proposed more certain in its grounds, more pregnant in its consequences, or that hath more harmonical reason within itself: and which is so connatural and essential to the genius and innate disposition of this nation, it being formed (silk-worm like) as that no other law can possibly regulate it – a law not to be derived from Alured, or Alfred, or Canute, or other elder or later promulgators of particular laws, but which might say of itself – When reason and the laws of God first came, then came I with them."[12]

As, according to an old saying, "an ill foreknown is half disarmed," I will here notice an inconvenience in our language, which, without a greater inconvenience, I could not avoid, in the use of the term *State*, in a double sense, a larger, in which it is equivalent to Realm and includes the Church, and a narrower, in which it is distinguished *quasi per antithesin* [as if through antithesis] from the Church, as in the phrase, Church and State. But the context, I trust, will in every instance prevent ambiguity.

CHAPTER II

The idea of a State in the larger sense of the term, introductory to the constitution of the State in the narrower sense, as it exists in this Country

A CONSTITUTION is the attribute of a state, *i.e.* of a body politic, having the principle of its unity within itself, whether by concentration of its forces, as a constitutional pure Monarchy, which, however, has hitherto continued to be *ens rationale* [rational entity], unknown in history[13]. . . or – with which we are alone concerned – by equipoise and interdependency: the *lex equilibrii* [law of balance] the principle prescribing the means and conditions by and under which this balance is to be established and preserved, being the constitution of the state. It is the chief of many blessings derived from the insular character and circumstances of our country, that our social institutions have formed themselves out of our proper needs and interests; that long and fierce as the birth-struggle and the growing pains have been, the antagonist powers have been of our own system, and have been allowed to work out their final balance with less disturbance from external forces, than was possible in the Continental states.

> O ne'er enchain'd nor wholly vile,
> O Albion! O my Mother Isle!
> Thy valleys fair as Eden's bowers
> Glitter green with sunny showers!
> Thy grassy uplands' gentle swells
> Echo to the bleat of flocks;
> Those grassy hills, those glittering dells,
> Proudly ramparted with rocks:

And OCEAN 'mid his uproar wild
Speaks safety to his ISLAND-CHILD!
Hence thro' many a fearless Age
Has social Freedom lov'd the Land,
Nor Alien Despot's jealous rage
Or warp'd thy growth or stamp'd the servile Brand.[14]

Now, in every country of civilized men, acknowledging the rights of property, and by means of determined boundaries and common laws united into one people or nation, the two antagonist powers or opposite interests of the state, under which all other state interests are comprised, are those of PERMANENCE and of PROGRESSION.*

It will not be necessary to enumerate the several causes that combine to connect the permanence of a state with the land and the landed property. To found a family, and to convert his wealth into land, are twin thoughts, births of the same moment, in the mind of the opulent merchant, when he thinks of reposing from his labours. From the class of the Novi Homines [new men] he redeems himself by becoming the staple ring of the chain, by which the present will become connected with the past; and the test and evidence of permanency afforded. To the same principle appertain primogeniture and hereditary titles, and the influence which these exert in accumulating large masses of property, and in counteracting the antagonist and dispersive forces, which the follies, the vices, and misfortunes of individuals can scarcely fail to supply. To this, likewise, tends the proverbial obduracy of prejudices characteristic of the humbler tillers of the soil, and their aversion even to benefits that are offered in the form of innovations. But why need I attempt to explain a fact which no thinking man will deny, and where the admission of the fact is all that my argument requires?

On the other hand, with as little chance of contradiction, I may assert, that the progression of a state, in the arts and comforts of

---

* Permit me to draw your attention to the essential difference between *opposite* and *contrary*. Opposite powers are always of the same kind, and tend to union, either by equipoise or by a common product. Thus the + and − poles of the magnet, thus positive and negative electricity are opposites. Sweet and sour are opposites; sweet and bitter are contraries. . . . Even so in the present instance, the interest of permanence is opposed to that of progressiveness; but so far from being contrary interests, they, like the magnetic forces, suppose and require each other. . . .

life, in the diffusion of the information and knowledge, useful or necessary for all; in short, all advances in civilization, and the rights and privileges of citizens, are especially connected with, and derived from the four classes of the mercantile, the manufacturing, the distributive, and the professional. To early Rome, war and conquest were the substitutes for trade and commerce. War was their trade. As these wars became more frequent, on a larger scale, and with fewer interruptions, the liberties of the plebeians continued increasing: for even the sugar plantations of Jamaica would (in their present state, at least), present a softened picture of the hard and servile relation, in which the plebeian formerly stood to his patrician patron.

Italy is supposed at present to maintain a larger number of inhabitants than in the days of Trajan or in the best and most prosperous of the Roman empire. With the single exception of the ecclesiastic state,[15] the whole country is cultivated like a garden. You may find there every gift of God – only not freedom. It is a country, rich in the proudest records of liberty, illustrious with the names of heroes, statesmen, legislators, philosophers. It hath a history all alive with the virtues and crimes of hostile parties, when the glories and the struggles of ancient Greece were acted over again in the proud republics of Venice, Genoa, and Florence. The life of every eminent citizen was in constant hazard from the furious factions of their native city, and yet life had no charm out of its dear and honored walls. All the splendors of the hospitable palace, and the favor of princes, could not soothe the pining of Dante or Machiavel, exiles from their free, their beautiful Florence. But not a pulse of liberty survives. It was the profound policy of the Austrian and the Spanish courts, by every possible means to degrade the profession of trade; and even in Pisa and Florence themselves to introduce the feudal pride and prejudice of less happy, less enlightened countries. Agriculture, meanwhile, with its attendant population and plenty, was cultivated with increasing success; but from the Alps to the Straits of Messina, the Italians are slaves.

We have thus divided the subjects of the state into two orders, the agricultural or possessors of land; and the merchant, manufacturer, the distributive, and the professional bodies, under the common name of citizens. And we have now to add that by the nature of things common to every civilized country, at all events by the course of events in this country, the first is subdivided into two classes, which, in imitation of our old law books, we may intitle the Major and Minor Barons; both these, either by their interests or by the very effect of their situation, circumstances, and the nature of their employment, vitally connected with the permanency of the state, its institutions, rights, customs, manners, privileges – and as such, opposed to the inhabitants of ports, towns, and cities, who are in like manner and from like causes more especially connected with its progression. I scarcely need say, that in a very advanced stage of civilization, the two orders of society will more and more modify and leaven each other, yet never so completely but that the distinct character remains legible, and to use the words of the Roman Emperor, even in what is struck out the erasure is manifest. At all times the lower of the two ranks, of which the first order consists, or the Franklins, will, in their political sympathies, draw more nearly to the antagonist order than the first rank. On these facts, which must at all times have existed, though in very different degrees of prominence or maturity, the principle of our constitution was established. The total interests of the country, the interests of the STATE, were entrusted to a great council or parliament, composed of two Houses. The first consisting exclusively of the Major Barons, who at once stood as the guardians and sentinels of their several estates and privileges, and the representatives of the common weal. The Minor Barons, or Franklins, too numerous, and yet individually too weak, to sit and maintain their rights in person, were to choose among the worthiest of their own body representatives, and these in such number as to form an important though minor proportion of a second House – the majority of which was formed by the representatives chosen by the cities, ports, and boroughs; which representatives ought on principle to have been elected not only by, but from among, the members of the manufacturing, mercantile, distributive, and professional classes.

These four classes, by an arbitrary but convenient use of the phrase, I will designate by the name of the Personal Interest, as the exponent of all moveable and personal possessions, including skill and acquired knowledge, the moral and intellectual stock in trade of the professional man and the artist, no less than the raw materials, and the means of elaborating, transporting, and distributing them.

Thus in the theory of the constitution it was provided, that even though both divisions of the Landed Interest should combine in any legislative attempt to encroach on the rights and privileges of the Personal Interest, yet the representatives of the latter forming the clear and effectual majority of the lower House, the attempt must be abortive: the majority of votes in both Houses being indispensable, in order to the presentation of a bill for the Completory Act, – that is, to make it a law of the land. By force of the same mechanism must every attack be baffled that should be made by the representatives of the minor landholders, in concert with the burgesses, on the existing rights and privileges of the peerage, and of the hereditary aristocracy, of which the peerage is the summit and the natural protector. Lastly, should the nobles join to invade the rights and franchises of the Franklins and the Yeomanry, the sympathy of interest, by which the inhabitants of cities, towns, and sea-ports, are linked to the great body of the agricultural fellow-commoners, who supply their markets and form their principal customers, could not fail to secure a united and successful resistance. Nor would this affinity of interest find a slight support in the sympathy of feeling between the burgess senators and the county representatives, as members of the same House; and in the consciousness, which the former have, of the dignity conferred on them by the latter. For the notion of superior dignity will always be attached in the minds of men to that kind of property with which they have most associated the idea of permanence: and the land is the synonime of country.

That the burgesses were not bound to elect representatives from among their own order, individuals bonâ fide belonging to one or other of the four divisions above enumerated; that the elective franchise of the towns, ports, &c., first invested with borough-rights, was not made conditional, and to a certain extent at least dependent on their retaining the same comparative wealth and independence, and rendered subject to a periodical revisal and re-adjustment; that in consequence of these and other causes, the very weights intended for the effectual counterpoise of the great land-holders, have, in the course of events, been shifted into the opposite scale; that they now constitute a large proportion of the political power and influence of the very class whose personal cupidity, and whose partial views of the landed interest at large they were meant to keep in check; these are no part of the constitution, no essential ingredients in the idea, but apparent defects and imperfections in its realization – which, however, we will neither regret nor set about amending, till we have seen whether an equivalent force had not arisen to supply the deficiency – a force great enough to have destroyed the equilibrium, had not such a transfer taken place previously to, or at the same time with, the operation of the new forces. Roads, canals, machinery, the press, the periodical and daily press, the might of public opinion, the consequent increasing desire of popularity among public men and functionaries of every description, and the increasing necessity of public character, as a means or condition of political influence – I need but mention these to stand acquitted of having started a vague and naked possibility in extenuation of an evident and palpable abuse.

But whether this conjecture be well or ill grounded, the *principle* of the constitution remains the same. That harmonious balance of the two great correspondent, at once supporting and counterpoising, interests of the state, its permanence, and its progression: that balance of the landed and the personal interests was to be secured by a legislature of two Houses; the first consisting wholly of barons or landholders, permanent and hereditary senators; the second of the knights or minor barons, elected by, and as the representatives of, the remaining landed community, together with the burgesses, the representatives of the commercial, manufacturing, distributive, and professional classes, – the latter (the elected burgesses) constituting the major number. The king, meanwhile, in whom the executive power is vested, it will suffice at present to consider as the beam of the constitutional scales. A more comprehensive view of the kingly office must be deferred, till the remaining problem (the idea of a national church) has been solved.

I must here intreat the reader to bear in mind what I have before endeavoured to impress on him, that I am not giving an historical account of the legislative body; nor can I be supposed to assert that such was the earliest mode or form in which the national council was constructed. My assertion is simply this, that its formation has advanced in this direction. The line of evolution, however sinuous, has still tended to this point, sometimes with, sometimes without, not seldom, perhaps, against, the intention of the individual actors, but always as if a power, greater, and better, than the men themselves, had intended it for them. Nor let it be forgotten that every new growth, every power and privilege, bought or extorted, has uniformly been claimed by an antecedent right; not acknowledged as a boon conferred, but both demanded and received as what had always belonged to them, though withheld by violence and the injury of the times. This too, in cases, where, if documents and historical records, or even consistent traditions, had been required in evidence, the monarch would have had the better of the argument. But, in truth, it was no more than a *practical* way of saying: this or that is contained in the *idea* of our government, and it is a consequence of the "Lex, Mater Legum," which, in the very first law of state ever promulgated in the land, was pre-supposed as the ground of that first law.

Before I conclude this part of my subject, I must press on your attention, that the preceding is offered only as the constitutional idea of the *State*. In order to correct views respecting the constitution, in the more enlarged sense of the term, viz. the constitution of the *Nation*, we must, in addition to a grounded knowledge of the *State*, have the right idea of the *National Church*. These are two poles of the same magnet; the magnet itself, which is constituted by them, is the CONSTITUTION of the nation.

CHAPTER III

On the Church; i.e. the National Church

THE reading of *histories*, my dear Sir, may dispose a man to satire; but the science of HISTORY, – History studied in the light of philosophy, as the great drama of an ever unfolding Providence, – has a very different effect. It infuses hope and reverential thoughts of man and his destination. To you, therefore, it will be no unwelcome result, though it should be made appear that something deeper and better than priestcraft and priest-ridden ignorance was at the bottom of the phrase, Church and State, and intitled it to be the form in which so many thousands of the men of England clothed the wish for their country's weal. But many things have conspired to draw off the attention from its true origin and import, and have led us to seek the reasons for thus connecting the two words, in facts and motives, that lie nearer the surface. I will mention one only, because, though less obvious than many other causes that have favoured the general misconception on this point, and though its action is indirect and negative, it is by no means the least operative. The immediate effect, indeed, may be confined to the men of education. But what influences these, will finally influence all. I am referring to the noticeable fact, arising out of the system of instruction pursued in all our classical schools and universities, that the annals of ancient Greece, and of republican and imperial Rome, though they are, in fact, but brilliant exceptions of history generally, do yet, partly from the depth and intensity of all early impressions, and in part, from the number and splendor of individual characters and particular events and exploits, so fill the imagination, as almost to be, – during the period, when the groundwork of our minds is principally formed and the direction given to our modes of thinking, – what we mean by HISTORY. Hence things, of which no instance or analogy is recollected in the customs, policy, and legisprudence of Greece and Rome, lay little hold on our attention. Among these, I know not one more worthy of notice, than the principle of the division of property, which, if not, as I however think, universal in the earliest ages, was, at all events, common to the Scandinavian, Celtic, and Gothic tribes, with the Semitic, or the tribes descended from Shem.

It is not the least among the obligations, which the antiquarian and the philosophic statist owe to a tribe of the last-mentioned race, the Hebrew I mean, that in the institutes of their great legislator, who first formed them into a *state* or nation, they have preserved for us a practical illustration of this principle in question, which was by no means peculiar to the Hebrew people, though in their case it received a peculiar sanction.[16]

To confound the inspiring spirit with the informing word, and both with the dictation of sentences and formal propositions; and to confine the office and purpose of inspiration to the miraculous immission, or infusion, of novelties, rebus nusquam prius visis, vel auditis [things nowhere previously seen or heard], – these, alas! are the current errors of Protestants without learning, and of bigots in spite of it; but which I should have left unnoticed, but for the injurious influence which certain notions in close connexion with these errors have had on the present subject. The notion, I mean, that the Levitical institution was not only enacted by an inspired Law-giver, not only a work of revealed *wisdom*, (which who denies?) but that it was a part of revealed *Religion*, having its *origin* in this particular revelation, as a something which could not have existed otherwise; yet, on the other hand, a part of the religion that had been *abolished* by Christianity. Had these reasoners contented themselves with asserting that it did not *belong* to the Christian Religion, they would have said nothing more than the truth; and for this plain reason, that it forms no part of *religion* at all, in the Gospel sense of the word, – that is, *Religion* as contra-distinguished from *Law*; spiritual, as contra-distinguished from temporal or political.

In answer to all these notions, it is enough to say, that not the principle itself, but the superior wisdom with which the principle was carried into effect, the greater perfection of the machinery, forms the true distinction, the *peculiar* worth, of the Hebrew constitution. The principle itself was common to Goth and Celt, or rather, I would say, to all the tribes that had not fallen off to either of the two *Aphelia*, or extreme distances from the generic character of man, the wild or barbarous state; but who remained either constituent parts or appendages of the *stirps generosa seu historica* [undegenerate or historic stock], as a philosophic friend has named that portion of the Semitic and Japetic races, that had not degenerated below the *conditions* of progressive civilization: – it was, I say, common to all the primitive races, that in taking possession of a new country, and in the division of the land into hereditable estates among the individual warriors or heads of families, a reserve should be made for the nation itself.

The sum total of these heritable portions, appropriated each to an individual Lineage, I beg leave to name the PROPRIETY; and to call the *reserve* above-mentioned the NATIONALTY; and likewise to employ the term wealth, in that primary and wide sense which it retains in the term, Commonwealth. In the establishment, then, of the landed *proprieties*, a *nationalty* was at the same time consti-tuted: as a *wealth* not consisting of lands, but yet derivative from the land, and rightfully inseparable from the same. These, the *Propriety* and the *Nationalty*, were the two constituent factors, the opposite, but correspondent and reciprocally supporting, counter-weights, of the *commonwealth*; the existence of the one being the condition, and the perfecting of the rightfulness of the other. Now as all polar forces, *i.e. opposite*, not *contrary*, powers, are necessarily *unius generis*, homogeneous, so, in the present instance, each is that which it is called, relatively, by *predominance* of the one character or quality, not by the absolute exclusion of the other. The wealth appropriated was not so entirely a property as not to remain, to a certain extent, national; nor was the wealth reserved so exclusively national, as not to admit of individual tenure. It was only necessary that the mode and origin of the tenure should be different, and in *antithesis*, as it were. *Ex. gr.* If the one be hereditary, the other must be elective; if the one be lineal, the other must be circulative.

CHAPTER IV

Illustration of the preceding Chapter from History, and principally that of the Hebrew Commonwealth

IN the unfolding and exposition of any idea, we naturally seek assistance and the means of illustration from the historical instance, in which it has been most nearly realized, or of which we possess the most exact and satisfactory records. Both of these recommendations are found in the formation of the Hebrew Commonwealth. But, in availing ourselves of examples from history, there is always danger, lest that, which was to assist us in attaining a clear insight into truth, should be the means of disturbing or falsifying it, so that we attribute to the object what was but the effect of flaws, or other accidents in the glass, through which we looked at it. To secure ourselves from this danger, we must constantly bear in mind, that in the actual realization of every great idea or principle, there will always exist disturbing forces, modifying the product, either from the imperfection of their agents, or from especial circumstances overruling them: or from the defect of the materials; or lastly, and which most particularly applies to the instances we have here in view, from the co-existence of some yet greater idea, some yet more important purpose, with which the former must be combined, but likewise subordinated. Nevertheless, these are no essentials of the idea, no exemplary parts in the particular construction adduced for its illustration. On the contrary, they are deviations from the idea, from which we must abstract, which we must put aside, before we can make a safe and fearless use of the example.

Such, for instance, was the settlement of the NATIONALTY in one tribe, which, to the exclusion of the eleven other divisions of the Hebrew confederacy, was to be invested with its rights, and to be capable of discharging its duties. This was, indeed, in some measure, corrected by the institution of the *Nabim*, or Prophets, who might be of any tribe, and who formed a numerous body, uniting the functions and three-fold character of the Roman

Censors, the Tribunes of the people, and the sacred college of Augurs; protectors of the Nation and privileged state-moralists, whom, you will recollect, our Milton has already compared* to the orators of the Greek Democracies. Still the most satisfactory justification of this exclusive policy, is to be found, I think, in the fact, that the Jewish Theocracy itself was but a means to a further and greater end; and that the effects of the policy were subordinated to an interest, far more momentous than that of any single kingdom or commonwealth could be. The unfitness and insufficiency of the Jewish character for the reception and execution of the legislator's scheme were not less important parts of the sublime purpose of Providence in the separation of the chosen people, than their characteristic virtues. Their frequent relapses, and the never-failing return of a certain number to the national faith and customs, were alike subservient to the ultimate object, the final cause, of the Mosaic dispensation.[18] Without pain or reluctance, therefore, I should state this provision, by which a particular lineage was made a necessary qualification for the trustees and functionaries of the reserved NATIONALTY, as the main cause of the comparatively little effect, which the Levitical establishment produced on the moral and intellectual character of the Jewish people, during the whole period of their existence as an independent state.

With this exception, however, the scheme of the Hebrew polity may be profitably made use of, as the diagram or illustrative model of a principle which actuated the primitive races generally under similar circumstances. With this and one other exception, likewise arising out of the peculiar purpose of Providence, as before stated, namely, the discouragement of trade and commerce in the Hebrew policy, a principle so inwoven in the whole fabric, that the revolution in this respect effected by Solomon had no small share

---

* The lines which our sage and learned poet puts in the Saviour's mouth, both from their truth and from their appositeness to the present subject, well deserve to be quoted: –

> Their orators thou then extoll'st, as those
> The top of eloquence: – Statists indeed
> And lovers of their country as may seem;
> But herein to our prophets far beneath,
> As men divinely taught and better teaching
> The solid rules of civil government,
> In their majestic, unaffected style,
> Than all the oratory of Greece and Rome.
> In them is plainest taught and easiest learnt
> What makes a nation happy, and keeps it so.[17]

in the quickly succeeding dissolution of the confederacy, it may be profitably considered even under existing circumstances.

And first, let me observe, with the Celtic, Gothic, and Scandinavian, equally as with the Hebrew tribes, Property by absolute right existed only in a tolerated alien;[19] and there was everywhere a prejudice against the occupation expressly directed to its acquirement, viz. the trafficking with the current representatives of wealth. Even in that species of possession, in which the right of the individual was the prominent relative character, the institution of the Jubilee provided against its degeneracy into the merely *personal*; reclaimed it for the state, – that is, for the *line*, the *heritage*, as one of the permanent units, or integral parts, the aggregate of which constitutes the STATE, in that narrower and especial sense, in which it has been distinguished from the *nation*.[20] And to these permanent units the calculating and governing *mind* of the state directs its attention, even as it is the depths, breadths, bays, and windings or reaches of a river, that are the subject of the hydrographer, not the water-drops, that at any one moment constitute the stream. And on this point the greatest stress should be laid; this should be deeply impressed, carefully borne in mind, that the abiding interests, the *estates*, and ostensible tangible properties, not the *persons* as *persons*, are the proper subjects of the *state* in this sense, or of the power of the parliament or supreme council, as the representatives and plenipotentiaries of the state, *i.e.* of the PROPRIETY, and in distinction from the commonwealth, in which I comprise both the Propriety and the Nationalty.

And here permit me, for the last time, I trust, to encroach on your patience, by remarking, that the records of the Hebrew policy are rendered far less instructive as lessons of political wisdom, by the disposition to regard the Jehovah in that universal and spiritual acceptation, in which we use the word as Christians. But relatively to the Jewish polity, the Jehovah was their covenanted king: and if we draw any inference from the former, the Christian sense of the term, it should be this – that God is the unity of every nation; that the convictions and the will, which are one, the same, and simultaneously acting in a multitude of individual agents, are not the birth of any individual; "that when the people speak loudly and unanimously, it is from their being strongly impressed by the godhead or the demon. Only exclude the (by no means extravagant) supposition of a demoniac possession, and *then* Vox Populi Vox Dei [the voice of the people is the voice of God]." So thought Sir

Philip Sydney,[21] who in the great revolution of the Netherlands considered the universal and simultaneous adoption of the same principles, as a proof of the divine presence; and on that belief, and on that alone, grounded his assurance of its successful result. And that I may apply this to the present subject, it was in the character of the king, as the majesty, or symbolic unity of the whole nation, both of the state and of the persons; it was in the name of the KING, in whom both the propriety and the nationalty ideally centered, and from whom, as from a fountain, they are ideally supposed to flow – it was in the name of the KING, that the proclamation throughout the land, by sound of trumpet, was made to all possessors: "The land is not your's, saith the Lord, the land is mine. To you I lent it."[22] The voice of the trumpets is not, indeed, heard in this country. But no less intelligibly is it declared by the spirit and history of our laws, that the possession of a property, not connected with especial duties, a property not fiduciary or official, but arbitrary and unconditional, was in the light of our forefathers the brand of a Jew and an alien; not the distinction, not the right, or honour, of an English baron or gentleman.

CHAPTER V

Of the Church of England, or National Clergy, according to the Constitution: its characteristic ends, purposes and functions: and of the persons comprehended under the Clergy, or the Functionaries of the National Church

AFTER these introductory preparations, I can have no difficulty in setting forth the right idea of a national church as in the language of Elizabeth the *third* great venerable estate of the realm.[23] The first being the estate of the land-owners or possessors of fixed property, consisting of the two classes of the Barons and the Franklins; the second comprising the merchants, the manufacturers, free artizans, and the distributive class. To comprehend, therefore, this third estate, in whom the reserved nationalty was vested, we must first ascertain the end, or national purpose, for which it was reserved.

Now, as in the former state, the permanency of the nation was provided for; and in the second estate its progressiveness, and personal freedom; while in the king the cohesion by interdependence, and the unity of the country, were established; there remains for the third estate only that interest, which is the ground, the necessary antecedent condition, of both the former. Now these depend on a continuing and progressive civilization. But civilization is itself but a mixed good, if not far more a corrupting influence, the hectic of disease, not the bloom of health, and a nation so distinguished more fitly to be called a varnished than a polished people; where this civilization is not grounded in *cultivation*, in the harmonious developement of those qualities and faculties that characterise our *humanity*. We must be men in order to be citizens.[24]

The Nationalty, therefore, was reserved for the support and maintenance of a permanent class or order, with the following duties. A certain smaller number were to remain at the fountain heads of the humanities, in cultivating and enlarging the knowledge already possessed, and in watching over the interests of physical and moral science; being, likewise, the instructors of such as constituted, or were to constitute, the remaining more numerous classes of the order. This latter and far more numerous body were to be distributed throughout the country, so as not to leave even the smallest integral part or division without a resident guide, guardian, and instructor; the objects and final intention of the whole order being these – to preserve the stores, to guard the treasures, of past civilization, and thus to bind the present with the past; to perfect and add to the same and thus to connect the present with the future; but especially to diffuse through the whole community, and to every native entitled to its laws and rights, that quantity and quality of knowledge which was indispensable both for the understanding of those rights, and for the performance of the duties correspondent. Finally, to secure for the nation, if not a superiority over the neighbouring states, yet an equality at least, in that character of general civilization, which equally with, or rather more than, fleets, armies, and revenue, forms the ground of its defensive and offensive power. The object of the two former estates of the realm, which conjointly form the STATE, was to reconcile the interests of permanence with that of progression – law with liberty. The object of the National Church, the third remaining estate of the realm, was to secure and improve that civilization, without which the nation could be neither permanent nor progressive.

That in all ages, individuals who have directed their meditations and their studies to the nobler characters of our nature, to the cultivation of those powers and instincts which constitute the man, at least separate him from the animal, and distinguish the nobler from the animal part of his own being, will be led by the *supernatural* in themselves to the contemplation of a power which is likewise super-*human*; that science, and especially moral science, will lead to religion, and remain blended with it – this, I say, will, in all ages, be the course of things. That in the earlier ages, and in the dawn of civility, there will be a twilight in which science and religion give light, but a light refracted through the dense and the dark, a superstition – this is what we learn from history, and what philosophy would have taught us to expect. But we affirm, that in the spiritual purpose of the word, and as understood in reference to a future state, and to the abiding essential interest of the individual as a person, and not as the citizen, neighbour, or subject, religion may be an indispensable ally, but is not the essential constitutive end of that national institute, which is unfortunately, at least improperly, styled a church – a name which, in its best sense is exclusively appropriate to the church of Christ. If this latter be ecclesia, the communion of such as are called out of the world, *i.e.* in reference to the especial ends and purposes of that communion; this other might more expressively have been entitled *enclesia*, or an order of men, chosen in and of the realm, and constituting an estate of that realm. And in fact, such was the original and proper sense of the more appropriately named CLERGY. It comprehended the learned of all names, and the CLERK was the synonyme of the man of learning. Nor can any fact more strikingly illustrate the conviction entertained by our ancestors, respecting the intimate connexion of this clergy with the peace and weal of the nation, than the privilege formerly recognized by our laws, in the well-known phrase, "benefit of clergy."[25]

Deeply do I feel, for clearly do I see, the importance of my Theme. And had I equal confidence in my ability to awaken the same interest in the minds of others, I should dismiss as affronting to my readers all apprehension of being charged with prolixity, while I am labouring to compress in two or three brief Chapters, the principal sides and aspects of a subject so large and multilateral as to require a volume for its full exposition. With what success will be seen in what follows, commencing with the Churchmen, or (a far apter and less objectionable designation,) the National CLERISY.

THE CLERISY of the nation, or national church, in its primary acceptation and original intention comprehended the learned of all denominations; – the sages and professors of the law and jurisprudence; of medicine and physiology; of music; of military and civil architecture; of the physical sciences; with the mathematical as the common *organ* of the preceding; in short, all the so called liberal arts and sciences, the possession and application of which constitute the civilization of a country, as well as the Theological. The last was, indeed, placed at the head of all; and of good right did it claim the precedence. But why? Because under the name of Theology, or Divinity, were contained the interpretation of languages; the conservation and tradition of past events; the momentous epochs, and revolutions of the race and nation; the continuation of the records; logic, ethics, and the determination of ethical science, in application to the rights and duties of men in all their various relations, social and civil; and lastly, the ground-knowledge, the prima scientia as it was named, – PHILOSOPHY, or the doctrine and discipline* of *ideas*.

Theology formed only a part of the objects, the Theologians formed only a portion of the clerks or clergy of the national church. The theological order had precedency indeed, and deservedly; but not because its members were priests, whose office was to conciliate the invisible powers, and to superintend the interests that survive the grave; not as being exclusively, or even principally, sacerdotal or templar, which, when it did occur, is to be considered as an accident of the age, a mis-growth of ignorance and oppression, a falsification of the constitutive principle, not a constituent part of the same. No! The Theologians took the lead, because the SCIENCE of Theology was the root and the trunk of the knowledges that civilized man, because it gave unity and the circulating sap of life

---

* That is, of knowledge immediate, yet real, and herein distinguished *in kind* from logical and mathematical truths, which express not realities, but only the necessary *forms* of conceiving and perceiving, and are therefore named the *formal* or *abstract* sciences. Ideas, on the other hand, or the truths of philosophy, properly so called, correspond to substantial beings, to objects the actual subsistence of which is *implied* in their idea, though only *by* the idea revealable. To adopt the language of the great philosophic Apostle, they are *"spiritual realities that can only spiritually be discerned"* and the inherent aptitude and moral *preconfigurations* to which constitutes what we mean by ideas, and by the presence of *ideal* truth and *ideal* power, in the human being. They, in fact, constitute his *humanity*. For try to conceive a *man* without the ideas of God, eternity, freedom, will, absolute truth, of the good, the true, the beautiful, the infinite. An *animal* endowed with a memory of appearances and of facts might remain. But the *man* will have vanished, and you will have instead a creature, "more subtle than any beast of the field, but likewise cursed above every beast of the field; upon the belly must it go and dust must it eat all the days of its life." [Genesis 3.] But I recall myself from a train of thoughts, little likely to find favour in this age of sense and selfishness.

to all other sciences, by virtue of which alone they could be contemplated as forming, collectively, the living tree of knowledge. It had the precedency, because, under the name theology, were comprised all the main aids, instruments, and materials of NATIONAL EDUCATION, the *nisus formativus* [formative impulse] of the body politic, the shaping and informing spirit, which *educing*, *i.e.* eliciting, the latent *man* in all the natives of the soil, *trains them up* to citizens of the country, free subjects of the realm. And lastly, because to divinity belong those fundamental truths, which are the common ground-work of our civil and our religious duties, not less indispensable to a right view of our temporal concerns, than to a rational faith respecting our immortal well-being. (Not without celestial observations, can even terrestrial charts be accurately constructed.) And of especial importance is it to the objects here contemplated, that only by the vital warmth diffused by these truths throughout the MANY, and by the guiding light from the philosophy, which is the basis of *divinity*, possessed by the FEW, can either the community or its rulers fully comprehend, or rightly appreciate, the permanent *distinction*, and the occasional *contrast*, between cultivation and civilization; or be made to understand this most valuable of the lessons taught by history, and exemplified alike in her oldest and her most recent records – that a nation can never be a too cultivated, but may easily become an over-civilized race.

CHAPTER VI

Secessions or offsets from the National Clerisy. Usurpations and abuses previous to the Reformation. Henry VIII. What he might and should have done. The main End and Final Cause of the Nationalty: and the duties, which the State may demand of the National Clerisy. A question, and the answer to it

As a natural consequence of the full development and expansion of the mercantile and commercial order, which in the earlier epochs of the constitution, only existed, as it were, potentially and in the bud; the students and possessors of those sciences, and those sorts of learning, the use and necessity of which were indeed constant and perpetual to the *nation*, but only accidental and occasional to *individuals*, gradually detached themselves from the nationalty and the national clergy, and passed to the order, with the growth and thriving condition of which their emoluments were found to increase in equal proportion. Rather, perhaps, it should be said, that under the common name of professional, the learned in the departments of law, medicine, &c., formed an intermediate link between the established clergy and the burgesses.

This circumstance, however, can in no way affect the principle, nor alter the tenure, nor annul the rights of those who remained, and who, as members of the permanent learned class, were planted throughout the realm, each in his appointed place, as the immediate agents and instruments in the great and indispensable work of perpetuating, promoting, and increasing the civilization of the nation, and who thus fulfilling the purposes for which the determinate portion of the total wealth from the land had been reserved, are entitled to remain its trustees, and usufructuary proprietors. But, remember, I do not assert that the proceeds from the nationalty cannot be rightfully vested, except in what we now mean by clergymen, and the established clergy. I have every where implied the contrary. But I do assert, that the nationalty cannot rightfully [be], and that without foul wrong to the nation it never has been, alienated from its original purposes. I assert that those who, being duly elected and appointed thereto, exercise the functions, and perform the duties, attached to the nationalty – that these collectively possess an unalienable, indefeasible title to the same – and this by a *Jure Divino* [divine law], to which the thunders from Mount Sinai might give additional authority, but not additional evidence.

COROLLARY. – During the dark times, when the incubus of superstition lay heavy across the breast of the living and the dying; and when all the familiar "tricksy spirits" in the service of an alien, self-expatriated and anti-national priesthood were at work in all forms, and in all directions, to aggrandize and enrich a "kingdom of this world;" large masses were alienated from the heritable proprieties of the realm, and confounded with the Nationality under the common name of church property. Had every rood, every peppercorn, every stone, brick, and beam, been re-transferred, and made heritable, at the Reformation, no right would have been invaded, no principle of justice violated. What the state, by law – that is, by the collective will of its functionaries at any one time assembled – can do or suffer to be done; that the state, by law, can undo or inhibit. And in *principle*, such bequests and donations were vitious *ab initio*, implying in the donor an absolute property in land, unknown to the constitution of the realm, and in defeasance of that immutable reason, which in the name of the nation and the national majesty proclaims: – "The land is not yours; it was vested in your *lineage* in trust for the nation." And though, in change of times and circumstances, the interest of progression, with the means and motives for the same – Hope, Industry, Enterprise – may render it the wisdom of the state to facilitate the transfer from line to line, still it must be within the same scale, and with preservation of the balance. The *most* honest of our English historians, and with no *superior* in industry and research, Mr. Sharon Turner, has labored successfully in detaching from the portrait of our first Protestant king the layers of soot and blood, with which pseudo-Catholic hate and pseudo-Protestant candour had coated it.[26] But the name of Henry VIII. would outshine that of Alfred, and with a splendor, which not even the ominous shadow of his declining life would have eclipsed – had he retained the will and possessed the power of effecting, what in part, he promised and proposed to do – if he had availed himself of the wealth, and landed masses that had been unconstitutionally alienated from the state, *i.e.* transferred from the scale of heritable lands and revenues, to purchase and win back whatever had been alienated from the opposite scale of the nationalty. *Wrongfully* alienated: for it was a possession, in which every free subject in the nation has a living interest, a permanent, and likewise a possible personal and reversionary interest! *Sacrilegiously* alienated: for it had been consecrated τῷ Θεῷ οἰκείῳ, to the potential divinity in every man, which is the ground and condition of his *civil* existence, that without which a man can be neither free nor obliged, and by which alone, therefore, he is capable of being a free subject – a citizen.

If, having thus righted the balance on both sides, HENRY had then directed the nationalty to its true national purposes, (in order to which, however, a different division and sub-division of the kingdom must have superseded the present barbarism, which forms an obstacle to the improvement of the country, of much greater magnitude than men are generally aware of) – if the Nationalty had been distributed in proportionate channels, to the maintenance, – 1, Of universities, and the great schools of liberal learning: 2, Of a pastor, presbyter, or *parson** in every parish: 3, Of a school-master in every parish, who in due time, and under condition of a faithful performance of his arduous duties, should succeed to the pastorate; so that both should be labourers in different compartments of the same field, workmen engaged in different stages of the same process, with such difference of rank, as might be suggested in the names pastor and sub-pastor, or as now exists between curate and rector, deacon and elder. Both alike, I say, members and ministers of the national clerisy or church, working to the same end, and determined in the choice of their means and the direction of their labours, by one and the same object – namely, in producing and re-producing, in preserving, continuing and perfecting, the necessary sources and conditions of national civilization; this being itself an indispensable condition of national safety, power and welfare, the strongest security and the surest provision, both for the permanence and the progressive advance of whatever (laws, institutions, tenures, rights, privileges, freedoms, obligations, &c. &c.) constitute the public weal: these parochial clerks being the great majority of the national clergy, and the comparatively small remainder, being principally† *in* ordine *ad hos*, Cleri doctores ut Clerus Populi [*in* order *to these*, teachers of the Clergy, as the Clergy are teachers of the people].

I may be allowed, therefore, to express the final cause of the whole by the office and purpose of the greater part – and this is, to form and train up the people of the country to obedient, free, useful, organizable subjects, citizens, and patriots, living to the benefit of the state, and prepared to die for its defence. The proper

* . . . the representative and exemplar of the *personal* character of the community or parish; of their duties and rights, of their hopes, privileges, and requisite qualifications, as moral *persons*, and not merely living things. But this the pastoral clergy cannot be other than imperfectly – they cannot be that which it is the paramount end and object of their establishment and distribution throughout the country, that they should be – each in his sphere the germ and nucleus of the progressive civilization – unless they are *in the rule* married men and heads of families. This, however, is adduced only as an accessory to the great principle stated in a following page, as an instance of its beneficial consequences, not as the grounds of its validity.

† Considered, I mean, in their national relations, and in that which forms their *ordinary*, their most *conspicuous* purpose and utility; for Heaven forbid, I should deny or forget, that the sciences, and not only the sciences both abstract and experimental, but the Literae Humaniores, the products of genial power, of whatever name, have an immediate and positive value, even in their bearings on the national interests.

object and end of the National Church is civilization with freedom; and the duty of its ministers, could they be contemplated merely and exclusively as officiaries of the *National* Church, would be fulfilled in the communication of that degree and kind of knowledge to all, the possession of which is necessary for all in order to their CIVILITY. By civility I mean all the qualities essential to a citizen, and devoid of which no people or class of the people can be calculated on by the rulers and leaders of the state for the conservation or promotion of its essential interests.

It follows therefore, that in regard of the grounds and principles of action and conduct, the State has a right to demand of the National Church, that its instructions should be fitted to diffuse throughout the people *legality*, that is, the obligations of a well-calculated self-interest, under the conditions of a common interest determined by common laws. At least, whatever of higher origin and nobler and wider aim the ministers of the National Church, in some other capacity, and in the performance of other duties, might labour to implant and cultivate in the minds and hearts of their congregations and seminaries, should include the practical consequences of the *legality* above mentioned. The State requires that the basin should be kept full, and that the stream which supplies the hamlet and turns the mill, and waters the meadow-fields, should be fed and kept flowing. If this be done, the State is content, indifferent for the rest, whether the basin be filled by the spring in its first ascent, and rising but a hand's-breadth above the bed; or whether drawn from a more elevated source, shooting aloft in a stately column, that reflects the light of heaven from its shaft, and bears the "Iris, Coeli decus, promissumque Iovis lucidum [Rainbow, glory of heaven, and Jove's bright promise]," on its spray, it fills the basin in its descent.

In what relation then do you place Christianity to the National Church? Though unwilling to anticipate what belongs to a part of my subject yet to come, namely, the idea of the Catholic or Christian church, yet I am still more averse to leave this question, even for a moment, unanswered. And this is my answer.

In relation to the National Church, Christianity, or the Church of Christ, is a blessed* accident, a providential boon, a grace of

---

* Let not the religious reader be offended with this phrase. The writer means only that Christianity is an aid and instrument which no State or Realm could have produced out of its own elements – which no State had a right to expect. It was, most awfully, a GOD-SEND!

God, a mightly and faithful friend, the envoy indeed and liege subject of another state, but which can neither administer the laws nor promote the ends of this other State, which is *not* of the world, without advantage, direct and indirect, to the true interests of the States, the aggregate of which is what we [note omitted] mean by the WORLD – *i.e.* the civilized world. As the olive tree is said in its growth to fertilize the surrounding soil; to invigorate the roots of the vines in its immediate neighbourhood, and to improve the strength and flavour of the wines – such is the relation of the Christian and the National Church. But as the olive is not the same plant with the vine, or with the elm or poplar (*i.e.* the State) with which the vine is wedded; and as the vine with its prop may exist, though in less perfection, without the olive, or prior to its implantation – even so is Christianity, and à fortiori any particular scheme of Theology derived and supposed (by its partizans) to be *deduced* from Christianity, no essential part of the *Being* of the *National* Church, however conducive or even indispensable it may be to its *well* being. And even so a National Church might exist, and has existed, without, because before the institution of the *Christian* Church – as the Levitical Church in the Hebrew Constitution, the Druidical in the Celtic, would suffice to prove.

But here I earnestly intreat, that two things may be remembered – first, that it is my object to present the *Idea* of a National Church, as the only safe criterion, by which the judgment can decide on the existing state of things; for when we are in full and clear possession of the ultimate aim of an Institution, it is comparatively easy to ascertain, in what respects this aim has been attained in other ways, arising out of the growth of the Nation, and the gradual and successive expansion of its germs; in what respects the aim has been frustrated by errors and diseases in the body politic; and in what respects the existing institution still answers the original purpose, and continues to be a mean to necessary or most important ends, for which no adequate substitute can be found. First, I say, let it be borne in mind, that my object has been to present the *idea* of a National Church, not the history of *the* Church established in this nation. Secondly, that two distinct functions do not necessarily imply or require two different functionaries. Nay, the perfection of each may require the union of both in the same person. And in the instance now in question, great and grievous errors have arisen from confounding the functions; and fearfully great and grievous will be the evils from the success of an attempt to separate them – an attempt long and passionately pursued, in many forms, and through many various channels, by a numerous party, who has already the ascendancy in the *State*; and which, unless far other minds and far other principles than the opponents of this party have hitherto allied with their cause, are called into action, *will* obtain the ascendancy in the *Nation*.[27]

I have already said, that the subjects, which lie right and left of my road, or even jut into it, are so many and so important, that I offer these Chapters but as a catalogue *raisonné* of texts and theses, that will have answered their purpose if they excite a certain class of readers to desire or to supply the commentary. But there will not be wanting among my readers men who are no strangers to the ways, in which my thoughts travel: and the jointless sentences that make up the following Chapter or Inventory of regrets and apprehensions, will suffice to possess them of the chief points that press on my mind.

The commanding knowledge, the *power* of truth, given or obtained by contemplating the subject in the fontal mirror of the Idea, is in Scripture ordinarily expressed by Vision: and no dissimilar gift, if not rather in its essential characters the same, does a great living Poet speak of, as

The Vision and the Faculty divine.[28]

And of the many political *ground-truths* contained in the Old Testament, I cannot recall one more worthy to be selected as the *Moral* and L'ENVOY of a Universal History, than the text in Proverbs, Where no Vision is, the People perisheth.[29]

It is now thirty years since the diversity of Reason and the Understanding, of an Idea and a Conception, and the practical importance of distinguishing the one from the other, were first made evident to me. And scarcely a month has passed during this long interval in which either books, or conversation, or the experience of life, have not supplied or suggested some fresh proof and instance of the mischiefs and mistakes, derived from that ignorance of this Truth, which I have elsewhere called the Queen-bee in the Hive of Error.

Well and truly has the understanding been defined; *Facultas mediata et Mediorum*: – the Faculty of means to medial Ends, that is to *Purposes*, or such ends as are themselves but means to some ulterior end.

My eye at this moment rests on a volume newly read by me, containing a well-written history of the Inventions, Discoveries, Public Improvements, Docks, Rail-ways, Canals, &c. for about the same period, in England and Scotland.[30] I closed it under the strongest impressions of awe, and admiration akin to wonder. We live, I exclaimed, under the dynasty of the understanding: and this is its golden age.

It is the faculty of means to medial ends. With these the age, this favoured land, teems: they spring up, the armed host, ("seges clypeata [the shield-bearing crop]") from the serpent's teeth sown by Cadmus: "mortalia semina, dentes [the man-producing seed, the teeth]."[31] In every direction they advance, conquering and to conquer. Sea, and Land, Rock, Mountain, Lake and Moor, yea Nature and all her Elements, sink before them, or yield themselves captive! But the *ultimate* ends? Where shall I seek for information concerning these? By what name shall I seek for the historiographer of REASON? Where shall I find the annals of *her* recent campaigns? the records of her conquests? In the facts disclosed of the Mendicant Society?[32] In the reports on the increase of crimes, commitments? In the proceedings of the Police? Or in the accumulating volumes on the horrors and perils of population?

> O voice, once heard
> Delightfully, *Increase and multiply!*
> Now death to hear! For what can we increase
> Or multiply, *but penury, woe and crime?*[33]

Alas! for a certain class, the following Chapter will, I fear, but too vividly shew "the burden of the valley of vision, even the burden upon the crowned isle, whose merchants are princes, whose traffickers the honourable of the earth; who stretcheth out her hand over the sea, and she is the mart of nations!"[34]

CHAPTER VII

Regrets and Apprehensions

THE National Church was deemed in the *dark age* of Queen Elizabeth, in the unenlightened times of Burleigh, Hooker, Spenser,

Shakspeare, and Lord Bacon, A GREAT VENERABLE ESTATE OF THE REALM; but now by "*all* the intellect of the kingdom," it has been determined to be one of the many theological sects, churches or communities, established in the realm; but distinguished from the rest by having its priesthood *endowed*, durante bene placito [during good pleasure], by favour of the legislature – that is, of the majority, for the time being, of the two Houses of Parliament. The Church being thus reduced to *a* religion, Religion *in genre* is consequently separated from the church, and made a subject of parliamentary determination, independent of this church. The poor withdrawn from the discipline of the church. The education of the people detached from the ministry of the church. Religion, a *noun of multitude*, or nomen collectivum, expressing the aggregate of all the different groups of notions and ceremonies connected with the invisible and supernatural. On the plausible (and in *this* sense of the word, unanswerable) pretext of the multitude and variety of *Religions*, and for the suppression of bigotry and negative persecution, National Education to be finally sundered from all religion, but speedily and decisively emancipated from the superintendence of the National Clergy. Education reformed. Defined as synonimous with Instruction. *Axiom of Education so defined.* Knowledge being power, those attainments, which give a man the power of doing what he wishes in order to obtain what he desires, are alone to be considered as knowledge, or to be admitted into the scheme of National Education. Subjects to be taught in the National Schools. Reading, writing, arithmetic, the mechanic arts, elements and results of physical science, but to be taught, as much as possible, empirically. For all knowledge being derived from the Senses, the closer men are kept to the fountain head, the *knowinger* they must become. – POPULAR ETHICS, *i.e.* a Digest of the Criminal Laws, and the evidence requisite for conviction under the same: Lectures on Diet, on Digestion, on Infection, and the nature and effects of a specific virus incidental to and communicable by living bodies in the intercourse of society. N.B. In order to balance the Interests of Individuals and the Interests of the State, the Dietetic and Peptic Text Books, to be under the censorship of the Board of Excise.

Shall I proceed with my chapter of hints? Game Laws, Corn Laws, Cotton Factories, Spitalfields, the tillers of the land paid by poor-rates, and the remainder of the population mechanized into engines for the manufactory of new rich men – yea, the machinery of the wealth of the nation made up of the wretchedness, disease and depravity of those who should constitute the strength of the nation! Disease, I say, and vice, while the wheels are in full motion; but at the first stop the magic wealth-machine is converted into an intolerable weight of pauperism! But this partakes of History. The head and neck of the huge Serpent are out of the den: the voluminous train is to come. What next? May I not whisper as a fear, what Senators have promised to demand as a right? Yes! the next in my filial bodings is Spoliation. – Spoliation of the NATIONALTY, half thereof to be distributed among the land-owners, and the other half among the stock-brokers, and stock-owners, who are to receive it in lieu of the interest formerly due to them.[35]

But enough! I will ask only one question. Has the national welfare, have the *weal* and happiness of the people, advanced with the increase of the circumstantial prosperity? Is the increasing number of wealthy individuals that which ought to be understood by the wealth of the nation?[36] In answer to this, permit me to annex the following chapter of contents of the moral history of the last 130 years.

A. Declarative act, respecting certain parts of the constitution, with provisions against further violation of the same, erroneously entitled, "THE REVOLUTION of 1688."

B. The Mechanico-corpuscular Theory raised to the Title of the Mechanic Philosophy, and espoused as a revolution in philosophy, by the actors and partizans of the (so called) Revolution in the state.[37]

C.[38] Result illustrated, in the remarkable contrast between the acceptation of the word, Idea, *before* the Restoration, and the *present* use of the same word. *Before* 1660, the magnificent SON OF COSMO was wont to discourse with FICINO, POLITIAN and the princely MIRANDULA on the IDEAS of Will, God, Freedom. SIR PHILIP SIDNEY, the star of serenest brilliance in the glorious constellation of Elizabeth's court, communed with SPENSER, on the IDEA of the beautiful: and the younger ALGERNON – Soldier, Patriot, and Statesman – with HARRINGTON, MILTON, and NEVIL on the IDEA of the STATE: and in what sense it may be more truly affirmed, that the people (*i.e.* the component particles of the body politic, at any moment existing as such) are in order to the state, than that the state exists for the sake of the people.[39]

PRESENT USE OF THE WORD

Dr. Holofernes, in a lecture on metaphysics, delivered at one of the Mechanics' Institutions, explodes all *ideas* but those of sensation; and his friend, Deputy Costard, has no *idea* of a better flavored haunch of venison, than he dined off at the London Tavern last week.[40] He admits, (for the deputy has travelled) that the French have an excellent *idea* of cooking in general; but holds that their most accomplished *Maitres du Cuisine* have no more *idea* of dressing a turtle, than the Parisian Gourmands themselves have any *real* idea of the true *taste* and *colour* of the fat.

D. Consequences exemplified. State of nature, or the Ouran Outang theology of the origin of the human race, substituted for the Book of Genesis, ch. I.–X.[41] Rights of nature for the duties and privileges of citizens. Idealess facts, misnamed proofs from history, grounds of experience, &c., substituted for principles and the insight derived from them. State-policy, a Cyclops with one eye, and that in the back of the head! Our measures of policy, either a series of anachronisms, or a truckling to events substituted for the science, that should command them; for all true insight is foresight. (Documents. The measures of the British Cabinet from the Boston Port-Bill, March 1774;[42] but particularly from 1789, to the Union of Ireland, and the Peace of Amiens.) Mean time, the true historical feeling, the immortal life of an historical Nation, generation linked to generation by faith, freedom, heraldry, and ancestral fame, languishing, and giving place to the superstitions of wealth, and newspaper reputation.

E. Talents without genius: a swarm of clever, well-informed men: an anarchy of minds, a despotism of maxims. Despotism of finance in government and legislation – of vanity and sciolism in the intercourse of life – of presumption, temerity, and hardness of heart, in political economy.

F. The Guess-work of general consequences substituted for moral and political philosophy, adopted as a text book in one of the Universities, and cited as authority, in the legislature:[43] Plebs pro Senatu Populoque [the populace for the Senate and the people]; the wealth of the nation (*i.e.* of the wealthy individuals thereof, and the magnitude of the Revenue) for the well-being of the people.

G. Gin consumed by paupers to the value of about eighteen millions yearly. Government by journeymen clubs;[44] by saint and sinner societies, committees, institutions; by reviews, magazines, and above all by newspapers. Lastly, crimes quadrupled for the whole country, and in some counties decupled.

Concluding address to the parliamentary leaders of the Liberalists and Utilitarians. I respect the talents of many, and the motives and character of some among you too sincerely to court the scorn, which I anticipate. But neither shall the fear of it prevent me from declaring aloud, and as a truth which I hold it the disgrace and calamity of a professed statesman not to know and acknowledge, that a permanent, nationalized, learned order, a national clerisy or church, is an essential element of a rightly constituted nation, without which it wants the best security alike for its permanence and its progression; and for which neither tract societies nor conventicles, nor Lancasterian schools, nor mechanics' institutions, nor lecture-bazaars under the absurd name of universities, nor all these collectively, can be a substitute. For they are all marked with the same asterisk of spuriousness,[45] shew the same distemper-spot on the front, that they are empirical specifics for morbid *symptoms* that help to feed and continue the disease.

But you wish for *general* illumination: you would spur-arm the toes of society: you would enlighten the higher ranks per ascensum ab imis [by ascent from the lowest levels]. You begin, therefore, with the attempt to *popularize* science: but you will only effect its *plebification*. It is folly to think of making all, or the many, philosophers, or even men of science and systematic knowledge. But it is duty and wisdom to aim at making as many as possible soberly and steadily religious; – inasmuch as the morality which the state requires in its citizens for its own well-being and ideal immortality, and without reference to their spiritual interest as individuals, can only exist for the people in the form of religion. But the existence of a true philosophy, or the power and habit of contemplating particulars in the unity and fontal mirror of the idea – this in the rulers and teachers of a nation is indispensable to a sound state of religion in all classes. In fine, Religion, true or false, is and ever has been the centre of gravity in a realm, to which all other things must and will accommodate themselves.

CHAPTER VIII

The subject resumed – viz. the proper aims and characteristic directions
and channels of the Nationalty. The Benefits of the National Church in
time past. The present beneficial influences and workings of the same.

THE deep interest which, during the far larger portion of my life
since early manhood, I have attached to these convictions, has, I
perceive, hurried me onwards as by the rush from the letting forth
of accumulated waters by the sudden opening of the sluice gates.
It is high time that I should return to my subject. And I have no
better way of taking up the thread of my argument, than by
restating my opinion, that our Eighth Henry would have acted in
correspondence to the great principles of our constitution, if having
restored the original balance on both sides, he had determined the
nationalty to the following objects: 1st. To the maintenance of
the Universities and the great liberal schools. 2ndly. To the
maintenance of a pastor and schoolmaster in every parish. 3rdly.
To the raising and keeping in repair of the churches, schools, &c.,
and, Lastly: To the maintenance of the proper, that is, the infirm,
poor whether from age or sickness: one of the original purposes
of the national Reserve being the alleviation of those evils, which
in the best forms of worldly states must arise and must have been
foreseen as arising from the institution of individual properties
and primogeniture. If these duties were efficiently performed, and
these purposes adequately fulfilled, the very increase of the
population, (which would, however, by these very means have
been prevented from becoming a vicious population,) would have
more than counterbalanced those savings in the expenditure of the
nationalty occasioned by the detachment of the practitioners of
law, medicine, &c., from the national clergy. That this transfer of
the national reserve from what had become national evils to its
original and inherent purpose of national benefits, instead of the
sacrilegious alienation which actually took place – that this was
impracticable, is historically true: but no less true is it philosophi-
cally that this impracticability, arising wholly from moral causes –
that is, from loose manners and corrupt principles – does not
rescue this wholesale sacrilege from deserving the character of the
first and deadliest wound inflicted on the constitution of the
kingdom: which term constitution in the body politic, as in bodies
natural, expresses not only what has been actually evolved, but

likewise whatever is potentially contained in the seminal principle of the particular body, and would in its due time have appeared but for emasculation or disease. Other wounds, by which indeed the constitution of the nation has suffered, but which much more immediately concern the constitution of the church, we shall perhaps find another place to mention.

The mercantile and commercial class, in which I here comprise all the four classes that I have put in antithesis to the Landed Order, the guardian, and depository of the *Permanence* of the Realm, as more characteristically conspiring to the interests of its progression, the improvement and general freedom of the country – this class did as I have already remarked, in the earlier states of the constitution, exist but as in the bud. But during all this period of potential existence, or what we may call the minority of the burgess order, the National Church was the substitute for the most important national benefits resulting from the same. The National Church presented the only breathing hole of hope. The church alone relaxed the iron fate by which feudal dependency, primogeniture, and entail would otherwise have predestined every native of the realm to be lord or vassal. To the Church alone could the nation look for the benefits of existing knowledge, and for the means of future civilization. Lastly, let it never be forgotten, that under the fostering wing of the church, the class of free citizens and burgers were reared. To the feudal system we owe the *forms*, to the church the *substance*, of our liberty. We mention only two of many facts that would form the proof and comment of the above; first, the origin of towns and cities, in the privileges attached to the vicinity of churches and monasteries, and which preparing an asylum for the fugitive Vassal and oppressed Franklin, thus laid the first foundation of a class of freemen detached from the land. Secondly, the holy war, which the national clergy, in this instance faithful to their national duties, waged against slavery and villenage, and with such success, that in the reign of Charles II., the law which declared every native of the realm free by birth, had merely to sanction an opus jam consummatum [work already completed].[46] Our Maker has distinguished man from the brute that perishes, by making hope first an instinct of his nature; and secondly, an indispensable condition of his moral and intellectual progression:

> For every gift of noble origin
> Is breathed upon by Hope's perpetual breath.
>   WORDSWORTH[47]

But a natural instinct constitutes a right, as far as its gratification is compatible with the equal rights of others. And this principle we may expand, and apply to the idea of the National Church.

Among the primary ends of a STATE, (in that highest sense of the word, in which it is equivalent to the nation, considered as one body politic, and therefore includes the National Church), there are two, of which the National Church (according to its idea), is the especial and constitutional organ and means. The one is, to secure to the subjects of the realm generally, the hope, the chance, of bettering their own or their children's condition. And though during the last three or four centuries, the National church has found a most powerful surrogate and ally for the effectuation of this great purpose in her former wards and foster-children, *i.e.* in trade, commerce, free industry, and the arts – yet still the nationalty, under all defalcations, continues to feed the higher ranks by drawing up whatever is worthiest from below, and thus maintains the principle of Hope in the humblest families, while it secures the possessions of the rich and noble. This is one of the two ends.

The other is, to develope, in every native of the country, those faculties, and to provide for every native that knowledge and those attainments, which are necessary to qualify him for a member of the state, the free subject of a civilized realm. We do not mean those degrees of moral and intellectual cultivation which distinguish man from man in the same civilized society, much less those that separate the Christian from the this-worldian; but those only that constitute the civilized man in contra-distinction from the barbarian, the savage, and the animal.

I have now brought together all that seemed requisite to put the intelligent reader in full possession of (what I believe to be) the right Idea of the National Clergy, as an estate of the realm. But I cannot think my task finished without an attempt to rectify the too frequent false feeling on this subject, and to remove certain vulgar errors, errors, alas! not confined to those whom the world call the vulgar. Ma nel mondo non è se non volgo [But in the world there are only the vulgar], says Machiavel.[48] I shall make no apology therefore, for interposing between the preceding statements, and the practical conclusion from them, the following paragraph, extracted from a work long out of print, and of such very limited circulation that I might have stolen from myself with little risk of detection, had it not been my wish to shew that the convictions expressed in the preceding pages, are not the offspring of the moment, brought forth for the present occasion; but an expansion of sentiments and principles publicly avowed in the year 1817.[49]

Among the numerous blessings of the English Constitution, the introduction of an established Church makes an especial claim on the gratitude of scholars and philosophers; in England, at least, where the principles of Protestantism have conspired with the freedom of the government to double all its salutary powers by the removal of its abuses.

That the maxims of a pure morality, and those sublime truths of the divine unity and attributes, which a Plato found hard to learn, and more difficult to reveal; that these should have become the almost hereditary property of childhood and poverty, of the hovel and the workshop; that even to the unlettered they sound as *common place*; this is a phenomenon which must withhold all but minds of the most vulgar cast from undervaluing the services even of the pulpit and the reading desk. Yet he who should *confine* the efficiency of an Established Church to these, can hardly be placed in a much higher rank of intellect. That to every parish throughout the kingdom there is transplanted a germ of civilization; that in the remotest villages there is a nucleus, round which the capabilities of the place may crystallise and brighten; a model sufficiently superior to excite, yet sufficiently near to encourage and facilitate, imitation; *this* unobtrusive, continuous agency of a Protestant Church Establishment, *this* it is, which the patriot, and the philanthropist, who would fain unite the love of peace with the faith in the progressive amelioration of mankind, cannot estimate at too high a price – "It cannot be valued with the gold of Ophir, with the precious onyx, or the sapphire. No mention shall be made of coral or of pearls: for the price of wisdom is above rubies."[50] – The clergyman is with his parishioners and among them; he is neither in the cloistered cell, nor in the wilderness, but a neighbour and family-man, whose education and rank admit him to the mansion of the rich landholder, while his duties make him the frequent visitor of the farmhouse and the cottage. He is, or he may become, connected with the families of his parish or its vicinity by marriage. And among the instances of the blindness or at best of the shortsightedness, which it is the nature of cupidity to inflict, I know few more striking, than the clamours of the farmers against church property. Whatever was not paid to the clergymen would inevitably at the next lease be paid to the landholder, while, as the case at present stands, the revenues of the church are in some sort the reversionary property of every family that may have a member educated for the church, or a daughter that may marry a clergyman. Instead of being *fore closed* and immoveable, it is, in fact, the only species of landed property that is essentially moving and circulative.[51] That there exist no inconveniencies, who will pretend to assert? But I have yet to expect the proof, that the inconveniences are greater in this than in any other species; or that either the farmers or the clergy would be benefited by forcing the latter to become either *trullibers* or salaried *placemen*.[52] Nay, I do not hesitate to declare my firm persuasion that whatever *reason* of discontent the farmers may assign, the true *cause* is that they may cheat the *Parson* but cannot cheat the steward; and they are disappointed if they should have been able to withhold only two pounds less than the legal claim, having expected to withhold five.

CHAPTER IX

Practical Conclusion: What unfits; and what excludes from the National Church

THE clerisy, or National Church, being an estate of the realm, the Church and State with the king as the sovereign head of both constituting the Body Politic, the State in the large sense of the word, or the NATION dynamically considered (ἐν δυνάμει κατά πνεῦμα [in power, according to the spirit], *i.e.* as an *ideal*, but not the less *actual* and abiding, unity); and in like manner, the Nationalty being one of the two constitutional modes or species, of which the common wealth of the nation consists; it follows by the immediate consequence, that of the qualifications for the trusteeship, absolutely to be required of the order collectively, and of every individual person as the conditions of his admission into this order, and of his liability to the usufruct or life-interest of any part or parcel of the Nationalty, the first and most indispensable qualification and pre-condition, that without which all others are null and void, – is that the National Clergy, and every member of the same from the highest to the lowest, shall be fully and exclusively citizens of the State, neither acknowledging the authority, nor within the influence of any other State in the world – full and undistracted subjects of this kingdom, and in no capacity, and under no pretences, owning any other earthly sovereign or visible head but the king, in whom alone the majesty of the nation is *apparent*, and by whom alone the unity of the nation in will and in deed is symbolically expressed and impersonated.

The full extent of this first and absolutely necessary qualification will be best seen in stating the contrary, that is, the absolute disqualifications, the existence of which in any individual, and in any class or order of men, constitutionally incapacitates such individual and class or order from being inducted into the National Trust: and this on a principle so vitally concerning the health and integrity of the body politic, as to render the voluntary transfer of the nationalty, whole or part, direct or indirect, to an order notoriously thus disqualified, a foul treason against the most fundamental rights and interests of the realm, and of all classes of its citizens and free subjects, the individuals of the very order itself, *as* citizens and subjects, not excepted. Now there are two things, and but two, which evidently and predeterminably disqualify for this great trust: the first absolutely, and the second, which in its collective operation, and as an attribute of the whole class, would, of itself, constitute the greatest possible unfitness for the proper ends and purposes of the National Church, as explained and specified in the preceding paragraphs, and the heaviest drawback from the civilizing influence of the National Clergy in their pastoral and parochial character – the second, I say, by implying the former, becomes likewise an *absolute* ground of disqualification. It is scarcely necessary to add, what the reader will have anticipated, that the first absolute disqualification is allegiance to a foreign power: the second, the abjuration – under the command and authority of this power, and as by the rule of their order its professed Lieges (Alligati) – of that bond, which more than all other ties connects the citizen with his country; which beyond all other securities affords the surest pledge to the state for the fealty of its citizens, and that which (when the rule is applied to any body or class of men, under whatever name united, where the number is sufficiently great to neutralize the accidents of individual temperament and circumstances) enables the State to calculate on their constant adhesion to its interests, and to rely on their faith and singleness of heart in the due execution of whatever public or national trust might be assigned to them.

But we shall, perhaps, express the nature of this security more adequately by the negative. The Marriage Tie is a Bond, the preclusion of which by an antecedent obligation, that overrules the accidents of individual character and is common to the whole order, deprives the State of a security with which it cannot dispense. I will not say, that it is a security which the State may rightfully demand of all its adult citizens, competently circumstanced, by positive enactment: though I might shelter the position under the authority of the great Publicists and State-Lawyers of the Augustan Age, who, in the Lex Julia Papia, enforced anew a principle common to the old Roman Constitution with that of Sparta.[53] But without the least fear of confutation, though in the full foresight of vehement contradiction, I do assert, that the State may rightfully demand of any number of its subjects united in one body or order the *absence* of all customs, initiative vows, covenants and by-laws in that order, precluding the members of the said body collectively and individually from affording this security. In strictness of principle, I might here conclude the sentence – though as it now stands it would involve the assertion of a right in the state to suppress any order confederated under laws so anti-civic. But I am no friend to any rights that can be disjoined from the *duty* of enforcing them. I therefore at once confine and complete the sentence thus: – The State not only possesses the right of demanding, but is in duty bound to demand, the above as a *necessary condition* of its entrusting to any order of men, and to any individual as a member of a known order, the titles, functions, and investments of the *National* Church.

But if any doubt could attach to the proposition, whether thus stated or in the perfectly equivalent *Converse, i.e.* that the existence and known enforcement of the injunction or prohibitory by-law, before described, in any Order or Incorporation constitutes an *a priori* disqualification for the Trusteeship of the Nationalty, and an insuperable obstacle to the establishment of such an order, or of any members of the same as a National Clergy – such doubt would be removed, as soon as the fact of this injunction, or vow exacted and given, or whatever else it may be, by which the members of the Order, collectively and as such, incapacitate themselves from affording this security for their full, faithful, and unbiassed application of a *National* Trust to its proper and national purposes, is found in conjunction with, and aggravated by, the three following circumstances. First, that this incapacitation originates in, and forms part of, the allegiance of the order to a foreign Sovereignty: Secondly, that it is notorious, that the Canon or Prescript, or which it is grounded, was first enforced on the secular clergy universally, after long and obstinate reluctation on their side, and on that of their natural sovereigns in the several realms, to which as subjects they belonged; and that it is still retained in force, and its revocation inflexibly refused, as the direct and only adequate means of *supporting* that usurped and foreign Sovereignty, and of securing by virtue of the expatriating and insulating effect of its operation, the devotion, and allegiance of the order [note omitted] to their visible Head, and Sovereign. And thirdly, that the operation of the interdict precludes one of the most constant and influencive ways and means of promoting the great paramount end of a National Church, the progressive civilization of the community. Emollit mores nec sinit esse feros [(A faithful study of the liberal arts) humanises character and permits it not to be cruel].[54]

And now let me conclude these preparatory Notices by compressing the sum and substance of my argument into this one sentence. Though many things may detract from the comparative fitness of individuals, or of particular classes, for the Trust and Functions of the NATIONALTY, there are only two *absolute* Disqualifications: and these are, Allegiance to a Foreign Power, or the Acknowledgement of any other visible HEAD OF THE CHURCH, but our Sovereign Lord the King: and compulsory celibacy in connection with, and in dependence on, a foreign and extra-national head.

CHAPTER X

On the King and the Nation

A TREATISE? why, the subjects might, I own, excite some apprehension of the sort. But it will be found like sundry Greek Treatises among the tinder-rolls of Herculaneum, with titles of as large promise, somewhat largely and irregularly abbreviated in the process of unrolling. In fact, neither my purpose nor my limits permit more than a few hints, that may prepare the reader for some of the positions assumed in the second part of this volume.

Of the King with the two Houses of Parliament, as constituting the STATE (in the special and antithetic sense of the word) we have already spoken: and it remains only to determine the proper and legitimate objects of its superintendence and control. On what is the power of the State rightfully exercised? Now, I am not arguing in a court of law; and my purpose would be grievously misunderstood if what I say should be taken as intended for an assertion of the *fact*. Neither of facts, nor of statutory and demandable rights do I speak; but exclusively of the STATE according to the *idea*. And, in accordance with the *idea* of the State, I do not hesitate to answer, that the legitimate objects of its power comprise all the interests and concerns of the PROPRIETAGE, both landed and personal, and whether inheritably vested in the lineage or in the individual citizen; and these alone. Even in the lives and limbs of the lieges, the King, as the head and arm of the State, has an interest of property: and in any trespass against them the King appears as plaintiff.

The chief object, for which men who from the beginning existed as a social bond, first formed themselves into a *State*, and on the social super-induced the political relation, was not the protection of their lives but of their property.[55] The natural man is too proud an animal to admit that he needs any other protection for his life than his own courage and that of his clan can bestow. Where the nature of the soil and climate has precluded all property but personal, and admitted that only in its simplest forms, as in Greenland for instance – there men remain in the domestic state and form neighbourhoods, not governments. And in North America, the chiefs appear to exercise government in those tribes only which possess individual landed property. Among the rest the chief is the general, a leader in war; not a magistrate. To property and to its necessary inequalities must be referred all human laws, that would not be laws without and independent of any conventional enactment: *i.e.* all State-legislation. – FRIEND, vol i. 351.

Next comes the King, as the Head of the National Church, or Clerisy, and the Protector and Supreme Trustee of the NATIONALTY: the power of the same in relation to its proper objects being exercised by the King and the Houses of Convocation, of which, as before of the State, the King is the head and arm. And here if it had been my purpose to enter at once on the development of this position, together with the conclusions to be drawn from it, I should need with increased earnestness remind the reader, that I am neither describing what the National Church now is, nor determining what it ought to be. My statements respect the idea alone, as deduced from its original purpose and ultimate aim: and of the *idea* only must my assertions be understood. But the full exposition of this point is not necessary for the appreciation of the late Bill which is the subject of the following part of the volume. It belongs indeed to the chapter with which I had intended to conclude this volume, and which, should my health permit, and the circumstances warrant it, it is still my intention to let follow the present work – namely, my humble contribution towards an answer to the question, What is to be done now? For the present, therefore, it will be sufficient, if I recall to the reader's recollection, that formerly the National Clerisy, in the two Houses of Convocation duly assembled and represented, taxed themselves. But as to the proper objects, on which the authority of the convocation with the King as its head was to be exercised – these the reader will himself without difficulty decypher by referring to what has been already said respecting the proper and distinguishing ends and purposes of a National Church.

I pass, therefore, at once to the relations of the Nation, or the State in the larger sense of the word, to the State especially so named, and to the Crown. And on this subject again I shall confine myself to a few important, yet, I trust, not common nor obvious, remarks respecting the conditions requisite or especially favorable to the health and vigor of the realm. From these again I separate those, the nature and importance of which cannot be adequately exhibited but by adverting to the consequences which have followed their neglect or inobservance, reserving them for another place: while for the present occasion I select two only; but these, I dare believe, not unworthy the name of Political Principles, or *Maxims*, *i.e.* regulae quae inter *maximas* numerari merentur [rules that deserve to be numbered among the *most important*]. And both of them forcibly confirm and exemplify a remark, often and in various ways suggested to my mind, that with, perhaps, one* exception, it would be difficult in the whole compass of language, to find a metaphor so commensurate, so pregnant, or suggesting so many points of elucidation, as that of *Body Politic*, as the exponent of a State or Realm. I admire, as little

---

* That namely of the Word (John I.1) for the Divine Alterity, the Deus Alter et idem [God other and the same] of Philo [Judaeus]; Deitas Objectiva [Objective Deity].

as you do, the many-jointed similitudes of Flavel, and other finders of moral and spiritual meanings in the works of Art and Nature, where the proportion of the likeness to the difference not seldom reminds us of the celebrated comparison of the Morning Twilight to a Boiled Lobster.[56] But the correspondence between the Body Politic to the Body Natural holds even in the detail of application. Let it not however be supposed, that I expect to derive any proof of my positions from this analogy. My object in thus prefacing them is answered, if I have shown cause for the use of the physiological terms by which I have sought to render my meaning intelligible.

The first condition then required, in order to a sound constitution of the Body Politic, is a due proportion of the free and permeative life and energy of the Nation to the organized powers brought within containing channels. What those vital forces that seem to bear an analogy to the imponderable agents, magnetic, or galvanic, in bodies inorganic, if indeed, they are not the same in a higher energy and under a differing law of action – what these, I say, are in the living body in distinction from the fluids in the glands and vessels – the same, or at least a like relation, do the indeterminable, but yet actual influences of intellect, information, prevailing principles and tendencies, (to which we must add the influence of property, or income, where it exists without right of suffrage attached thereto), hold to the regular, definite, and legally recognised Powers, in the Body Politic. But as no simile runs on all four legs (*nihil simile est idem* [nothing similar is the same]), so here the difference in respect of the Body Politic is, that in sundry instances the former, *i.e.* the permeative, species of force is capable of being converted into the latter, of being as it were organized and rendered a part of the vascular system, by attaching a measured and determinate political right, or privilege thereto.

What the exact proportion, however, of the two kinds of force should be, it is impossible to pre-determine. But the existence of a disproportion is sure to be detected, sooner or later, by the effects. Thus: the ancient Greek democracies, the *hot-beds* of Art, Science, Genius, and Civilization, fell into dissolution from the excess of the former, the permeative power deranging the functions, and by explosions shattering the organic structures, they should have enlivened. On the contrary, the Republic of Venice fell by the contrary extremes. All political power was confined to the determinate vessels, and these becoming more and more rigid, even to an ossification of the arteries, the State, in which the people were nothing, lost all power of resistance ad extra.

Under this head, in short, there are three possible sorts of malformation to be noticed, namely, – The adjunction or concession of direct political power to *personal* force and influence, whether physical or intellectual, existing in classes or aggregates of individuals, without those fixed or tangible possessions, freehold, copyhold, or leasehold, in land, house, or stock. The power resulting from the acquisition of knowledge or skill, and from the superior developement of the understanding is, doubtless, of a far nobler kind than mere physical strength and fierceness, the one being *peculiar* to the animal *Man*, the other common to him with the Bear, the Buffalo, and the Mastiff. And if superior Talents, and the mere possession of knowledges, such as can be learnt at Mechanics' Institutions,[57] were regularly accompanied with a Will in harmony with the Reason, and a consequent subordination of the appetites and passions to the ultimate ends of our Being: if intellectual gifts and attainments were infallible signs of wisdom and goodness in the same proportion, and the knowing, clever, and *talented* (a vile word!) were always *rational*; if the mere facts of science conferred or superseded the soft'ning humanizing influences of the moral world, that habitual presence of the beautiful or the seemly, and that exemption from all familiarity with the gross, the mean, and the disorderly, whether in look or language, or in the surrounding objects, in which the main efficacy of a liberal education consists; and if, lastly, these acquirements and powers of the understanding could be shared equally by the whole class, and did not, as by a necessity of nature they ever must do, fall to the lot of two or three in each several group, club, or neighbourhood; – then, indeed, by an enlargement of the Chinese system, political power might not unwisely be conferred as the honorarium or privilege on having passed through all the forms in the National Schools, without the security of political ties, without those fastenings and radical fibres of a collective and registrable property, by which the Citizen inheres in and belongs to the Commonwealth, as a constituent part either of the Proprietage, or of the Nationalty; either of the State, or of the National Church. But as the contrary of all these suppositions may be more safely assumed, the practical conclusion will be – not that the requisite means of intellectual developement and growth should be withheld from any native of the soil, which it was at all times wicked to wish, and which it would be now silly to attempt; but – that the gifts of the understanding, whether the boon of a genial nature, or the reward of more persistent application, should be allowed fair play in the acquiring of that proprietorship, to which a certain portion of political power belongs, as its proper function. For in this way there is at least a strong probability, that intellectual power will be armed with political power, only where it has previously been combined with and guarded by the moral qualities of prudence, industry, and self-control. And this is the first of the three kinds of mal-organization in a state: viz. direct political power without cognizable possession.

The second is: the exclusion of any class or numerous body of individuals, who have notoriously risen into possession, and the influence inevitably connected with known possession, under pretence of impediments that do not directly or essentially affect the character of the individuals as citizens, or absolutely disqualify them for the performance of civic duties. Imperfect, yet oppressive, and irritating ligatures that peril the trunk, whose circulating current they would withhold, even more than the limb which they would fain excommunicate!

The third and last is: a gross incorrespondency of the proportion of the antagonistic interests of the Body Politic in the representative body – *i.e.* (in relation to our own country,) in the two Houses of Parliament – to the actual proportion of the same interests, and of the public influence exerted by the same in the Nation at large. Whether in consequence of the gradual revolution which has transferred to the Magnates of the Landed Interest so large a portion of that Borough Representation which was to have been its counterbalance; whether the same causes which have deranged the equilibrium of the Landed and the *Monied Interests in the Legislation, have not likewise deranged the balance between the

---

* *Monied*, used arbitrarily, as in preceding pages the words, *Personal* and *Independent*, from my inability to find any one self-interpreting word, that would serve for the generic name of the four classes, on which I have stated the Interest of *Progression* more especially to depend, and with it the Freedom which is the indispensable *condition* and propelling force of all national progress: even as the Counter-pole, the other great Interest of the Body Politic, its *Permanency*, is more especially committed to the Landed Order, as its natural Guardian and Depository. I have therefore had recourse to the convenient figure of speech, by which a conspicuous part or feature of a subject is used to express the whole; and the reader will be so good as to understand, that the Monied Order in this place comprehends and stands for, the Commercial, Manufacturing, Distributive, and Professional classes of the Community. . . .

two unequal divisions of the Landed Interest itself, viz. the Major Barons, or great Land-owners, with or without title, and the great body of the Agricultural Community, and thus giving to the real or imagined interests of the comparatively few, the imposing name of the Interest of the whole – the landed Interest! – these are questions, to which the obdurate adherence to the jail-crowding Game Laws, (which during the reading of our Church Litany, I have sometimes been tempted to include, by a sort of *subintellige*, in the petitions – "from envy, hatred, and malice, and all uncharitableness; from battle, murder, and sudden death, Good Lord, deliver us!") to which the Corn Laws,[58] the exclusion of the produce of our own colonies from our distilleries, &c., during the war, against the earnest recommendation of the government, the retention of the Statutes against Usury, and other points, of minor importance or of less safe handling, may seem at a first view to suggest an answer in the affirmative; but which, for reasons before assigned, I shall leave unresolved, content if only I have made the Principle itself intelligible. . . .

CHAPTER XI

The relations of the potential to the actual. The omnipotence of Parliament: of what kind

So much, in explanation of the first of the two *Conditions* of the health and vigour of a Body Politic: and far more, I must confess, than I had myself reckoned on.[59] I will endeavour to indemnify the reader, by despatching the second in a few sentences, which could not so easily have been accomplished, but for the explanations given in the preceding paragraphs. For as we have found the first condition in the due proportion of the free and permeative Life of the State to the Powers organized, and severally determined by their appropriate and containing, or conducting nerves, or vessels; the Second Condition is –

A due proportion of the *potential* (latent, dormant) to the *actual* Power. In the first Condition both Powers alike are awake and in act. The Balance is produced by the *polarization* of the Actual Power, *i.e.* the opposition of the Actual Power organized, to the Actual Power free and permeating the organs. In the Second, the Actual

Power, *in toto*, is opposed to the Potential. It has been frequently and truly observed, that in England, where the ground plan, the skeleton, as it were, of the government is a monarchy, at once buttressed and limited by the Aristocracy, (the assertions of its popular character finding a better support in the harangues and theories of popular men, than in state-documents and the records of clear History), a far greater degree of liberty is, and long has been enjoyed, than ever existed in the ostensibly freest, that is, most democratic, Commonwealths of ancient or of modern times – greater, indeed, and with a more decisive predominance of the Spirit of Freedom, than the wisest and most philanthropic states-men of antiquity, or than the great Commonwealth's-men (the stars of that narrow interspace of blue sky between the black clouds of the first and second Charles's reigns) believed compatible, the one with the safety of the State, the other with the interests of Morality.[60]

Yes! for little less than a century and a half Englishmen have collectively, and individually, lived and acted with fewer restraints on their free-agency, than the citizens of any known *Republic, past or present. The fact is certain. It has been often boasted of, but never, I think, clearly explained. The solution of the phenomenon must, it is obvious, be sought for in the combination of circumstances, to which we owe the insular privilege of a self-evolving Constitution: and the following will, I think, be found the main cause of the fact in question. Extremes meet – an adage of inexhaustible exemplification. A democratic Republic and an Absolute Monarchy agree in this; that in both alike, the Nation, or People, delegates its whole power. Nothing is left obscure, nothing suffered to remain in the Idea, unevolved and only acknowledged as an existing, yet indeterminable Right. A Constitution such states can scarcely be said to possess. The whole Will of the Body Politic is in act at every moment. But in the Constitution of England according to the Idea, (which in this instance has demonstrated its actuality by its practical influence, and this too though counter-worked by fashionable errors and maxims, that left their validity

---

* It will be thought, perhaps, that the United States of North America should have been excepted. But the identity of Stock, Language, Customs, Manners and Laws scarely allows me to consider this an exception: even though it were quite certain both that it is and that it will continue such. It was, at all events, a remark worth remembering, which I once heard from a traveller (a prejudiced one I must admit), that where every man may take liberties, there is little Liberty for any man – or, that where every man takes liberties, no man can enjoy any.

behind in the Law-Courts, from which they were borrowed) the Nation has delegated its power, not without measure and circumscription, whether in respect of the duration of the Trust, or of the particular interests entrusted.

The Omnipotence of Parliament, in the mouth of a lawyer, and understood exclusively of the restraints and remedies within the competence of our Law-courts, is objectionable only as bombast. It is but a puffing pompous way of stating a plain matter of fact. Yet in the times preceding the Restoration, even this was not universally admitted. And it is not without a fair show of reason, that the shrewd and learned author of "THE ROYALIST'S DEFENCE;" printed in the year 1648, (a tract of 172 pages, small quarto, from which I now transcribe) thus sums up his argument and evidences:[61]

"Upon the whole matter clear it is, the Parliament itself (that is, the King, the Lords, and Commons) although unanimously consenting, are *not boundless*: the Judges of the Realm by the *fundamental* Law of *England* have power to determine which Acts of Parliament are binding and which void." p. 48. – That a unanimous declaration of the Judges of the realm, that any given Act of Parliament was against right reason and the fundamental law of the land (*i.e.* the Constitution of the realm), render such Act null and void, was a principle that did not want defenders among the lawyers of elder times. And in a state of society in which the competently informed and influencive members of the community, (the National Clerisy not included), scarcely perhaps trebled the number of the members of the two Houses, and Parliaments were so often tumultuary congresses of a victorious party rather than representatives of the State, the right and Power here asserted might have been wisely vested in the Judges of the realm: and with at least equal wisdom, under change of circumstances, has the right been suffered to fall into abeyance. Therefore let the potency of Parliament be that highest and uttermost, beyond which a court of Law looketh not: and within the sphere of the Courts quicquid Rex cum Parliamento voluit, *Fatum* sit [whatever the King with Parliament has decided, let it be pronounced]!

But if the strutting phrase be taken, as from sundry recent speeches respecting the fundamental institutions of the realm it may be reasonably inferred that it has been taken, *i.e.* absolutely, and in reference, not to our Courts of Law exclusively, but to the Nation, to England with all her venerable heir-looms, and with all her germs of reversionary wealth – thus used and understood, the Omnipotence of Parliament is an hyperbole, that would contain mischief in it, were it only that it tends to provoke a detailed analysis of the materials of the joint-stock company, to which so terrific an attribute belongs, and the competence of the shareholders in this earthly omnipotence to exercise the same. And on this head the observations and descriptive statements given in Chap. v. of the old tract, just cited, retain all their force; or if any have fallen off, their place has been abundantly filled up by new growths. The degree and sort of knowledge, talent, probity, and prescience, which it would be only too easy, were it not too invidious, to prove from acts and measures presented by the history of the last half century, are but *scant measure* even when exerted within the sphere and circumscription of the constitution, and on the matters properly and peculiarly appertaining to the State according to the idea – this portion of moral and mental endowment placed by the side of the plusquam-gigantic height and amplitude of power, implied in the unqualified use of the phrase, Omnipotence of Parliament, and with its dwarfdom exaggerated by the contrast, would threaten to distort the countenance of truth itself with the sardonic laugh of irony [note omitted].

The non-resistance of successive generations has ever been, and with evident reason, deemed equivalent to a tacit consent, on the part of the nation, and as finally legitimating the act thus acquiesced in, however great the dereliction of principle, and breach of trust, the original enactment may have been. I hope, therefore, that without offence I may venture to designate the Septennial Act,[62] as an act of usurpation, tenfold more dangerous to the true Liberty of the Nation, than the pretext for the measure, viz. the apprehended Jacobite leaven from a new election, was at all likely to have proved: and I repeat the conviction, I have expressed in reference to the practical suppression of the CONVOCATION,[63] that no great principle was ever invaded or trampled on, that did not sooner or later avenge itself on the country, and even on the governing classes themselves, by the consequences of the precedent. The statesman who has not learnt this from history, has missed its most valuable result, and might in my opinion as profitably, and far more delightfully have devoted his hours of study to Sir Walter Scott's Novels [note omitted].

But I must draw in my reins. Neither my limits permit, nor does my present purpose require that I should do more than exemplify the limitation resulting from that latent or *potential* Power, a due proportion of which to the actual powers I have stated as the second condition of the health and vigor of a body politic, by an instance bearing directly on the measure, which in the following section I am to aid in appreciating, and which was the occasion of the whole work. The principle itself, which, as not contained within the rule and compass of law, its practical manifestations being indeterminable and inappreciable *a priori*, and then only to be recorded as having manifested itself, when the predisposing causes and the enduring effects prove the unific mind and energy of the nation to have been in travail; when they have made audible to the historian that Voice of the People which is the Voice of God – this Principle, I say, (or the Power, that is the subject of it) which by its very essence existing and working as an *Idea* only, except in the rare and predestined epochs of Growth and Reparation, might seem to many fitter matter for verse than for sober argument, I will, by way of compromise, and for the amusement of the reader, sum up in the rhyming prose of an old Puritan Poet, consigned to contempt by Mr. Pope, but whose writings, with all their barren flats and dribbling common-place, contain nobler principles, profounder truths, and more that is properly and peculiarly *poetic* than are to be found in his* own works. The passage in question, however, I found occupying the last page on a flying-sheet of four leaves, entitled *England's Misery and Remedy, in a judicious Letter from an Utter-Barrister to his Special Friend, concerning Lieut.-Col. Lilburne's Imprisonment in Newgate, Sept.* 1745;[64] and I beg leave to borrow the introduction, together with the extract, or that part at least, which suited my purpose.

"Christian Reader, having a vacant place for some few Lines, I have made bold to use some of Major GEORGE WITHERS, his verses out of Vox PACIFICA, *page* 199.

---

* If it were asked whether the Author then considers the works of the one of equal value with those of the other, or holds George Withers to be as great a writer as Alexander Pope? his answer would be, that he is as little likely to do so, as the Querist would be to put no greater value on a highly wrought vase of pure silver from the hand of a master, than on an equal weight of Copper Ore that contained a small per centage of separable Gold scattered through it. The Reader will be pleased to observe, that in the stanza here cited, the "STATE" is used in the largest sense, and as synonymous with the Realm, or entire Body Politic, including Church and *State*, in the narrower and special sense of the latter term. . . .

> Let not your King and Parliament in *One*,
> Much less apart, mistake themselves for that
> Which is most worthy to be thought upon:
> Nor think they are, essentially, the STATE.
> Let them not fancy, that th' Authority
> And Priviledges upon them bestown,
> Conferr'd are to set up a MAJESTY,
> A POWER, or a GLORY of their own!
> But let them know, 'twas for a deeper life,
> Which they but *represent* –
> That there's on earth a yet auguster Thing,
> Veil'd tho' it be, than Parliament and King."[65]

CHAPTER XII

*The preceding position exemplified. The origin and rationale of the
Coronation Oath, in respect of the National Church. In what its moral
obligation consists. Recapitulation*

AND here again the "Royalist's Defence" furnishes me with the
introductory paragraph: and I am always glad to find in the words
of an elder writer, what I must otherwise have said in my own
person – *otium simul et autoritatem* [(it gives me) at the same time
leisure and authority].

"All Englishmen grant, that Arbitrary power is destructive of
the best purposes for which power is conferred: and in the
preceding chapter it has been shown, that to give an unlimited
authority over the fundamental Laws and Rights of the nation,
even to the King and two Houses of Parliament jointly, though
nothing so bad as to have this boundless power in the King
alone, or in the Parliament alone, were nevertheless to deprive
Englishmen of the Security from Arbitrary Power, which is their
birth right.

"Upon perusal of former statutes it appears, that the Members
of both Houses have been *frequently* drawn to consent, not only to
things *prejudicial* to the Commonwealth, but, (even in matters of
greatest weight) to alter and contradict what formerly themselves
had agreed to, and that, as it happened to please the fancy of the
present Prince, or to suit the passions and interests of a prevailing

Faction. Witness the statute by which it was enacted that the Proclamation of King Henry VIII. should be equivalent to an Act of Parliament; another declaring both Mary and Elizabeth bastards; and a third statute empowering the King to dispose of the Crown of England by Will and Testament. Add to these the several statutes in the times of King Henry VIII. Edward VI. Queen Mary, and Queen Elizabeth, setting up and pulling down each other's religion, every one of them condemning even to death the profession of the one before established."[66]

So far my anonymous author, evidently an old Tory Lawyer of the genuine breed, too enlightened to obfuscate and incense-blacken the shrine, through which the kingly Idea should be translucent, into an Idol to be worshipped in its own right; but who, considering both the reigning Sovereign and the Houses, as limited and representative functionaries, thought they saw reason, in some few cases, to place more confidence in the former than in the latter: while there were points, which they wished as little as possible to trust to either. With this experience, however, as above stated, (and it would not be difficult to increase the catalogue,) can we wonder that the nation grew sick of parliamentary *Religions?* or that the Idea should at last awake and become operative, that what virtually concerned their humanity, and involved yet higher relations, than those of the citizen to the state, duties more awful, and more precious privileges, while yet it stood in closest connection with all their *civil* duties and rights, as their indispensable condition and only secure ground – that this was not a matter to be voted up or down, off or on, by fluctuating majorities! that it was too precious an inheritance to be left at the discretion of an Omnipotency, that had so little claim to Omniscience? No interest of a single generation, but an entailed Boon too sacred, too momentous, to be shaped and twisted, pared down or plumped up, by any assemblage of Lords, Knights, and Burgesses for the time being? Men perfectly competent, it may be, to the protection and management of those interests, in which, as having so large a stake they may be reasonably presumed to feel a sincere and lively concern, but who, the experience of ages might teach us, are not the class of persons most likely to study, or feel a deep concern in, the interests here spoken of, in either sense of the term CHURCH; *i.e.* whether the interests be of a kingdom "not of the World,"[67] or those of an Estate of the Realm, and a constituent part, therefore, of the same System with the State, though as the opposite

Pole. The results at all events have been such, whenever the Representatives of the One Interest have assumed the direct control of the other, as gave occasion long ago to the rhyming couplet, quoted as proverbial by Luther:

> Cum Mare siccatur, cum Daemon ad astra levatur,
> Tunc Clero Laicus fidus Amicus erit.[68]

[When the sea dries up, when the Devil is raised to the stars,
Then the Laity will be a true friend to the Clergy.]

But if the nation willed to withdraw the religion of the realm from the changes and revolutions incident to whatever is subjected to the suffrages of the representative assemblies, whether of the state or of the church, the trustees of the proprietage or those of the nationalty, the first question is, how this reservation is to be declared, and by what means to be effected. These means, the security for the permanence of the established religion, must, it may be foreseen, be imperfect; for what can be otherwise, that depends on human will? but yet it may be abundantly sufficient to declare the aim and intention of the provision. Our ancestors did the best it was in their power to do. Knowing by recent experience that multitudes never blush, that numerous assemblies, however respectably composed, are not exempt from temporary hallucinations, and the influences of party passion; that there are things, for the conservation of which –

> Men safelier trust to heaven, than to themselves,
> When least themselves, in storms of loud debate
> Where folly is contagious, and too oft
> Even wise men leave their better sense at home
> To chide and wonder at them, when returned.[69]

Knowing this, our ancestors chose to place their reliance on the honour and conscience of an individual, whose comparative height, it was believed, would exempt him from the gusts and shifting currents, that agitate the lower region of the political atmosphere. Accordingly, on a change of dynasty they bound the person, who had accepted the crown in trust – bound him for himself and his successors by an oath, to refuse his consent (without which no change in the existing law can be effected), to any measure subverting or tending to subvert the safety and independence of the National Church, or which exposed the realm to the danger of a return of that foreign usurper, misnamed spiritual, from which it had with so many sacrifices emancipated itself. However unconstitutional therefore the royal veto on a Bill presented by the Lords and Commons may be deemed in all ordinary cases, this is clearly an exception. For it is no additional power conferred on the king; but a limit imposed on him by the constitution itself for its own safety. Previously to the ceremonial act, which announces him the only lawful and sovereign head of both church and the state, the oath is administered to him *religiously* as the representative person and crowned majesty of the nation. *Religiously*, I say, for the mind of the nation, existing only as an *Idea*, can act *distinguishably* on the ideal powers alone – that is, on the reason and conscience.[70]

It only remains then to determine, what it is to which the Coronation Oath obliges the conscience of the king. And this may be best determined by considering what in reason and in conscience the Nation had a right to impose. Now that the Nation had a right to decide for the King's conscience and reason, and for the reason and conscience of all his successors, and of his and their counsellors and ministers, laic and ecclesiastic, on questions of theology, and controversies of faith – *ex. gr.* that it is not allowable in directing our thoughts to a departed Saint, the Virgin Mary for instance, to say O*ra* pro nobis, Beata Virgo [Pray for us, bless Virgin], though there would be no harm in saying, O*ret* pro nobis, precor, beata Virgo [Let the blessed Virgin pray for us, I beseech thee]; whether certain books are to be held canonical; whether the text, "They shall be saved as through fire," refers to a purgatorial process in the body, or during the interval between its dissolution and the day of judgment; whether the words, "this is my body," are to be understood literally, and if so, whether it is by consubstantiation with, or transubstantiation of, bread and wine; and that the members of both Houses of Parliament, together with the Privy Counsellors and all the Clergy shall abjure and denounce the theory last mentioned – this I utterly deny. And if this were the whole and sole object and intention of the Oath, however large the number might be of the persons who imposed or were notoriously favorable to the imposition, so far from recognising the Nation in their collective number, I should regard them as no other than an aggregate of intolerant mortals, from bigotry and presumption forgetful of their fallibility, and no less ignorant of their own rights, than callous to those of succeeding generations. If the articles of faith therein disclaimed and denounced were the substance and proper intention of the Oath, and not to be understood, as in all common sense they ought to be, as temporary marks because the known accompaniments of other and legitimate grounds of disqualification; and which only in reference to *these*, and only as long as they implied their existence, were fit objects of political interference; it would be as impossible for me, as for the late Mr. Canning,[71] to attach any such sanctity to the Coronation Oath, as should prevent it from being superannuated in times of clearer light and less heat. But that these theological articles, and the open profession of the same by a portion of the king's subjects as parts of their creed, are not the evils which it is the true and legitimate purpose of the oath to preclude, and which constitute and define its obligation on the royal conscience; and what the real evils are, that do indeed disqualify for offices of national trust, and give the permanent obligatory character to the engagement – this, in which I include the exposition of the essential characters of the Christian or Catholic Church. . . .

And now I may be permitted to look back on the road, we have past: in the course of which, I have placed before you, patient fellow-traveller! a small part indeed of what might, on a suitable occasion, be profitably said; but it is all, that for my present purpose, I deem it necessary to say respecting three out of the five themes that were to form the subject of the first part of this – small volume, shall I call it? or large and dilated epistle? But let me avail myself of the pause, to repeat my apology to the reader for any *extra* trouble I may have imposed on him, by employing the same term (the State, namely) in two senses; though I flatter myself, I have in each instance so guarded it as to leave scarcely the possibility, that a moderately attentive reader should understand the word in one sense, when I had meant it in the other, or confound the STATE as a *whole*, and comprehending the Church, with the State as one of the two constituent parts, and in contra-distinction from the Church.

BRIEF RECAPITULATION

First then, I have given briefly but, I trust, with sufficient clearness the right idea of a STATE, or Body Politic; "State" being here synonimous with a *constituted* Realm, Kingdom, Commonwealth, or Nation, *i.e.* where the integral parts, classes, or orders are so balanced, or interdependent, as to constitute, more or less, a moral unit, an organic whole; and as arising out of the Idea of a State I have added the Idea of a Constitution, as the informing principle of its coherence and unity. But in applying the above to our own kingdom (and with this qualification the reader is requested to understand me as speaking in all the following remarks), it was necessary to observe, and I willingly avail myself of this opportunity to repeat the observation – that the Constitution, in its widest sense as the Constitution of the Realm, arose out of, and in fact consisted in, the co-existence of the Constitutional STATE (in the second acceptation of the term) with the King as its head, and of the CHURCH (*i.e.* the *National* Church), likewise the King as its head; and lastly of the King, as the Head and Majesty of the whole Nation. The reader was cautioned therefore not to confound it with either of its constituent parts; that he must first master the true idea of each of these severally; and that in the synopsis or conjunction of the three, the Idea of the English Constitution, the Constitution of the Realm, will rise of itself before him. And in aid of this purpose and following this order, I have given according to my best judgment, first, the Idea of the State, (in the second or *special* sense of the term;) of the State-legislature; and of the two constituent orders, the landed, with its two classes, the Major Barons, and the Franklins; and the Personal, consisting of the mercantile, or commercial, the manufacturing, the distributive and the professional; these two orders corresponding to the two great all-including INTERESTS of the State, – the landed, namely, to the PERMANENCE, – the Personal to the PROGRESSION. The Possessions of both orders, taken collectively, form the PROPRIETAGE [note omitted] of the Realm. In contra-distinction from this and as my second theme, I have explained (and as being the principal object of this work, more diffusely) the NATIONALTY, its nature and purposes, and the duties and qualifications of its Trustees and Functionaries. In the same sense as I at once oppose and conjoin the NATIONALTY to the PROPRIETAGE; in the same antithesis and conjunction I use and understand the phrase, CHURCH and STATE.

Lastly, I have essayed to determine the Constitutional Idea of the CROWN, and its relations to the Nation, to which I have added a few sentences on the relations of the Nation to the State.

To the completion of this first part of my undertaking, two subjects still remain to be treated of – and to each of these I shall devote a small section . . . "On the Idea of the Christian Church". . . .

IDEA OF THE CHRISTIAN CHURCH

"WE, (said Luther), tell our Lord God plainly: If he will have his Church, then He must look how to maintain and defend it; for we can neither uphold nor protect it. And well for us, that it is so! For in case we could, or were able to defend it, we should become the proudest Asses under heaven. Who is the Church's Protector, that hath promised to be with her to the end, and the gates of Hell shall not prevail against her? Kings, Diets, Parliaments, Lawyers? Marry, no such cattle."[72]

THE practical conclusion from our enquiries respecting the origin and Idea of the National Church, the paramount end and purpose of which is the continued and progressive civilization of the community (*emollit mores nec sinit esse feros*), was this: that though many things may be conceived of a tendency to diminish the *fitness* of particular men, or of a particular class, to be chosen as trustees and functionaries of the same; though there may be many points more or less adverse to the perfection of the establishment; there are yet but two absolute disqualifications; namely, allegiance to a foreign power, or an acknowledgment of any other visible head of the Church, but our sovereign lord the king; and compulsory celibacy in connection with, and dependence on, a foreign and extra-national head. We are now called to a different contemplation, to the Idea of the Christian Church.

Of the Christian *Church*, I say, not of Christianity. To the ascertainment and enucleation of the latter, of the great redemptive process which began in the separation of light from Chaos (*Hades, or the Indistinction*), and has its end in the union of life with God, the whole summer and autumn, and now commenced winter of my life have been dedicated. HIC labor, HOC opus est [This is the toil, this is the task], on which alone the author rests his hope, that he shall be found not to have lived altogether in vain. Of the Christian *Church* only, and of this no further than is necessary for the distinct understanding of the National Church, it is my purpose now to speak: and for this purpose it will be sufficient to enumerate the essential characters by which the Christian church is distinguished.

FIRST CHARACTER. – The Christian Church is not a KINGDOM, REALM, (*royaume*), or STATE, (*sensu latiori* [in a wider sense]) of the WORLD, that is, of the aggregate, or total number of the kingdoms, states, realms, or bodies politic, (these words being as far as our present argument is concerned, perfectly synonimous), into which civilized man is distributed; and which, collectively taken, constitute the civilized WORLD. The Christian Church, I say, is no state, kingdom, or realm of this world; nor is it an Estate of any such realm, kingdom or state; but it is the appointed Opposite to them all *collectively* – the *sustaining, correcting, befriending* Opposite of the world! the compensating counterforce to the inherent [note omitted] and inevitable evils and defects of the STATE, *as* a State, and without reference to its better or worse construction as a particular state; while whatever is beneficent and humanizing in the aims, tendencies, and proper objects of the state, the Christian Church collects in itself as in a focus, to radiate them back in a higher quality: or to change the metaphor, it completes and strengthens the edifice of the state, without interference or commixture, in the mere act of laying and securing its own foundations. And for these services the Church of Christ asks of the state neither wages nor dignities. She asks only protection, and *to be let alone.* These indeed she demands; but even these only on the ground, that there is nothing in her constitution, nor in her discipline, inconsistent with the interests of the state, nothing resistant or impedimental to the state in the exercise of its rightful powers, in the fulfilment of its appropriate duties, or in the effectuation of its legitimate objects. It is a fundamental principle of all legislation, that the state shall leave the largest portion of personal free agency to each of its citizens, that is compatible with the free agency of all, and not subversive of the ends of its own existence as a state.[73] And though a negative, it is a most important distinctive character of the Church of Christ, that she asks nothing for her members as

Christians, which they are not already entitled to demand as citizens and subjects.

SECOND CHARACTER. – The Christian Church is not a secret community. In the once current (and well worthy to be re-issued) terminology of our elder divines, it is objective in its nature and purpose, not mystic or subjective, *i.e.* not like reason or the court of conscience, existing only in and for the individual. Consequently the church here spoken of is not "the kingdom of God which is *within*, and which cometh not with observation, . . . but most observable . . ." – A city built on a hill, and not to be hid – an institution consisting of visible and public communities.[74] In one sentence, it is the Church visible and militant under Christ. And this visibility, this *publicity*, is its second distinctive character. The

THIRD CHARACTER – reconciles the two preceding, and gives the condition, under which their co-existence in the same subject becomes possible. Antagonist forces are necessarily of the same kind. It is an old rule of logic, that only concerning two subjects of the same kind can it be properly said that they are opposites. Inter res heterogeneas non datur oppositio [Between things of different kinds there is no opposition], *i.e.* contraries cannot be opposites. Alike in the primary and the metaphorical use of the word, Rivals (Rivales) are those only who inhabit the opposite banks of *the same stream*.

Now, in conformity to character the first, the Christian Church dare not be considered as a counter-pole to any particular STATE, the word, State, here taken in the largest sense. Still less can it, like the national clerisy, be opposed to the STATE in the narrower sense. The *Christian* Church, as such, has no *nationalty* entrusted to its charge. It forms no counter-balance to the collective *heritage* of the realm. The phrase, Church and State, has a sense and a propriety in reference to the *National* Church alone. The Church of Christ cannot be placed in this conjunction and antithesis without forfeiting the very name of Christian. The true and only contra-position of the Christian Church is to the world. Her paramount aim and object, indeed, is *another* world, not a world *to come* exclusively, but likewise *another world that now is* . . . and to the concerns of which alone the epithet spiritual, can without a mischievous abuse of the word, be applied. But as the necessary consequence and accompaniments of the means by which she seeks to attain this especial end; and as a collateral object, it is her office to counteract the evils that result by a common necessity from all Bodies Politic, the system or aggregate of which is the WORLD. And observe that the nisus, or counter-agency, of the Christian Church is against the evil *results* only, and not (directly, at least, or by primary intention) against the defective institutions that may have caused or aggravated them.

But on the other hand, by virtue of the second character, the Christian Church is to exist in every kingdom and state of the world, in the form of public communities, is to exist as a real and ostensible power. The consistency of the first and second depends on, and is fully effected by, the

THIRD CHARACTER

of the Church of Christ: namely, the absence of any visible head or sovereign – by the non-existence, nay the utter preclusion, of any local or personal centre of unity, of any single source of universal power. This fact may be thus illustrated. Kepler and Newton, substituting the idea of the infinite for the conception of a finite and determined world, assumed in the Ptolemaic Astronomy, superseded and drove out the notion of a one central point or body of the Universe. Finding a centre in every point of matter and an absolute circumference no where, they explained at once the unity and the distinction that co-exist throughout the creation by focal instead of central bodies: the attractive and restraining power of the sun or focal orb, in each particular system, supposing and resulting from an actual power, present in all and over all, throughout an indeterminable multitude of systems. And this, demonstrated as it has been by science, and verified by observation, we rightly name the true system of the heavens. And even such is the scheme and true idea of the Christian Church. In the primitive times, and as long as the churches retained the form given them by the Apostles and Apostolic men, every community, or in the words of a father of the second century, (for the pernicious fashion of assimilating the Christian to the Jewish, as afterwards to the Pagan, Ritual, by false analogies, was almost coeval with the church itself,) every altar had its own bishop, every flock its own pastor, who derived his authority immediately from Christ, the universal Shepherd, and acknowledged no other superior than the same Christ, speaking by his spirit in the unanimous decision of any number of bishops or elders, according to his promise, *"Where* *two or three are gathered together in my name, there am I in the midst of them."**

Hence the unitive relation of the churches to each other, and of each to all, being equally *actual* indeed, but likewise equally IDEAL, *i.e.* mystic and supersensual, as the relation of the whole church to its one invisible Head, the church with and under Christ, as a one kingdom or state, is hidden: while from all its several component monads, (the particular visible churches I mean,) Caesar receiving the things that are Caesar's, and confronted by no rival Caesar, by no authority, which existing locally, temporally, and in the person of a fellow mortal, must be essentially of the same *kind* with his own, notwithstanding any attempt to belie its true nature under the perverted and contradictory name of *spiritual*, sees only so many loyal groups, who, claiming no peculiar rights, make themselves known to him as Christians, only by the more scrupulous and exemplary performance of their duties as citizens and subjects. And here let me add a few sentences on the use, abuse, and misuse of the phrase, *spiritual* Power. In the only appropriate sense of the words, *spiritual* power is a power that acts on the *spirits* of men. Now the spirit of a man, or the spiritual part of our being, is the intelligent Will: or (to speak less abstractly) it is the capability, with which the Father of Spirits hath endowed man of being determined to action by the *ultimate ends*, which the reason alone can present. (The Understanding, which derives all its materials from the Senses, can dictate *purposes* only, *i.e.* such ends as are in their turn *means* to other ends.) The ultimate ends, by which the will is to be determined, and by which alone the will, not corrupted, *"the spirit made perfect," would* be determined, are called, in relation to the Reason, moral *Ideas*. Such are the Ideas of the Eternal, the Good, the True, the Holy, the Idea of God as the Absoluteness and Reality (or real ground) of all these, or as the Supreme Spirit in which all these substantially *are*, and are ONE. Lastly, the idea of the responsible will itself; of duty, of guilt, or evil in itself

---

* Questions of dogmatic divinity do not enter into the purpose of this enquiry; . . . but when I contemplate the whole system [of the Romish religion], as it affects the great fundamental principles of morality, the *terra firma*, as it were, of our humanity; then trace its operation on the sources and conditions of national strength and well-being; and lastly, consider its woeful influences on the innocence and sanctity of the female mind and imagination, on the faith and happiness, the gentle fragrancy and unnoticed ever-present verdure of domestic life, – I can with difficulty avoid applying to it what the Rabbins fable of the fratricide CAIN, after the curse: that *the firm earth trembled wherever he strode, and the grass turned black beneath his feet.*[75] . . .

without reference to its outward and separable consequences, &c. &c.

A power, therefore, that acts on the appetites and passions, which we possess in common with the beasts, by motives derived from the senses and sensations, has no pretence to the name; nor can it without the grossest abuse of the word be called a *spiritual* power. Whether the man expects the *auto de fè*, the fire and faggots, with which he is threatened, to take place at Lisbon or Smithfield, or in some dungeon in the centre of the earth, makes no difference in the *kind* of motive by which he is influenced; nor of course in the nature of the power, which acts on his passions by means of it. It would be strange indeed, if ignorance and superstition, the dense and rank fogs that most strangle and suffocate the light of the spirit in man, should constitute a spirituality in the power, which takes advantage of them!

This is a gross *abuse* of the term, spiritual. The following, sanctioned as it is by custom and statute, yet (speaking exclusively as a philologist and without questioning its legality) I venture to point out, as a *misuse* of the term. Our great Church dignitaries sit in the Upper House of the Convocation, as *Prelates* of the National Church: and as *Prelates*, may exercise *ecclesiastical* power. In the House of Lords they sit as *barons*, and by virtue of the baronies which, much against the will of those haughty prelates, our kings forced upon them: and as such, they exercise a *Parliamentary* power. As bishops of the Church of Christ only can they possess, or exercise (and God forbid! I should doubt, that as such, many of them do faithfully exercise) a *spiritual* power, which neither king can give, nor King and Parliament take away. As Christian *bishops*, they are spiritual *pastors*, by power of the spirit ruling the flocks committed to their charge; but they are *temporal* peers and prelates. The

FOURTH CHARACTER

of the Christian Church, and a necessary consequence of the first and third, is its Catholicity, *i.e.* universality. It is neither Anglican, Gallican, nor Roman, neither Latin nor Greek. Even the Catholic and Apostolic Church *of* England is a less safe expression than the Churches of Christ in England: though the Catholic Church *in* England, or (what would be still better,) the Catholic Church under Christ throughout Great Britain and Ireland, is justifiable and appropriate: for through the presence of its only head and sovereign, entire in each and one in all, the Church universal is spiritually perfect in every true Church, and of course in any number of such Churches, which from circumstance of place, or the community of country or of language, we have occasion to speak of collectively. (I have already, here and elsewhere, observed, and scarcely a day passes without some occasion to repeat the observation, that an equivocal term, or a word with two or more different meanings, is never quite harmless. Thus, it is at least an inconvenience in our language, that the term Church, instead of being confined to its proper sense, Kirk, Aedes Kyriacae, or the Lord's House, should likewise be the word which our forefathers rendered the ecclesia, or the eccleti (ἔκκλητοι) i.e. evocati, the called out of the world, named collectively, and likewise our term for the clerical establishment. To the Called at Rome – to the Church of Christ at Corinth – or in Philippi – such was the language of the apostolic age; and the change since then has been no improvement.) The true Church *of* England is the National Church, or Clerisy. There exists, God be thanked! a Catholic and Apostolic church *in* England: and I thank God also for the Constitutional and Ancestral Church *of* England.

These are the four distinctions, or peculiar and essential marks, by which the church with *Christ* as its head is distinguished from the National Church, and *separated* from every possible counterfeit, that has, or shall have, usurped its name. And as an important comment on the same, and in confirmation of the principle which I have attempted to establish, I earnestly recommend for the reader's perusal, the following transcript from Dr. Henry More's *Modest Enquiry, or True Idea of Anti-christianism.*

"We will suppose some one prelate, who had got the start of the rest, to put in for the title and authority of Universal Bishop: and for the obtaining of this sovereignty, he will first pretend, that it is unfit that the visible Catholic Church, being one, should not be united under one visible head, which reasoning, though it makes a pretty shew at first sight, will yet, being closely looked into, vanish into smoke. For this is but a quaint concinnity urged in behalf of an impossibility. For the erecting such an office for one man, which no one *man* in the world is able to perform, implies that to be possible which is indeed impossible. Whence it is plain that the *head* will be *too little for the body;* which therefore will be a piece of mischievous assymmetry or inconcinnity also. No one mortal can be a competent head for that church which has a right to be *Catholic*, and to overspread the face of the whole earth. There can be no such head but Christ, who is not mere man, but God in the Divine humanity, and therefore present with every part of the church, and every member thereof, at what distance soever. But to set some one mortal bishop over the whole church, were to suppose that great bishop of our spirit absent from it, who has promised that he *will be with her to the end of the world*. Nor does the Church Catholic on earth lose her unity thereby. For rather hereby only is or can she be one.["] "As rationally might it be pretended, that it is not the Life, the *Rector Spiritus praesens per totum et in omni parte*, but the Crown of the skull, or some one Convolute of the brain, that causes and preserves the unity of the Body Natural."[76]

Such and so futile is the first pretence. But if this will not serve the turn, there is another in reserve. And notwithstanding the demonstrated impossibility of the thing, still there must be one visible head of the church universal, the successor and vicar of Christ, *for the slaking of controversies*, for the determination of disputed points! We will not stop here to expose the weakness of the argument (not alas! peculiar to the sophists of Rome, nor employed in support of *papal* infallibility only), that this or that *must be*, and consequently *is*, because sundry inconveniences would result from the want of it! and this without considering whether these inconveniences *have been* prevented or removed by its (pretended) presence; whether they do not continue in spite of this pretended remedy or antidote; whether these inconveniences were *intended* by providence to be precluded, and not rather for wise purposes permitted to continue; and lastly, whether the remedy may not be worse than the disease, like the sugar of lead administered by the Empiric, who cured a fever fit by exchanging it for the dead palsy. Passing by this sophism, therefore, it is sufficient to reply, that all points necessary are so plain and so widely known, that it is impossible that a Christian, who seeks those aids which the true head of the church has promised shall never be sought in vain, should err therein from lack of knowing better. And those who, from defects of head or heart, are blind to this widely diffused light, and who neither seek nor wish those aids, are still less likely to be influenced by a minor and derivative authority. But for other things, whether ceremonies or conceits, whether matters of discipline or of opinion, their diversity does not at all break the unity of the outward and visible church, as long as they do not subvert the fundamental laws of Christ's kingdom, nor contradict the terms of admission into his church, nor contravene the essential characters, by which it subsists, and is distinguished as the Christian Catholic Church.

To these sentiments, borrowed from one of the most philosophical of our learned elder Divines, I have only to add an observation as suggested by them – that as many and fearful mischiefs have ensued from the confusion of the Christian with the National Church, so have many and grievous practical errors, and much unchristian intolerance, arisen from confounding the outward and visible church of Christ, with the spiritual and invisible church, known only to the Father of all Spirits. The perfection of the former is to afford every opportunity, and to present no obstacle, to a gradual advancement in the latter. The different degrees of progress, the imperfections, errors and accidents of false perspective, which lessen indeed with our advance – spiritual *advance* – but to a greater or lesser amount are inseparable from all progression: these, the interpolated half-truths of the twilight, through which every soul must pass from darkness to the spiritual sunrise, belong to the visible church as objects of Hope, Patience, and Charity alone.

6

A Few Late Reflections: Coleridge on the 1832 Reform Act

In the last few years of his life Coleridge commented on the debates over, and the terms of, the Representation of the People Act that was passed in 1832. It will be noted from the extracts printed below that Coleridge was not hostile to the idea of parliamentary reform as such; the conception of 'idea' which he applied to Church and State could, as he himself noted, open up possibilities for refoim of the system of representation.[1] Coleridge's comments on the 1832 Act do not close off these possibilities, but they indicate that he thought the terms of the debate confused, and that he condemned what he saw as the rhetoric and rabble-rousing of extreme proponents of reform. In addition, he considered that the terms of the various proposals put before Parliament ignored the long-established relationship between property and political power in the English Constitution. Coleridge was especially concerned about the impact of a reformed House of Commons on the role of the House of Lords and, more significantly, given the argument of Church and State, on that of the Church of England.

(a) *Table Talk*, 21 November 1830: "House of Commons"

. . . It is a melancholy thing to live when there is no vision in the land. Where are our statesmen to meet this emergency? I see no reformer who asks himself the question, *What* is it that I propose to myself to effect in the result?

Is the House of Commons to be re-constructed on the principle of a representation of interests, or of a delegation of men? If on the former, we may, perhaps, see our way; if on the latter, you can never, in reason, stop short of universal suffrage; and in that case, I am sure that women have as good a right to vote as men.[2]

(b) *Table Talk*, 20 March 1831: "Government"

Government is not founded on property, taken merely as such, in

221

the abstract; it is founded on *unequal* property; the inequality is an essential term in the position. The phrases – higher, middle, and lower classes, with reference to this point of representation – are delusive; no such divisions as classes actually exist in society. There is an indissoluble blending and interfusion of persons from top to bottom; and no man can trace a line of separation through them, except such a confessedly unmeaning and unjustifiable line of political empiricism as 10l. householders.[3] I cannot discover a ray of principle in the government plan, – not a hint of the effect of the change upon the balance of the estates of the realm, – not a remark on the nature of the constitution of England, and the character of the property of so many millions of its inhabitants. Half the wealth of this country is purely artificial, – existing only in and on the credit given to it by the integrity and honesty of the nation.[4] This property appears, in many instances, a heavy burthen to the numerical majority of the people, and they believe that it causes all their distress: and they are now to have the maintenance of this property committed to their good faith – the lamb to the wolves!

(c) *Table Talk*, 25 June 1831: "Popular Representation"

. . . In that imperfect state of society in which our system of representation began, the interests of the country were pretty exactly commensurate with its municipal divisions. The counties, the towns, and the seaports, accurately enough represented the only interests then existing; that is to say, – the landed, the shop-keeping or manufacturing, and the mercantile. But for a century past, at least, this division has become notoriously imperfect, some of the most vital interests of the empire being now totally unconnected with any English localities. Yet now, when the evil and the want are known, we are to abandon the accommodations which the necessity of the case had worked out for itself, and begin again with a rigidly territorial plan of representation![5] The miserable tendency of all is to destroy our nationality, which consists, in a principal degree, in our representative government, and to convert it into a degrading delegation of the populace. There is no unity for a people but in a representation of national interests; a delegation from the passions or wishes of the individuals themselves is a rope of sand.

Undoubtedly it is a great evil, that there should be such an evident discrepancy between the law and the practice of the constitution in the matter of the representation. Such a direct, yet clandestine, contravention of solemn resolutions and established laws is immoral, and greatly injurious to the cause of legal loyalty and general subordination in the minds of the people. But then a statesman should consider that these very contraventions of law in practice point out to him the places in the body politic which need a remodelling of the law. You acknowledge a certain necessity for indirect representation in the present day, and that such representation has been instinctively obtained by means contrary to law; why then do you not approximate the useless law to the useful practice, instead of abandoning both law and practice for a completely new system of your own?

(d) *Table Talk*, 20 November 1831: "Conduct of Ministers on the Reform Bill. – The Multitude"

The present ministers have, in my judgment, been guilty of two things pre-eminently wicked, *sensu politico*, in their conduct upon this Reform Bill. First, they have endeavoured to carry a fundamental change in the material and mode of action of the government of the country by so exciting the passions, and playing upon the necessary ignorance of the numerical majority of the nation, that all freedom and utility of discussion, by competent heads, in the proper place, should be precluded. In doing this they have used, or sanctioned the use of, arguments which may be applied with equal or even greater force to the carrying of any measure whatever, no matter how atrocious in its character or destructive in its consequences. They have appealed directly to the argument of the greater number of voices, no matter whether the utterers were drunk or sober, competent or not competent; and they have done the utmost in their power to rase out the sacred principle in politics of a representation of interests, and to introduce the mad and barbarizing scheme of a delegation of individuals. And they have done all this without one word of thankfulness to God for the manifold blessings of which the constitution as settled at the Revolution, imperfect as it may be, has been the source or vehicle or condition to this great nation, – without one honest statement of the manner in which the anomalies in the practice grew up, or any manly declaration of the inevitable necessities of government which those anomalies have met. With no humility, nor fear, nor reverence, like Ham the accursed, they have beckoned, with grinning faces, to a vulgar mob, to come and insult over the nakedness of a parent; when it had become them, if one spark of filial patriotism had burnt within their breasts, to have marched with silent steps and averted faces to lay their robes upon his destitution!

Secondly, they have made the *king* the prime mover in all this political wickedness:[6] they have made the *king* tell his people that they were deprived of their rights, and, by direct and necessary implication, that they and their ancestors for a century past had been slaves: they have made the king vilify the memory of his own brother and father. Rights! There are no rights whatever without corresponding duties. Look at the history of the growth of our constitution, and you will see that our ancestors never upon any occasion stated, as a ground for claiming any of their privileges, an abstract right inherent in themselves; you will nowhere in our parliamentary records find the miserable sophism of the Rights of Man. No! they were too wise for that. They took good care to refer their claims to custom and prescription, and boldly – sometimes very impudently – asserted them upon traditionary and constitutional grounds. The Bill is bad enough, God knows; but the arguments of its advocates, and the manner of their advocacy, are a thousand times worse than the Bill itself; and you will live to think so.

I am far, very far, from wishing to indulge in any vulgar abuse of the vulgar. I believe that the feeling of the multitude will, in most cases, be in favour of something good; but this it is which I perceive, that they are always under the domination of some one feeling or view; – whereas truth, and above all, practical wisdom, must be the result of a wide comprehension of the more and the less, the balance and the counterbalance.

(e) *Table Talk*, 22 February 1832: "Ministers and the Reform Bill"

I could not help smiling, in reading the report of Lord Grey's speech in the House of Lords, the other night, when he asked

Lord Wicklow whether he seriously believed that he, Lord Grey, or any of the ministers, intended to subvert the institutions of the country. Had I been in Lord Wicklow's place, I should have been tempted to answer this question something in the following way: – "Waiving the charge in an offensive sense of personal consciousness against the noble earl, and all but one or two of his colleagues, upon my honour, and in the presence of Almighty God, I answer, Yes! You have destroyed the freedom of parliament; you have done your best to shut the door of the House of Commons to the property, the birth, the rank, the wisdom of the people, and have flung it open to their passions and their follies. You have disfranchised the gentry, and the real patriotism of the nation: you have agitated and exasperated the mob, and thrown the balance of political power into the hands of that class (the shopkeepers) which, in all countries and in all ages, has been, is now, and ever will be, the least patriotic and the least conservative of any. You are now preparing to destroy for ever the constitutional independence of the House of Lords; you are for ever displacing it from its supremacy as a co-ordinate estate of the realm; and whether you succeed in passing your bill by actually swamping our votes by a batch of new peers, or by frightening a sufficient number of us out of our opinions by the threat of one, – equally you will have superseded the triple assent which the constitution requires to the enactment of a valid law, and have left the king alone with the delegates of the populace!"

(f) *Table Talk*, 3 March 1832: "Disfranchisement"

I am afraid the Conservative party see but one half of the truth. The mere extension of the franchise is not the evil; I should be glad to see it greatly extended; – there is no harm in that *per se*; the mischief is that the franchise is nominally extended, but to such classes, and in such a manner, that a practical disfranchisement of all above, and a discontenting of all below, a favoured class are the unavoidable results.

(g) *Table Talk*, 4 April 1832: "Moral Law of Polarity"

It is curious to trace the operation of the moral law of polarity in the history of politics, religion, &c. When the maximum of one tendency has been attained, there is no gradual decrease, but a direct transition to its minimum, till the opposite tendency has attained its maximum; and then you see another corresponding revulsion. With the Restoration came in all at once the mechanico-corpuscular philosophy, which, with the increase of manufactures, trade, and arts, made every thing in philosophy, religion, and poetry objective; till, at length, attachment to mere external worldliness and forms got to its maximum, – when out burst the French revolution: and with it every thing became immediately subjective, without any object at all. The Rights of Man, the Sovereignty of the People, were subject and object both. We are now, I think, on the turning point again. This Reform seems the *ne plus ultra* of that tendency of the public mind which substitutes its own undefined notions or passions for real objects and historical actualities. There is not one of the ministers – except the one or two revolutionists among them – who has ever given us a hint, throughout this long struggle, as to *what* he really does believe will be the product of the bill; what sort of House of Commons it will make for the purpose of governing this empire soberly and safely. No; they have actualized for a moment a wish, a fear, a passion, but not an idea.

(h) *Table Talk*, 21 May 1832: "Professor Park. – English Constitution. – Democracy"

Professor Park talks about its being very *doubtful* whether the constitution described by Blackstone ever in fact existed.[7] In the same manner, I suppose, it is doubtful whether the moon is made of green cheese, or whether the souls of Welchmen do, in point of fact, go to heaven on the backs of mites. Blackstone's was the age of shallow law. Monarchy, aristocracy, and democracy, as *such*, exclude each the other: but if the elements are to interpenetrate, how absurd to call a lump of sugar, hydrogen, oxygen, and carbon! nay, to take three lumps, and call the first, hydrogen: the second, oxygen; and the third, carbon! Don't you see that each is in all, and all in each?

The democracy of England, before the Reform Bill, was, where it ought to be, in the corporations, the vestries, the joint-stock companies, &c. The power, in a democracy, is in focal points, without a centre; and in proportion as such democratical power is strong, the strength of the central government ought to be intense – otherwise the nation will fall to pieces.

We have just now incalculably increased the democratical action of the people, and, at the same time, weakened the executive power of the government. . . .

(i) The Reform Bill in Caricature (letter of 1832)[8]

. . . I should like to suggest to some Artists what seems to me no bad subject for a Caricature – viz. the REFORM BILL, allegorized as a Loco-motive Steam-Engine, with all it's smoke & fury – & a long train of Waggons, carts, &c dragged on by it, one or two huge Caravans containing the ministerial Majorities, &c – while on the road two or three poor Devils, – the Church, chancery, the Colonial Interests, &c – symbolically characterized, lie with broken limbs – Each of the Waggons should represent some one of the dead weights, and dead blunders of the present Ministry – Belgium, Holland, Portugal, Irish Tythes, Miss *Budget* with Lord Althorp pouting, Deficient Revenues – &c &c – all dragged on, with a *broken* rail-road, or perhaps, with the title, the Steam-Engine *run mad*, over hedge & ditch, toward a precipice – between which and the loco-motive-Engine, with Brougham & Durham atop of it, should be seen part of a herd of swine, the ᴄne fronting the Engine & the Train with a Devil across his Rump, & half a Devil, with tail & legs *below*, as half-entered into the Pig. . . .

Notes

Introduction

1. Kathleen Coburn's succinct summary of Coleridge's achievements runs thus: 'Author of *The Ancient Mariner* and other unforgettable poems. Great literary critic, psychologist, philosopher, theologian, lecturer, journalist, constructive critic of church and state . . .' – Kathleen Coburn (ed.), *Coleridge: A Collection of Critical Essays* (Englewood Cliffs, NJ, 1967) p. 2.
2. See for example C. V. Le Grice, 'College Reminiscences of Mr. Coleridge', *Gentleman's Magazine*, n.s., II (1834) 605–7. On Unitarianism at Jesus College see J. C. D. Clark, *English Society, 1688–1832* (Cambridge, 1985) pp. 313–14; and Frida Knight, *University Rebel: The Life of William Frend 1751–1841* (1971) chs 1–2.
3. *Religious Musings* is particularly marked by millenarian themes; see Clarke Garrett, *Respectable Folly* (Baltimore, 1975) p. 143. On the pantisocracy scheme see Sister Eugenia, 'Coleridge's Scheme of Pantisocracy and American Travel Accounts', *PMLA*, 1930, pp. 1069–84; and J. R. MacGillivray, 'The Pantisocracy Scheme and its Immediate Background', in M. W. Wallace (ed.), *Studies in English* (Toronto, 1931) pp. 131–69.
4. *Life and Correspondence of Robert Southey*, ed. C. C. Southey, 6 vols (1849–51) I, 221.
5. See Frank E. and Fritzie P. Manuel, *Utopian Thought in the Western World* (Cambridge, Mass., 1979) p. 736.
6. Six out of sixteen volumes of the Princeton *Collected Works* are wholly or mainly made up of social and political writings.
7. For Coleridge's Unitarianism see J. Robert Barth, *Coleridge and Christian Doctrine* (Cambridge, Mass., 1969) ch. 1; and Basil Willey, *Samuel Taylor Coleridge* (1972) chs 2 and 3.
8. This appeared in the Prospectus for the 'Lectures on Revealed Religion'; see *Lectures 1795*, p. 83.
9. Ibid., pp. 215ff.
10. See the Introduction to *Lectures 1795*, pp. lviii–lxxx; and Leonard W. Deen, 'Coleridge and the Sources of Pantisocracy: Godwin, the Bible and Hartley', *Boston University Studies in English*, 5 (1961) 232–45.
11. See note 9.
12. See below, p. 33.
13. This seems to be John Colmer's position in *Coleridge: Critic of Society* (Oxford, 1959) pp. 12–30, and also that of the editors of *Lectures 1795* (see pp. xxi–xxxiii). Cf. Marilyn Butler, *Romantics, Rebels and Reactionaries* (Oxford, 1981) pp. 77–8; David V. Erdman, 'Coleridge as Editorial Writer', in Conor Cruise O'Brien and William Dean Vanech (eds), *Power and Consciousness* (New York, 1969) pp. 183–5; Nicholas Roe, *Coleridge and Wordsworth: The Radical Years* (Oxford, 1988); E. P.

Thompson, 'Disenchantment or Default?', ibid., pp. 149–81. The discussion below seeks to establish a sense in which Coleridge's early writings were radical in terms of the context in which they were produced.

14. The radical implications of Unitarianism in the context of the late eighteenth century are discussed in Clark's important study, *English Society, 1688–1832*, pp. 277ff.

15. Joseph Priestley, *An Essay on the First Principles of Government, and on the Nature of Political, Civil and Religious Liberty* (1768), cited by Clark in *English Society*, p. 334; Edmund Burke, *Reflections on the Revolution in France* (1790), Penguin edn (Harmondsworth, 1968) p. 96ff.

16. See below, p. 26.

17. Cf. *Lectures 1795*, p. 5, note 3.

18. See below, pp. 29–32.

19. On the importance of hierarchy in English thought at this time see Clark, *English Society*, ch. 4. Horsley's remark is quoted by Coleridge in *Lectures 1795*, p. 285; it was made in the House of Lords on 11 Nov 1795. Samuel Horsley (1733–1806) was Bishop of St David's at the time, but was later translated to the sees of Rochester and St. Asaphs.

20. See below, pp. 38–40.

21. See below, pp. 37–8.

22. On the anti-war movement see John Cookson, *The Friends of Peace* (Cambridge, 1982) *passim*; on Frend see Knight, *University Rebel*, ch. 8.

23. See below, p. 43.

24. See below, pp. 26–7.

25. See below, pp. 45–6.

26. See Willey, *Samuel Taylor Coleridge*, pp. 113ff.

27. See below, pp. 54ff.

28. Erdman, 'Coleridge as Editorial Writer', in O'Brien and Vanech, *Power and Consciousness*, p. 185. See also Thompson, 'Disenchantment or Default?'.

29. See below, pp. 54–5.

30. On this tradition see J. G. A. Pocock, *The Machiavellian Moment* (Princeton, NJ, 1974) chs 11–12; and for Coleridge's place in it see John Morrow, 'The National Church in Coleridge's *Church and State*: A Response to Allen', *JHI*, 47 (1986) 640–7.

31. See below, p. 62.

32. See below, p. 68.

33. See below, pp. 77–8; and Morrow, 'The National Church', pp. 644–7.

34. *CL*, III, 143 (14 Aug 1808).

35. *Friend*, II, 140. The best account of *The Friend* is Deirdre Coleman, *Coleridge and 'The Friend' (1809–10)* (Oxford, 1988).

36. See below, p. 92.

37. See below, p. 85n.

38. *Friend*, II, 137.

39. Coleridge claimed that the ends of government were of 'two kinds, negative and positive. The negative ends . . . are the protection of Life, of personal Freedom, of Property, of Reputation and of Religion, from foreign and from domestic attacks. The positive ends are, 1st. to

make the means of subsistence more easy to each individual: 2d. that in addition to the necessaries of life he should derive from the union and division of labour a share of the comforts and conveniences, which humanize and ennoble his nature; and at the same time the power of perfecting himself in his own branch of industry by having those things which he needs, provided for him by others among his fellow-citizens; including the tools and raw or manufactured materials, necessary for his own Employment. . . . 3rdly. The hope of bettering his own condition and that of his children. . . . [Lastly] the development of those faculties which are essential to his human nature by the knowledge of his moral and religious duties, and the increase of his intellectual powers in as great a degree as is compatible with the other ends of the social union, and does not involve a contradiction' (*Friend*, II 201–2). See also *A Lay Sermon*, below, p. 143. John Colmer regards Coleridge's statement of positive ends for government as one of the most important features of his theory; see his 'Coleridge and Politics', in R. L. Brett (ed.), *S. T. Coleridge* (1972) pp. 258–9.

40. I am indebted to Mark Francis for this interpretation of Paley, which explains why Coleridge treated him with Hobbes; see 'Paley's Naturalism', *History of European Ideas*, 10 (1989) 203–20. Francis agrees with Coleridge about Paley's politics, but not his moral theory.
41. See below, p. 95.
42. See *Friend*, II, 132; and *CN*, III, no. 3835.
43. See R. J. White's Introduction to *LS*, pp. xli–xlii; and Arthur S. Link, 'Samuel Taylor Coleridge and the Economic and Political Crisis in Great Britain', *JHI*, 9 (1948) 323–38.
44. *LS*, pp. 29, 25, 17, 105–7.
45. See below, p. 117n. For arguments about commerce and freedom see Pocock, *The Machiavellian Moment*, chs 13–14.
46. See below, pp. 117ff.
47. See below, p. 118.
48. See below, pp. 138ff., and also *CL*, IV, 710, where Coleridge describes the gentry as Jacobinism's '*Quality Cousin*'.
49. See below, pp. 119ff.
50. See below, p. 129.
51. See John Colmer's Introduction to *C & S*, pp. xxxv–xxxvii; this essay, and Colmer's earlier discussion in *Coleridge: Critic of Society*, p. 153ff., are the best treatments of Coleridge's arguments. See also David P. Calleo, *Coleridge and the Idea of the Modern State* (New Haven, Conn., 1966); and Nigel Leask, *The Politics of Imagination in Coleridge's Critical Thought* (1988).
52. See below, p. 154.
53. See below, pp. 161ff.
54. *C & S*, p. 31, n. 2.
55. Unpublished Notebook 44, ff.75–6 (c. 1830), cited in *C & S*, p. lx.
56. See below, p. 172.
57. See below, pp. 198ff.
58. See below, pp. 204ff.
59. See below, p. 166.

60. See below, p. 168.
61. See below, pp. 77, 172, 184. See also *CL*, II, pp. 803 and 806.
62. See below, p. 173.
63. See below, pp. 212ff.
64. See below, p. 213.
65. *Table Talk*, p. 110 (19 Sep 1830).
66. See below, pp. 180–1.
67. *C & S*, pp. xxxvi–xxxviii.
68. John Stuart Mill, 'Coleridge', in *Mill on Bentham and Coleridge*, ed. F. R. Leavis (1967) pp. 99–100.
69. For a fuller statement of this interpretation see the concluding chapter of John Morrow, *Coleridge's Political Thought: Property, Morality and the Limits of Traditional Discourse* (1990).

Chapter 1   The Politics of Radical Religion: The Bristol Lectures of 1795

1. This work contains revised versions of material used by Coleridge in his Bristol lectures of early 1795. For full details of delivery and publication see *Lectures 1795*, pp. 22–4.
2. See below, p. 33.
3. This motto appears originally in Greek; the present translation is Coleridge's – see *Friend*, I, 326. The editors of *Lectures 1795* have been unable to trace the source of the motto.
4. An allusion to Arthur Young's *The Example of France, a Warning to Britain* (1793).
5. Milton, *Samson Agonistes*, ll. 1649–54 (modified).
6. Originally based on a deputation from the Gironde, this group, led by J. P. Brissot (1754–93), formed a focus for moderate members of the French National Assembly. The Girondists clashed with the extreme republican group, the Jacobins, led by Maximilien de Robespierre (1758–94). By the summer of 1793 the Jacobins were portraying the Girondists as a significant and cohesive party which threatened the popular forces of the Revolution. Brissot and many other Girondists were executed in Oct 1793 during a Jacobin-inspired purge of 'enemies of the Revolution'.
7. Milton, *Paradise Regained*, III, ll. 52–3; *Samson Agonistes*, ll. 1265–6, 1039–40.
8. That is, those who supported the existing political, social and ecclesiastical structures and opposed reform.
9. 'Constitutionalists' shared Montesquieu's admiration for the British Constitution. 'Dough-baked': 'imperfect, badly finished . . . feeble' (*OED*).
10. Milton, *Paradise Lost*, I, 10.
11. In July 1791 a Birmingham 'Church and King' mob burned down the houses of the Unitarian and scientist Joseph Priestley, and a number of other leading Dissenters.

12. William Godwin, *Enquiry Concerning Political Justice*, 2 vols (1793) I, 207.
13. Godwin assumed that 'private attachments' blinded individuals to the requirements of universal benevolence.
14. See above, p. 3. According to the 'Principle of Association', ideas came into the mind either from an external stimuli, or because they were linked to ideas that already existed there.
15. From Brissot de Warville (alias J. P. Brissot; see note 6 above), *New Travels in the United States Performed in 1788* (Dublin, 1792) pp. xvi–xvii. Coleridge and Southey used Brissot's work as a source of information about North America when planning their pantisocratic settlement.
16. An adaptation of St Paul's words in 1 Corinthians 16:13–14.
17. This pamphlet is based on material which was originally used in a lecture given in February 1795. The version printed here is abridged.
18. 'Six Lectures on Revealed Religion, Its Corruptions and Political Views', *Lectures 1795*.
19. Fast days were proclaimed during the war in order to seek God's blessing for the British war effort.
20. William Crowe, 'Verses Intended to Have Been Spoken in the Theatre to the Duke of Portland at His Installation as Chancellor of the University of Oxford, in the Year 1793', *Lewesdon Hill . . . with Other Poems* (1804) pp. 60–1.
21. In response to a motion put by the Duke of Bedford in the House of Lords, 27 Jan 1795.
22. In a letter of May 1793 Samuel Horsley, Bishop of St Asaph's, had instructed his clergy to aid and assist refugee priests from France. He claimed that they were more worthy of brotherly treatment than many Protestant Dissenters, who used a concern for civil liberty as a cloak for the advancement of radical political and religious notions. An extract from Horsley's letter is printed in *Lectures 1795*, p. 210 n. 1.
23. Richard Hurd, *A Discourse, by Way of General Preface to . . . Bishop Warburton's Works, Containing Some Account of the Life, Writings, and Character of the Author* (1794). Hurd was Bishop of Worcester.
24. Catholics, Dissenters and especially Unitarians were subject to a variety of penalties under the Test and Corporation Acts. 'Benefit of clergy' allowed those who could claim it to escape some penalties for criminal actions; the traditional test was of the individual's ability to read.
25. Sir William Blackstone, *Commentaries on the Laws of England*, 4 vols (1783) I, 171.
26. The large-scale expenditure of funds on either direct bribery, electoral expenses or the provision of public utilities was common in eighteenth-century elections.
27. William Paley, *The Principles of Moral and Political Philosophy*, 2 vols (1794) II, 220–1. The last sentence is a paraphrase, not a direct quotation. Coleridge's information on representation was derived from *The State of the Representation of England, Scotland, and Wales . . .* (1793) pp. 36–9.

28. Paley (1743–1805) is reputed to have made the remark in excusing himself from signing a petition against the rule that those taking a degree at Oxford or Cambridge should subscribe to the Thirty-Nine Articles of the Church of England. Paley was actually sympathetic to the cause, but depended on the University, and hence also the Church, for his livelihood; he was a fellow and tutor of Christ's College Cambridge, and Archdeacon of Carlisle (*DNB*). The story is recounted in *Lectures 1795*, pp. 310–11, n. 3.
29. See above, Introduction, pp. 6–7 and note 30.
30. James Burgh, *Political Disquisitions*, 3 vols (1776–8) III, pp. 438–9.

Chapter 2   The Retreat from Radicalism, 1798–1802

1. *CL*, I, 395–7 (10 Mar 1798).
2. 1 Kings 19:11–13.
3. This poem was later retitled 'France: An Ode'.
4. *Morning Post*, 7, 26, 27, 31 Dec 1799. Abridged. The relevant details of the new constitution are as follows. The executive was to be made up of three consuls, of whom Napoleon was the first; he had the exclusive right to appoint and dismiss members of the Council of State, ministers, ambassadors, military and naval officers, and members of the national and local systems of administration. The other two consuls had advisory functions only. There was to be a Senate which would eventually contain eighty members; the original thirty-one members were appointed by the consuls, and these men then selected a further twenty-nine members. Two additional members were to be added each year until the full complement was reached. The Senate's major role was to select a hundred-member Tribunate, and a Corps Législatif of 300, from lists produced by a complex system of indirect elections in cantons, municipalities, districts and departments. A tenth of the candidates at each stage moved on to the next list; the Senate selected members of the legislative chambers from the final lists. The Tribunate could discuss legislation and accept or reject it, but had no powers of amendment. The Législatif could not discuss legislative measures; it merely voted on proposals sent to it by the Tribunate. These details are taken from Owen Connelly, *French Revolution: Napoleonic Era* (New York, 1979), pp. 214–15.
5. Emanuel Joseph Sieyès (1748–1836), an abbé in pre-revolutionary France, was famous in the 1790s for his constitution-framing.
6. 'Ephorism': the supervision exercised by Spartan magistrates (ephors) over the king.
7. That is, the process of election whereby a tenth of the participants at any one stage were elected to advance to the next stage as delegates; see note 4 above.
8. *Morning Chronicle*, 26 Dec 1798. Erdman writes that Coleridge 'somewhat misrepresented' this paper's remarks; see *EOT*, I, 51, n. 6.
9. See also *A Lay Sermon*, below, p. 118.
10. Coleridge's support for a free press appeared in his earliest and latest

political writings: see *The Plot Discovered*, above, pp. 47–8; and *Church and State*, below, p. 165.

11. A series of three articles appeared in four issues of the *Morning Post*, on 21, 25, 29 Sep and 2 Oct 1802. The material printed here is abridged from the first two articles.

12. On the commercial spirit see also *A Lay Sermon*, below, pp. 118ff., and *Church and State*, below, pp. 189–90. Coleridge generally used the term 'commerce' to convey a broader range of activities than is now usually embraced by it. It included not only the production and/or distribution of goods and services, but also involvement in the system of debt-funding of government activities that had developed during the eighteenth century, and in the provision of other services to the government and its agencies, particularly the armed forces. For similar uses of the term see J. G. A. Pocock, *The Machiavellian Moment* (Princeton, NJ, 1974) chs 13–14. Coleridge's 'spirit of commerce' describes the sort of concern with maximising financial returns that is usually associated with capitalism; this use of the term is particularly apparent in *A Lay Sermon* and *Church and State* – see below, pp. 118ff., 189–90.

13. Coleridge's point here is obscure, but he seems to be claiming that, because 'republics' are based on a wide suffrage, property is widely distributed, and hence agrarian laws (which set a maximum on land-holdings and redistributed the balance to the landless) are necessary to re-establish the material basis of a 'republic'. A 'society', by contrast, contains wide variations in property-holding and a corresponding differentiation of political power and function; in that context, an agrarian law would undermine the social and economic basis of such a society.

14. By the terms of the Act of Union of 1707 it was decided that there was to be one parliament for the United Kingdoms of England and Scotland. Scotland was to be represented in the House of Lords by sixteen members of the Scottish peerage chosen by the peers themselves, and in the House of Commons by forty-five members elected by the Scottish shires and burghs.

15. The article originally appeared in the *Morning Post* for 21 Oct 1802; Coleridge used a modified version in *The Friend*. The title alludes to a remark attributed to William Pitt: a 'mind tainted by Jacobinism can never be wholly free from that taint'. See *EOT*, i, 367, n. 2.

16. Cf. 'On the French Constitution', above, pp. 54–5.

17. *CL*, ii, 803 and 805–6 (3 June and 1 July 1802). These letters also appear in *Unpublished Letters of Samuel Taylor Coleridge*, ed. Earl Leslie Griggs, 2 vols (1932) i, 198, 200–1.

18. In some late-seventeenth- and eighteenth-century arguments 'Standing Armies', which existed during peace time and were made up of professionals, were seen as a threat to the Constitution. They provided the Crown with an independent coercive capacity that was removed from the control of the landed classes, who were seen as forming the backbone of Parliament and the best defenders of the Constitution.

See John Morrow, 'The National Church in Coleridge's *Church and State*: A Response to Allen', *JHI*, 47 (1986) 646–7.
19. See also *Church and State*, below, pp. 77, 172, 184.

Chapter 3   Principles and Prudence in Politics: *The Friend* (1809–10)

1. *The Friend* first appeared in a periodical form in 1809–10; it was reprinted in 1812 and again in 1818 in a much revised and rearranged 'rifacciamento', although in these editions the sections printed below remained unchanged in substance. The text here follows that of the 1809–10 edition adopted here. These selections are abridged.
2. That is, contrary to sense and reason (*OED*).
3. Robert Burns, 'The Author's Earnest Cry and Prayer', ll. 163–74 (modified).
4. Shakespeare, *Hamlet*, iii.i.83 (modified).
5. Sir Alexander Ball (1757–1809), Rear Admiral, British High Commissioner of Malta 1801–9 (*DNB*). In 1804–5 Coleridge served first as Under-Secretary to Ball and then as Acting Public Secretary in the administration of Malta; see Donald Sultana, *Samuel Taylor Coleridge in Malta and Sicily* (1969).
6. The response to Hobbes is a gloss on a more involved statement by James Harrington in his *Oceana* (1656); see *The Political Writings of James Harrington*, ed. J. G. A. Pocock (Cambridge, 1977) p. 165.
7. See also *Church and State*, below, pp. 154–6, where Coleridge offers a similar account of the significance of the idea of social contract. The band-of-robbers analogy is found in St Augustine's *City of God*; see *The City of God*, ed. David Knowles (Harmondsworth, 1972) iv.iv: 'Remove justice, and what are kingdoms but gangs of criminals on a large scale' (p. 139).
8. The distinction between reason and understanding was a very important one for Coleridge; it is dealt with on a number of occasions in *The Friend*. Basil Willey's elaboration of the distinction is very useful: 'Reason seeks ultimate ends; Understanding studies means. Reason is the "source and substance of truths above sense"; Understanding, the faculty which judges "according to sense". Reason is the eye of the spirit, the faculty whereby spiritual reality is spiritually discerned; Understanding is the "mind of the flesh"' – *Nineteenth Century Studies* (1949); *Samuel Taylor Coleridge* (1972) p. 128.
9. The physiocrats developed a social philosophy that rested heavily on their observations about behaviour in capitalist economies; their philosophy was utilitarian in character and they were much concerned with formulating a role for professional administrators. They looked to free competition to advance human perfectibility, and thought of the state as a 'legal despot' whose role was to maintain security, guarantee property rights and establish and maintain the conditions for free competition. Foremost among the physiocrats were Dr Quesnay and Mercier de la Rivière; Turgot, the King's Minister just prior

to the Revolution of 1789, was also a member of the school.
10. See 'Once a Jacobin', above, pp. 72–6.
11. Coleridge's main target here is, as the title suggests, Rousseau, but his account of that philosopher's work, and especially his favourable comments on aspects of it, are marked by Kantian language.
12. See above, note 8.
13. Shakespeare, *Troilus and Cressida*, i.iii.122–9.
14. J. J. Rousseau, *Du contrat social* (1762) i.vi.
15. Ibid., ii.iii.
16. Rousseau is here glossed in the language of Kant: 'There is therefore only a single categorical imperative and it is this: *"Act only on that maxim through which you can at the same time will that it should become a universal law"* – *The Moral Law: Kant's Groundwork of the Metaphysics of Morals*, tr. H. J. Paton (1972) p. 84.
17. 'I mean, practically and with the inequalities inseparable from the actual existence of Property. Abstractedly, the Right to Property is deducible from the Free-agency of man. If to act freely be a Right, a *sphere* of action must be so too.' This note is an addition from the 1818 edition; see *Friend*, i, 200.
18. From John Cartwright, *The People's Barrier againt Undue Influence* (1780) p. 7. The rest of the paragraph summarises Cartwright. Major John Cartwright (1740–1824) had been involved in the Yorkshire Petitioning Movement in the 1780s, and continued to have an active interest in a reform of the parliamentary franchise. He was an advocate of annual parliaments, universal suffrage and the secret ballot. On Coleridge's view of Cartwright as a 'state moralist', see above, Introduction, p. 11.
19. The Levellers of the Civil War period in seventeenth-century England did not in fact believe in the equality of property, but smaller groups, one of which was known as 'True Levellers' or 'Diggers', did.

Chapter 4   Property and Responsibility: *A Lay Sermon* (1817)

1. Originally published in 1817, this sermon was the second in a projected series of three; the first, *The Statesman's Manual or The Bible; the Best Guide to Political Skill and Foresight: A Lay Sermon Addressed to the Higher Classes of Society*, was published in 1816, while the third (to be addressed to 'the lower and labouring Classes of society') was never written. These sermons were set against the background of economic dislocation and widespread hardship and discontent which followed the end of the war in 1815; for an account of this context see R. J. White's Introduction to *LS*. The version produced here is slightly abridged. The text for the sermon is from Isaiah 32:20. Coleridge's *Courier* articles 'To Mr. Justice Fletcher' (1814) and 'Children in the Cotton Factories' (1818), for which see *EOT*, ii, 373ff. and 473ff., are useful supplements to the work printed below.
2. The first motto is partly a translation of, and partly an improvisation on Heraclitus in Theodoret, *Opera* (Paris, 1642) iv, 716; the second is

adapted from Fulke Greville, *A Treatise of Warres*, stanzas 66–7, in *Certaine Learned and Elegant Works* (1633) p. 82.

3. This note nicely summarises the argument of *The Statesman's Manual*; there is a very interesting discussion of this work in R. J. White's Introduction to *The Political Tracts of Wordsworth, Coleridge and Shelley* (Cambridge, 1953).

4. Proverbial; originally in Latin, the translation is taken from *LS*, pp. 123–4, n. 5.

5. Cf. Romans 2:1; 1 Peter 3:15; 1 Corinthians 10:31; Colossians 3:17, 23.

6. See *Friend*, II, 28.

7. Isaiah in 2 Kings 19:30 and Isaiah 37:31 (modified).

8. Hebrews 5:12 (modified).

9. A reference to *The Statesman's Manual*; see above, note 3.

10. Isaiah 22:5; 24:16.

11. Coleridge concluded the Introduction with a version of an 'Allegoric Vision' which had been used in the 'Lectures on Revealed Religion' and in a number of his other writings; see *LS*, pp. 131–2 n. 1, for details. The allegory (which contrasts true religion with the sensuality and blasphemy of atheism and the superstition and mystery of religions such as Roman Catholicism) was designed to 'guard myself and my Readers from extremes of all kinds' (p. 131).

12. Adapted from Jeremiah 8:11, 15.

13. Isaiah 32:5–8 (modified).

14. Revelation 9:3–10.

15. Adapted from Fulke Greville, *Alaham*, LI, 72, in *Workes* (1633).

16. Jeremiah 23:15. The particular targets of Coleridge's remarks here have been identified as Samuel Whitbread MP, the journalist William Cobbett, Henry ('Orator') Hunt, Horne Tooke and Henry Brougham MP; see *LS*, pp. 144–5 and nn.

17. 1 John 3:15 (modified).

18. Ecclesiastes 10:13 (modified).

19. Cf. *Conciones ad Populum*, above, p. 32.

20. Exodus 12:8 (modified).

21. Ecclesiastes 1:9 (modified).

22. Isaiah 32:6.

23. Adapted from Milton, *Paradise Lost*, IV, 804, 802–3, 806–8. Coleridge listed eleven components that made up the poison offered to the public by radical reformers and publicists: they include a general disregard for, or misuse of, facts; the use of facts divorced from their context; a concentration on and condemnation of disadvantages (especially those of a short-term kind); complete disregard for advantages of existing social and political arrangements; and the use of language that veers between flattering *bonhomie* and manipulative superiority. For Coleridge's full list see *LS*, pp. 152–5.

24. Jeremiah 9:3, 8; 23:26, 32, 16, 15; 5:31.

25. That is, poetry. The defence of taxation which follows is based upon the essay 'On the Vulgar Errors Respecting Tales and Taxation', which appeared in *Friend* (I, 159ff.).

26. The image of occupied tables first appeared in the Revd Thomas

Malthus's *Essay on Population;* see *An Essay on the Principle of Population,*
2nd edn (1803) p. 531.

27. At this point the second edition included a reference to 'cash
    payments' – that is, to payments in gold rather than in paper currency.
28. Adapted from Numbers 16:46; Genesis 49:7; James 3:5; Ecclesiastes
    28:14.
29. On the social and political implications of credit-financing of
    government activity see *Friend,* II, 159ff.
30. See 'France and Rome', above, pp. 68–9.
31. See also *Church and State,* below, pp. 166ff.
32. This was the motto over the door of the Platonic Academy in Athens.
33. Cf. Coleridge's views in 1795; see above, pp. 38–40.
34. Taken from *Friend* I, 213.
35. Hebrews 5:12–14.
36. Ephesians 3:16, 18 (modified); 1 John 2:27.
37. Adapted from Psalm 119:34, 66, 96–7, 130, 147, 148.
38. Translation from *LS,* p. 183 n. 1; no source has been traced.
39. Source untraced by the editor of *LS.*
40. 1 John 5:5.
41. Isaiah 5:8.
42. Matthew 6:13.
43. Adapted from Milton, *The Reason of Church-Government,* II, Intro-
    duction, in *Complete Prose Works of John Milton,* 8 vols (New Haven,
    Conn., 1953) I, 803.
44. The wars of William III's reign (1689–1702) were partly financed by
    loans which were to be serviced by future taxation; this is usually
    regarded as the first systematic use of debit-financing of government
    activity, and gave rise to arguments about the growing importance of
    a 'commercial interest' in English politics; see above, Ch. 2, note 2.
45. That is, the revolution of 1688–9, the 'Glorious Revolution'.
46. That is, 1537 to 1688–9.
47. Dr John Donne (1573–1631), the poet and divine, was Dean of St
    Paul's. Jeremy Taylor (1613–67), Bishop of Down and Connor, had
    been a protégé of Archbishop Laud (*DNB*).
48. Izaak Walton (1593–1683), author of the *Lives* (subjects of which include
    Donne, and another favourite of Coleridge's, Richard Hooker) and
    The Compleat Angler (1653).
49. Source untraced.
50. Founded in 1804 by Church of England members to produce and
    distribute cheap, accurate copies of the Bible.
51. Syncretists aimed to reconcile all theological differences between
    Lutherans, Calvinists and Roman Catholics.
52. John Milton, *Paradise Lost,* II, 929–31, 932–3.
53. This could refer to Adam Smith's *An Inquiry into the Nature and Causes
    of the Wealth of Nations* (1776) I. vii, viii.
54. 'Bristled bear': a species of barley; 'pink haver': a species of oats.
55. Cf. above, pp. 229–30.
56. See Coleridge's earlier claims about the necessary relationship between
    property and free agency: *Friend,* above, p. 236, note 18.

57. *The Agricultural State of the Kingdom, in February, March and April, 1816; Being the Substance of the Replies to a Circular Letter Sent by the Board of Agriculture to Every Part of the Kingdom* (1816).
58. See previous note.

Chapter 5   The Idea of the Constitution: *On the Constitution of the Church and State, According to the Idea of Each* (1829)

1. The present work was published in Dec 1829, and thus, while it was occasioned by the debate over Catholic emancipation, it appeared after the issue had been settled. Coleridge began working on this material in 1825 when an Emancipation Bill was introduced into the Commons by the radical Sir Francis Burdett. The 'absent friend' mentioned in the first paragraph is John Hookham Frere (1769–1846), a Cambridge contemporary of Coleridge who was a resident of Malta but had visited England in 1825–6. For a full account of the development of *Church and State* see John Colmer's Introduction to *C & S*. The version produced here is slightly abridged; it follows the second edition of 1830. Two further sections ('On the Third Possible Church, or The Church of Anti-Christ' and 'Aids to a Right Appreciation of the Act Admitting Roman Catholics to Sit in Both Houses of Parliament') have been omitted.
2. Adapted from Shakespeare, *Troilus and Cressida*, III.iii. 202–5.
3. 10 Geo. IV c. 7: 'An Act for the relief of His Majesty's Roman Catholic subjects'. Introduced in the House of Commons by Sir Robert Peel on 5 Mar 1829, and in the Lords by the Duke of Wellington on the last day of the month; it received the royal assent on 13 Apr 1829.
4. The issue of securities was crucial in the consideration of Catholic emancipation, since it raised the question of how the Church of England was to be protected when the legislature that controlled it included adherents of a hostile faith. Coleridge thought that the Church would not be endangered provided that the granting of political rights to Roman Catholics was conditional upon a declaration that they would not seek to deprive the Church of its property; see 'Aids', *C & S*, 149ff.
5. Not in Bacon.
6. See also *Friend*, above, p. 83.
7. See also above, pp. 88–9.
8. Edinburgh was, of course, associated with the *Edinburgh Review*; there were well-known dissenting institutions at Hackney. Jonathan Edwards (1703–58) was the author of *Enquiry into . . . Freedom of Will* (1754); Alexander Crombie (1762–1840) wrote *A Defence of Philosophic Necessity* (1793); and William Lawrence (1783–1867) was the author of *On the Physiology, Zoology, and Natural History of Man* (1819), which was regarded as materialistic and atheistic. On these men see *C & S*, pp. 17–18, nn. 3–5.
9. St Augustine, *Confessions*, XI.xiv.
10. Thomas Paine, *The Rights of Man* (1792), II.iv.

11. High Church Tories were reluctant to accept the constitutional propriety of replacing James II by William and Mary in 1689. Coleridge's treatment of the Constitution as an idea meant that the Constitution was not necessarily damaged by a change to its form; this was his view with respect to Catholic emancipation.

12. From Sir John Davies, *Irish Reports* (1615), and Andrew Horn, *The Mirrour of Justices* (1646). Coleridge's use of Davies makes his position sound similar to the form of 'ancient constitutionalism' found in Edmund Burke – see J. G. A Pocock, 'Burke and the Ancient Constitution: A Problem in the History of Ideas', *Politics, Language and Time* (New York, 1971) pp. 202–32 – but in fact Coleridge's idea of the Constitution is far less static than Burke's; see J. D. Coates, 'Coleridge's Debt to Harrington: A Discussion of *Zapolya*', *JHI*, 38 (1977) 501–8.

13. See Spinoza, *Tractatus politicus* (1677) vi.iii.5; in *The Political Works of Benedict de Spinoza*, tr. A. G. Wernham (Oxford, 1958) pp. 315–17.

14. Coleridge, 'Ode to the Departing Year', *PW*, i, 166–7 (var).

15. That is, the Papal States, those territories in central Italy that were under the temporal authority of the Pope; the Vatican City is the remnant of those territories, most of which were lost during the wars of Italian unification in the mid-nineteenth century and absorbed into the kingdom of Italy. The references in the following sentences to 'the Austrians' refers to the central and northern Italian principalities and duchies which were subject to the House of Habsburg.

16. See the discussion of the Jewish constitution in the 'Lectures on Revealed Religion', *Lectures 1795*, pp. 124ff.

17. Milton, *Paradise Regained*, iv, 353–62.

18. That is, the old testament or covenant, granted to the Jews by God and transmitted by Moses. It distinguished the Jews from all other races and tribes who had not been chosen to receive a dispensation from God, the purpose of which (from a Christian point of view) was to prepare for the coming of Christ. Coleridge provides a very full discussion of the Mosaic dispensation in his 'Lectures on Revealed Religion', *Lectures 1795*, pp. 89ff.

19. See also *A Lay Sermon*, above, pp. 141–2.

20. See also 'Lectures on Revealed Religion', *Lectures 1795*, pp. 125–6. The Jubilee cancelled all debts and nullified all transfers of land that had taken place in the last fifty years.

21. Sir Philip Sidney (1554–86), English humanist; see also below, note 37.

22. Based on Leviticus 25:23: 'The land is mine saith the Lord . . . .'

23. See also *CL*, ii, 803, 806; and John Morrow, 'The National Church in Coleridge's *Church and State*: A Response to Allen', *JHI*, 47 (1986) 644–7.

24. See also *Friend*, i, 216: 'in order to be men we must be patriots'.

25. The clergy were exempt from arrest to stand trial in the King's Court, and were subject solely to Church courts. Benefit of clergy was not finally abolished until 1827.

26. Sharon Turner (1768–1847), *A History of the Reign of Henry VIII* (1826).

27. The Whig Party, Nonconformists and religious sceptics associated by Coleridge with the *Edinburgh Review*.
28. Wordsworth, *The Excursion*, I, 79; *WPW*, v, p. 10.
29. Proverbs 19.18 (modified).
30. That is, Francis Sellon White, *A History of Inventions and Discoveries* (1827).
31. Ovid, *Metamorphoses*, III.110, 105; translation from *C & S*, p. 59, note 4.
32. The Society for the Suppression of Mendicity was founded in 1818 to investigate those begging for relief in order to distinguish the 'deserving' from the 'undeserving' poor or from professional beggars. It published annual reports on the cases it had dealt with.
33. Milton, *Paradise Lost*, x, 729–32 (modified).
34. Isaiah 22–3.
35. See above, note 27.
36. See also *A Lay Sermon*, above, pp. 136–7.
37. An attack on John Locke and his followers; see also *Friend*, I, 446–7, from which this is taken.
38. See also Appendix E to the *Statesman's Manual*, *LS*, pp. 101–2.
39. The people mentioned in this paragraph are Lorenzo the Magnificent (1449–92), Duke of Florence; Marsilio Ficino (1433–99), philosopher and translator of Plato; Angelo Politian (1454–94), humanist scholar; Giovanni Pico della Mirandola (1463–94), philosopher in the forefront of the revival of Platonism. The English names comprise the most important of the English humanists of the late-sixteenth and seventeenth centuries. The people listed by Coleridge are Sir Philip Sidney (1554–86), Edmund Spenser (1552–99), Algernon Sidney (1622–83), James Harrington (1611–77), and his friend and follower Henry Neville (1620–94).
40. The schoolmaster and clown in Shakespeare's *Love's Labour's Lost*.
41. Theories of the development of mankind out of primitive forms predated the Darwinian controversy of the mid-nineteenth century; see *C & S*, p. 66, n. 2, for details.
42. The Boston Port Bill of 1774 closed the Port of Boston until reparation had been made for the dumping of tea in the harbour in the notorious Boston Tea Party of December 1773. Coleridge greatly regretted the union of Britain and Ireland in 1801 on the grounds that it made Irish problems British ones. He implied that the question of Catholic emancipation would have been far less troublesome if it had been confined to Ireland, as it could have been if the Irish Parliament had not been abolished. See *Table Talk*, p. 154 (17 Dec 1831).
43. William Paley's *Principles of Moral and Political Philosophy* (1785) was adopted as a textbook at Cambridge University.
44. 'Clubs of journeymen' refers to working-class, and often radically inclined, debating societies; Coleridge also refers to various societies for promoting moral improvement that were established by Evangelicals.
45. Classical scholars used asterisks to designate corrupt or conjectural passages in texts.
46. 12 Ch. II c. 24.

47. Wordsworth, *WPW*, III, 119.
48. Niccolò Machiavelli, *The Prince*, ch. 18.
49. Coleridge, *Biographia Literaria*, *CC*, 7, ed. James Engell and W. Jackson Bate, I, 226–7.
50. Job 28:16, 18.
51. That makes it particularly important in relation to that hope which it is one of the ends of the state to foster; see *A Lay Sermon*, above, p. 142.
52. Parson Trulliber, the oafish, unlearned part-cleric, part-farmer ('a parson on Sundays, but all the other six might more properly be called a farmer') who offered to fight the mild-mannered Parson Adams in Henry Fielding's *Joseph Andrews*, II.xiv.
53. A law of 9 AD which, like an earlier one of 18 BC, discouraged celibacy and childlessness, forbade misalliances and regulated divorces. Severe penalties for celibacy were laid down in Spartan law.
54. Ovid, *Epistulae ex Ponto*, II.ix.48; translation from A. L. Wheeler's edn in the Loeb Classical Library (1924) p. 363.
55. See also *Friend*, above, pp. 94–5.
56. Samuel Butler, *Hudibras*, II.ii.29–32.
57. See above, note 44.
58. The second part of the fifth petition of the Litany in the Book of Common Prayer.
59. See above, p. 198.
60. Coleridge no doubt has in mind men such as James Harrington, Algernon and Philip Sidney, and John Milton; see above, note 39.
61. Written by Charles Dallison; for Coleridge's marginal comments on this work see *CM*, II, 113ff.
62. The Septennial Act of 1716 extended the term of Parliament from three to seven years. Coleridge objected to the fact that the Act of 1716 applied to the sitting, as well as to any future, parliament.
63. The Convocation of the Church of England had two houses, a lower in which sat the representatives of the ordinary clergy, and an upper, comprised of bishops. It was prorogued in 1717 and did not resume its powers until 1852. Coleridge described the suppression of Convocation as 'a bitter disgrace & wrong' (*CM*, I, 359) and commented in a notebook entry that 'in good policy not to say common Justice, the Clergy, as a Property *sui generis*, ought either to have their Convocation restored or . . . elect a Parliamentary Representative in each diocese or one from two or three Dioceses according to number' (*C & S*, p. 99, n. 3). Coleridge's remarks on Convocation reflect his view that the clergy had a special kind of property that was neither private, nor granted them by the government; see John Morrow, 'The National Church, *JHI*, 47, p. 650.
64. *England's Miserie and Remedie . . . 6 Sept: 1645*.
65. A variation on George Wither's *Vox Pacifica* (1645) IV.
66. Charles Dallison, *The Royalist's Defence* (1648) p. 41. See above, note 61.
67. John 18:36 (modified); Revelation 11:15 (modified).
68. Martin Luther, *Colloquia Mensalia* (1652) p. 298; translation from *C& S*, p. 130, n. 2.

69. Coleridge, *Zapolya* (1816), *PW*, II, 895. On the political bearing of this play see Coates, 'Coleridge's Debt to Harrington', *JHI*, 38.
70. The Coronation Oath allowed George III and his son George IV to scruple about giving their assent to a piece of legislation they in any case disliked. The section of the oath which had, or was made to have, a special bearing on the Catholic emancipation question read, 'Will you to the utmost of your power, maintain . . . the Protestant reformed religion established by law . . .?' (cited in *C & S*, p. xxxvi, n. 2).
71. That is, since the oath was not a theological statement, objections to emancipation that depended upon it were not theological but were concerned about its effect on the nature and role of the Established Church. George Canning (1770–1827) had succeeded Lord Liverpool as Prime Minister in February 1827 but died in August of the same year. Canning did not think that the Coronation Oath precluded Catholic emancipation.
72. Luther, *Colloquia Mensalia*, p. 265. 'Who is . . . such cattle' is Coleridge's addition; it alludes to Matthew 28:20.
73. See *A Lay Sermon*, above, p. 151.
74. Luke 17:20–1 (modified); 21:29–31.
75. 'Rabbins fable': derived from rabbinical lore. In his discussion of 'The Church of Anti-Christ', omitted from this collection, Coleridge attacks the confusion of the spiritual and temporal, the conflation of the Church of Christ with particular political and social institutions, which he sees as a feature of the Papacy; see *C & S*, pp. 129ff.
76. Based on Henry More (1614–87), *A Modest Inquiry into the Mystery of Iniquity*, II.ix, in *Theological Works* (1708) pp. 486–7.

Chaper 6   A Few Late Reflections: Coleridge on the 1832 Reform Act

1. See above, p. 157.
2. Cf. the discussion of Rousseau, above, pp. 93–4.
3. The Reform Act gave votes to 40-shilling freeholders, £10 p.a. copyholders, £50 p.a. leaseholders with twenty-year leases, £10 p.a. leaseholders with sixty-year leases and £50 tenants-at-will in the counties; in the boroughs existing resident electors retained the vote, and those occupying houses worth £10 p.a. gained it. For details see Michael Brock, *The Great Reform Act* (1973) pp. 138–9.
4. A reference to debt-funding; see above, p. 110.
5. Cf. *The Plot Discovered*, above, pp. 44–5.
6. Legislation for the forthcoming session and the reasons for embarking on it form the substance of the Speech from the Throne at the opening of Parliament. Although the speech is delivered by the monarch it is written by ministers. The ministers most closely connected with the passage of the Reform Act were the Prime Minister, Earl Grey; Henry Brougham, the Lord Chancellor; Viscount Althorp, Chancellor of the Exchequer and Leader of the House; and the Earl of Durham, Lord Privy Seal.

7. John James Park was Professor of Law and Jurisprudence at King's College, London. His *Dogmas of the Constitution* (1832) was annotated by Coleridge; see S. T. Coleridge, *Notes, Theological, Political and Miscellaneous*, ed. Derwent Coleridge (1853). Blackstone is, of course, William Blackstone, author of *Commentaries on the Laws of England* (Oxford, 1765-9).

8. To Charles Aders, 11 Feb 1832: *CL*, vi, p. 883.

Select Bibliography

This bibliography is intended to provide a guide to editions of Coleridge's writings, and to some of the more important secondary works dealing with his social and political theory. For editions referred to by abbreviations, consult the List of Abbreviations (p. xiii).

Primary Works

The definitive edition of Coleridge's writings is the Princeton *Collected Works* (*CC*), in which the main sources for Coleridge's social and political theory are *Lectures 1795*, *The Watchman*, *EOT*, *Friend*, *LS* and *C & S*; the *Marginalia* in this edition (*CM*), the editions of the notebooks (*CN*, etc.) and the letters (*CL*, etc.) are also very useful, although the relevant matter is more dispersed than in the other works mentioned here. Material relating to Coleridge's social and political thought may also be found in the following works.

Coleridge, S. T., *On the Constitution of the Church and State According to the Idea of Each*, ed. John Barrell (1972).
Jackson, H. J. (ed.), *Samuel Taylor Coleridge* (Oxford, 1985).
Richards, I. A. (ed.), *The Portable Coleridge* (New York, 1950).
White, R. J. (ed.), *The Political Thought of Samuel Taylor Coleridge* (1938).
——, *Political Tracts of Wordsworth, Coleridge and Shelley* (Cambridge, 1953).

Secondary Works

The introductions to the various volumes of *CC* contain excellent scholarly studies. The works listed below may also prove useful.

(a) BOOKS ON, OR CONTAINING SUBSTANTIAL DISCUSSIONS OF, COLERIDGE'S SOCIAL AND POLITICAL THOUGHT

Appleyard, J. A., *Coleridge's Philosophy of Literature* (Cambridge, Mass., 1965).
Barth, J. Robert, *Coleridge and Christian Doctrine* (Cambridge, Mass., 1969).
Bowle, John, *Politics and Opinion in the Nineteenth Century* (1954).
Brinton, Crane, *The Political Ideas of the English Romanticists* (Oxford, 1926).
Butler, Marilyn, *Romantics, Rebels and Reactionaries: English Literature and its Background 1760–1830* (Oxford, 1981).
Calleo, David P., *Coleridge and the Idea of the Modern State* (New Haven, Conn., 1966).

245

Chandler, James K., *Wordsworth's Second Nature: A Study of the Poetry and Politics* (Chicago, 1984).
Cobban, Alfred, *Edmund Burke and the Revolt against the Eighteenth Century* (1929; 2nd edn 1960).
Coleman, Deirdre, *Coleridge and The Friend (1809–10)* (Oxford, 1988).
Colmer, John, *Coleridge: Critic of Society* (Oxford, 1959).
——, *From Coleridge to Catch-22* (1978).
Everest, Kelvin, *Coleridge's Secret Ministry* (Hassocks, Sussex, 1967).
Harding, Anthony John, *Coleridge and the Idea of Love* (Cambridge, 1974).
Kennedy, William F., *Humanist versus Economist: The Economic Thought of Samuel Taylor Coleridge* (Berkeley, Calif., 1958).
Knights, Ben, *The Idea of the Clerisy in the Nineteenth Century* (Cambridge, 1978).
Leask, Nigel J., *The Politics of Imagination in Coleridge's Critical Thought* (1988).
Morrow, John, *Coleridge's Political Thought: Property, Morality and the Limits of Traditional Discourse* (London, 1990).
Muirhead, J. H., *Coleridge as Philosopher* (1930).
Roe, Nicholas, *Coleridge and Wordsworth: The Radical Years* (Oxford, 1988).
Sanders, Charles Richard, *Coleridge and the Broad Church Movement* (Durham, NC, 1942).
Smith, Olivia, *The Politics of Language 1791–1819* (Oxford, 1984).
Stafford, William, *Socialism, Radicalism and Nostalgia* (Cambridge, 1987).
Turk, Christopher, *Coleridge and Mill* (Andover, 1988).
Willey, Basil, *Nineteenth-Century Studies* (1949).
——, *Samuel Taylor Coleridge* (1972).
Williams, Raymond, *Culture and Society* (1958).
Woodring, Carl R., *Politics in the Poetry of Coleridge* (Madison, Wis., 1961).

(b) ESSAYS AND ARTICLES

Allen, Peter, 'S. T. Coleridge's *Church and State* and the Idea of an Intellectual Establishment', *JHI*, 46 (1985) 89–106.
Beeley, Harold, 'The Political Thought of Coleridge', in Edmund Blunden and Earl Leslie Griggs (eds), *Coleridge Studies by Several Hands on the Hundredth Anniversary of his Death* (1934) pp. 159–75.
Beer, John, 'The "Revolutionary Youth" of Wordsworth and Coleridge: Another View', *Critical Quarterly*, 19, no. 2 (1977) 79–87.
Coates, J. D., 'Coleridge's Debt to Harrington: A Discussion of *Zapolya*', *JHI*, 38 (1977) 501–8.
Colmer, John, 'Coleridge and Politics', in R. L. Brett (ed.), *S. T. Coleridge* (1972) pp. 244–70.
Deen, Leonard W., 'Coleridge and the Sources of Pantisocracy: Godwin, the Bible and Hartley', *Boston University Studies in English*, 5 (1961) 232–45.
——, 'Coleridge and the Radicalism of Religious Dissent', *Journal of English and Germanic Philology*, 61 (1962) 496–510.
Erdman, David V., 'Coleridge as Editorial Writer', in Conor Cruise O'Brien

and William Dean Vanech (eds), *Power and Consciousness* (New York, 1969) pp. 183–201.

Eugenia, Sister, 'Coleridge's Scheme of Pantisocracy and American Travel Accounts', *PMLA*, 1930, pp. 1069–84.

Landess, Thomas H., 'The Politics of Samuel Taylor Coleridge', *Sewanee Review*, 81 (1973) 847–59.

Levy, David, 'S. T. Coleridge Replies to Adam Smith's "Pernicious Opinion": A Study in Hermetic Social Engineering', *Interpretation*, 14 (1986) 89–114.

Link, Arthur S., 'Samuel Taylor Coleridge and the Economic and Political Crisis in Great Britain, 1816–1820', *JHI*, 9 (1948) 323–38.

MacGillivray, J. R., 'The Pantisocracy Scheme and its Immediate Background', in M. W. Wallace (ed.), *Studies in English* (Toronto, 1931) pp. 131–69.

Morrow, John, 'The National Church in Coleridge's *Church and State*: A Response to Allen', *JHI*, 47 (1986) 640–52.

——, 'Coleridge and the English Revolution', *Political Science*, 40 (1988) 128–41.

Sanderson, David R., 'Coleridge's Political "Sermons": Discursive Language and the Voice of God', *Modern Philology*, 70 (1972–3) 318–30.

Stafford, William, 'Religion and the Doctrine of Nationalism in England at the Time of the French Revolution', *Studies in Church History*, 18 (1982) 381–95.

Thompson, E. P., 'Disenchantment or Default? A Lay Sermon', in Conor Cruise O'Brien and William Dean Vanech (eds), *Power and Consciousness* (New York, 1969) pp. 149–81.

Watson, George, 'The Revolutionary Youth of Wordsworth and Coleridge', *Critical Quarterly*, 18, no. 3 (1976) 49–66.

Werkmeister, Lucyle, 'Coleridge's *The Plot Discovered*: Some Facts and a Speculation', *Modern Philology*, 56 (1958–9) 254–63.

——, 'Coleridge and Godwin on the Communication of Truth', *Modern Philology*, 55 (1957–8) 170–7.

Whalley, George, 'Coleridge and Southey in Bristol, 1795', *Review of English Studies*, n.s., 1 (1950) 324–40.

Index